The Search for

Paradise

The Search for
Paradise

An Interpretation of the Song of Songs

Roger Young

Nenge Books

The Search for Paradise - An Interpretation of the Song of Songs
by Roger Young

Text & cover photo - Copyright: © Roger Young 2021.
All rights reserved.

This book or parts thereof may not be reproduced in any form, stored in a retrieval system or transmitted in any form by any means - electronic, mechanical, photocopy or otherwise - without prior written permission of the publisher.

Published by Nenge Books, Australia, February 2022.

ABN 26809396184 www.nengebooks.com, nengebooks1@gmail.com

Nenge Books publishes quality books for independant authors using print-on-demand technology. Author enquiries welcomed.

The primary reference Bibles used for the interpretation of the Song of Songs which is presented here are the transliterated Hebrew/Greek Bible provided with QuickVerse For Windows (Parson's Technology computer software) together with The Interpreter's Bible published by Abingdon Press, Nashville, Tenn., USA. 1956.

Scripture quotations marked (NIV) are taken from the Holy Bible, New International Version®, NIV®. Copyright © 1973, 1978, 1984, 2011 by Biblica, Inc.™ Used by permission of Zondervan. All rights reserved worldwide. www.zondervan.com The "NIV" and "New International Version" are trademarks registered in the United States Patent and Trademark Office by Biblica, Inc.™

Scripture quotations marked (AV) from The Authorized (King James) Version. Rights in the Authorized Version in the United Kingdom are vested in the Crown. Reproduced by permission of the Crown's patentee, Cambridge University Press.

Scripture quotations indicated (ASV) are from the American Standard Version, 1901, as used in Parsons Technology QuickVerse for Windows.

Scriptures marked (GNB) are from the Good News Bible © 1994 published by the Bible Societies/HarperCollins Publishers Ltd UK, Good News Bible© American Bible Society 1966, 1971, 1976, 1992. Used with permission.

Scripture quotations indicated "Jerusalem Bible" or (JB) are from the from The Jerusalem Bible © 1966 by Darton Longman & Todd Ltd and Doubleday and Company Ltd.

Scripture quotations marked (NASB) taken from the (NASB®) New American Standard Bible®, Copyright © 1960, 1971, 1977, 1995, 2020 by The Lockman Foundation. Used by permission. All rights reserved. www.lockman.org

Scripture quotations marked (NEB) are taken from the New English Bible, copyright © Cambridge University Press and Oxford University Press 1961, 1970. All rights reserved.

Scripture quotations marked (NLT) are taken from the Holy Bible, New Living Translation, copyright ©1996, 2004, 2015 by Tyndale House Foundation. Used by permission of Tyndale House Publishers, Carol Stream, Illinois 60188. All rights reserved.

Scripture quotations marked (NRSV) are taken from New Revised Standard Version Bible: Catholic Edition, copyright © 1989, 1993 National Council of the Churches of Christ in the United States of America. Used by permission. All rights reserved worldwide.(as used in Parsons Technology QuickVerse for Windows).

Scripture quotations indicated (RSV) are from the Revised Standard Version, 1957, published by Thomas Nelson Publishers.

Scripture quotations marked (TLB) are taken from The Living Bible copyright © 1971. Used by permission of Tyndale House Publishers, Carol Stream, Illinois 60188. All rights reserved.

ISBN 978-0-6488889-3-2

Contents

PREFACE	vii
THE SEARCH FOR PARADISE	1
Language and Style of Writing of Songs	5
Authorship - Who? When? and Why?	7
Interpretation	17
OUTLINE	21
ACT 1 AFFIRMATION	22
ACT 1, Scene 1	23
ACT 1, Scene 2	32
ACT 1 Scene 3	48
ACT 2 ANTICIPATION	59
ACT 2	60
Something to Think About	76
ACT 3 IMAGINATION	79
The Songs, Sex, and Pornography	82
The Biblical Acceptance of "Naked"	89
The Confusion Between Love and Lust	100
Sex, Prayer and Intimacy	102
ACT 4 CELEBRATION	104
The Ecstacy of Relationship	129
ACT 5 SEPARATION	133
Assessing the Value of a Relationship	156
ACT 6 RESTORATION	159
ACT 7 REVELATION	192
ACT 7 Scene 1	194
ACT 7 Scene 2	200
Healthy Boundaries, Healthy Relationships	204
Summary	214
APPENDIX 1 Is Eros Evil?	216
A brief history of J-C attitudes regarding sex & marriage	216
Hebrew Theology of Sexuality	218
New Testament Teaching on Sex and Marriage	226
APPENDIX 2 Other Interpretations of the Song of Songs	239
BIBLIOGRAPHY	244

PREFACE

Most of the research for this book was done in the last 2 decades of the 20th Century (1980 to 1998) but the manuscript was put aside because of other issues needing attention. However, attitudes to marriage and family have changed so much since then that I feel compelled to make this book available for public reading in the hope that it might be helpful to some married couples and perhaps even many who are just simply hoping some day to be married.

Although my wife Rose has contributed material for this book, done much proof reading and offered constructive criticism, where the pronoun "I" has been used it refers to Roger as writer/typist.

There are many different interpretations of the *Song of Songs* and this is often reflected in the way that the many difficult and obscure verses in the book have been translated. For this reason, some of the text from the Songs that is presented on the following pages has been paraphrased. These paraphrases are based on a study of the very technical exegesis given in *The Interpreter's Bible*, together with reference to *Strong's Analytical Concordance* as included in *Quick Verse for Windows* computer software and a comparison of all available English translations.

Where appropriate, the commentary explains why a certain word or form of expression has been used. A summary of the various other interpretations which have been suggested and explored in the past has been included as an appendix to this volume.

Roger Young,
Ballarat, Victoria
November 2021

THE SEARCH FOR PARADISE

Hidden deep within many people's heart there is a desire to discover Paradise. For many people if such a place ever can be found then they would like to live there. It is even possible that many couples enter into a marriage relationship believing that somehow in their life together they will discover such joy and contentment that it will be like paradise for them. But to achieve any goal requires not just a desire of the heart but also some idea, or even a specific definition, of what that goal really is.

So we need to ask, "What does the word paradise mean for you?"

Has anyone ever really discovered or described a real paradise? There are some books and films whose very title suggests that the characters are living in some kind of utopia, or paradise, because they have the freedom to do almost anything that their heart desires. But, when we examine that film or book, we find that the writer has deceived us for these people are still troubled by jealousy, heartache, selfish ambition, greed, and every imaginable failure of human emotions. This may be paradise for some, but not for everyone.

Possibly the best known book that gives any sort of description of a realistic paradise would be the Holy Bible, for in that book-of-books we find several word-pictures describing paradise. One is the description of Heaven in the book of Revelation. This is the record of a vision that had been given to a saintly Christian man named John.

At the time in history when John lived it was not safe to be a Christian. There were a number of reasons for this, but it was not uncommon for Christians to suddenly find themselves issued with a free ticket to the Roman Circus. Not just a ringside seat either. These unfortunate folk were right in the main arena, where they were expected to give a display of lion feeding – they became the lion's meal – or a fight-to-the-death with well armed gladiators. The Roman's called this "entertainment".

Because he was so outspoken about his Christian faith John was sent to live in exile on the island of Patmos. It was while he was there that he experienced a series of visions which God told him were a revelation of future events. The book he wrote describing these visions is known as *The Revelation to John*, or sometimes simply as the book of *Revelation*. Part of John's vision was a picture of Heaven. And it is fairly obvious to most readers that the man was having difficulty finding suitable words to describe the awesome beauty of that place, for we read in Revelation 21:11 that "it shone with the glory of God, and its brilliance was like that of a very precious jewel, like a jasper, clear as crystal".

Not only is Heaven a place of almost indescribable beauty, but John also tells us that this paradise is a place of emotional security and perfect peace. There will be no tears there, for we are also told that [God] "will wipe away every tear from their eye". There will be no more death, or mourning, or crying, or pain; There will be unlimited access to the River of Life, and also to the Tree of Life. This place is so perfect and peaceful that nothing impure or evil will ever be permitted enter that wonderful city.

The text in Revelation 21:27 states that "Nothing evil will be allowed to enter, nor anyone who practises shameful idolatry and dishonesty." (NLT). John concluded his description by declaring that the gates of that wonderful city will never be closed because there will be no night there.

As most people already know, the book of Revelation is the last book in the Bible. But at the other end of the Bible, in the first two chapters of the book of Genesis, the Garden of Eden is probably a better known picture of paradise in. We are actually told very little specific detail about this place within the narrative itself but the scene is always understood to be a place of wonderful beauty and perfect peace.

Many ideas about the Garden of Eden are actually based more on tradition, but some specific details the writer does mention are that there was nothing to fear. There was vegetation and animals but no fear of those animals. And there is no mention of problems like sunburn even though the couple who dwelt in this place of paradise had no clothes – they were both totally naked and there was no embarrassment or shame.

However, the Bible also has some other word-pictures describing paradise but these are not so well known. One of these is found almost at the very centre of the Bible in a delightful little book entitled *The Song of Songs*, although some people refer to it as *The Song of Solomon*.

For centuries people have debated and questioned many aspects of this book. There is no clear evidence for who wrote these lyrics, nor has there been any agreement about why they were written. Some seem to have been frankly scared of the Songs, because they seem to talk about human love, and for some reason there have always been people who believe that the Bible should not address such an issue. For them the subject of sex and human relationships, even within marriage, is somehow sordid, carnal, or ungodly. There are even others who, when they encounter the obviously sexual inferences in the *Song of Songs*, simply discard the book as ancient pornography. For a similar reason others try desperately to spiritualise everything that they read in these eight brief chapters. And some tell us that this book is merely an allegory of the history of the nation of Israel.

So strongly were these ideas held by some leaders during the first few centuries of the Christian church that when Theodore of Mopsuetia (AD360 – 429) even suggested that the *Song of Songs* may be a collection of love songs, or a love story rather than an allegory of some sort, the official reaction of the Church was to anathematise the man and his writings.[1]

Perhaps Dr G. Campbell Morgan was very close to the truth when he wrote in his commentary on the *Song of Songs* that:

> "There are men and women who would find indecencies in heaven – if they could ever get there – but they would take those impurities in their own corrupt souls. To those who live lives of simple purity, these songs are full of beauty. ...
>
> The calculating man who dislikes this book has never been in love, and probably never will be." [2]

But it is not only the human-love interpretations of the Songs that have inspired rebuke. Jeanne Guyon (1648-1717) lived in France during the reign of the brutal King Louis XIV, and when she produced her commentary on the *Song of Songs*, which she interpreted as an allegory of the relationship between Christ and the individual believer, she wrote from the depths of her own spiritual experience. However, for her efforts in suggesting that a mere human being could have such a personal relationship with God, she was condemned (of heresy?) and sent to the infamous Bastille prison.[3]

Nowadays, however, many people interpret this book at its face value. They recognise that the *Song of Songs* gives some very good teaching on relationships and also presents some extremely

---

1. Theophile J Meek, "Introduction to The *Song of Songs*", The Interpreter's Bible, Vol. V p94.
2. Dr. G Campbell Morgan, *Living Messages of the Books of the Bible Vol 2*, pp74-75.
3. From the Introduction to *Song of Songs* by Jeanne Guyon. Refer to bibliography.

wholesome attitudes to the subject of lovemaking within the relationship of marriage. As H T Kerr says in *The Interpreter's Bible*, "Love, such as is displayed in the *Song of Songs*, glorifies God".[4]

Because we can discover in these writings evidence of an (almost) perfect relationship, some describe this book as yet another picture of paradise.

As I have studied this book for many years, and have read what others have to say about the writing, I have become increasingly impressed with a sense of awe and wonder with the growing realisation that the writer of this work was obviously trying to teach us things that modern marriage and relationship counsellors seem to be only just discovering.

Language and Style of Writing of Songs

In the past, many people who read the *Songs of Songs* believed the book was just a random collection of simple romantic lyrics rather than the studied work of a professional writer. And many scholars in the past seem to have accepted the book as little more than that.

But when we recognize that there is a definite unity and a consistent theme presented throughout the entire book, and when we discover the extremely clever use of words and phrases that have a double meaning, then we have to acknowledge that the *Song of Songs* is the work of a genius.

The book has a style and vocabulary all of its own, and in many ways the writing is absolutely unique. This is the only book in the Bible that reads like the script for a stage play, where the entire text is put into the mouths of speakers.

Most of the story is reported in the present tense, as though the woman is describing to a group of friends or onlookers events

---

4. Hugh Thomson Kerr, *Exposition of The Song of Songs*, The Interpreter's Bible, Vol V p101.

that are actually happening. When she describes her lover she speaks in the third person. For example she says, "His eyes are like doves." But when there is dialogue between these two lovers then this is recorded as though we are listening to the actual words as they are spoken. Similarly, the lover's various descriptions of the woman are always addressed directly to her. Thus we frequently read statements such as, "You are beautiful, my darling".

We find an elaborate use of sensuous imagery as the bride and groom sing of the delights of love, and we encounter at least forty different words that are found nowhere else in the Bible.

The style of writing is very personal, with an abundant use of pronouns such as *me*, *my*, and *mine* and yet it is often difficult to determine who the speakers are, for they are never specifically identified or introduced.

We also need to understand that the headings "lover" and "beloved" (or "the man" and "the woman") are not part of the original text. These have been added by translators who have based this division on the gender of the words used. Obviously the story is told by the woman, for it is the feminine voice which introduces and concludes the dialogue.

It is the woman who describes her experience as the one who loves and also as the one who is loved. Nevertheless, in spite of this evidence, there are a number of technical reasons why it is often difficult to determine precisely who is making some of the statements.

Another obvious feature of the *Songs* is the choral background, or chorus. This appears to be a group of onlookers who interrupt with brief comments or questions, to which the woman, as the storyteller, always gives some reply. This concept of antiphonal question and response is a common feature of Hebrew prose, and is frequently used throughout the Psalms, as also is the use of parallelism, where an idea is repeated using slightly different imagery in the repetition. There are also some refrains that are repeated throughout the songs, and the writer seems to have used these as a literary device to move from one scene to the next.

Authorship - Who? When? and Why?

So it seems logical to ask: who originally wrote these songs and why were they written? Who was this dusky maiden with the beautiful flowing black hair and perfect smile; this one who moved with such poise and dignity that she captured the heart of a king? Who is this man of whom she speaks with such admiration? Was he a shepherd, or was he a king? Was King Solomon the author, or was it someone else? But the answers to these questions are not easy to find.

Although the book has been attributed to Solomon who, in the tenth century BC came to the throne as third king of Israel and who is credited with having written more than one thousand other songs or poems, there has been no unanimous agreement that he actually wrote these particular lyrics.

Admittedly the first verse of the book, in English translations, does give the title as *The Song of Songs which is Solomon's*, and the name of Solomon does appear seven times. (Songs 1:1; 1:5; 3:7; 3:9; 8:11; 8:12.)

But many commentary writers tell us that the reference to Solomon is simply an editorial note. Just because the title contains his name does not necessarily mean that he was the author. It could simply mean that the book was found in his library, or that the writing had been dedicated to him or in memory of him.

It is highly likely that the original writer may have been a woman, since it is the feminine voice which basically tells the story. It might be the storyteller who refers to herself as *Shulammite* or *Shunnamite* (6:13). But even this does not really identify who she is, for there are a number of different interpretations of the name she has used. It may be possible that this is just a reference to "wife of Solomon" for some authorities claim that *Shulammite* is the feminine form of Solomon. However, others tell us that the title simply derives from the Hebrew word *shalom* (closely related in Hebrew to the name Solomon) and hence may simply mean "the one who brings peace". This interpretation would be consistent with Songs 8:10 where the woman describes herself as one who finds (or brings) peace and satisfaction. Or she may simply be a woman from Shunam[5]. Still others tell us that the name could be a reference to Shalmanitu, a Mesopotamian goddess.

Nevertheless, the idea that the original writer was a woman does have some merit. In his letter to Titus, the Apostle Paul instructed this young pastor to "bid the older women to ... teach what is good, and so train the younger women to love their husbands and children." (Titus 2:3-4). It is possible that Paul was passing on an already recognised practice of the Hebrew people and that these songs are evidence that somebody had already put the idea into writing.

For the ancient Hebrew people this business of learning the art of a happy marriage was certainly not a one-sided responsibility, for they also had a law which required a new husband, during the first year of marriage, to learn to make his wife happy. (Deut 24:5). And the very existence of the book of Proverbs indicates that at least some Hebrew fathers (or mothers in the case of Proverbs 31) took seriously their responsibility of passing on to their sons and daughters some helpful guidelines for living.

Captain Cook, who explored many islands in the South Pacific during the eighteenth century, recorded incidents which suggest that the people who lived in some of those islands accepted it as normal that the more mature women in the tribe would teach the younger ones how to enjoy their relationship with a man.

For the people of Solomon's time this education would almost certainly have included the physical and sexual aspects of marriage, for we have also been told that the ancient rabbis were

---

5. Abishag, of King David's harem, came from Shunam. Refer 1 Kings 1:3.

outspoken in all matters of sex education and in techniques for enhancing the knowledge and mastery of the subject. The idea of prudery was foreign to them.[6]

The expression *"Song of Songs"* is a Hebrew idiom meaning "the most superlative song" or "the best of all songs." We see a similar concept with the well-known expression "King of kings and Lord of lords."

The name *Solomon*, as has been already mentioned, is derived from the Hebrew word *shalom*. (See: 1 Chronicles 22:9. Solomon will be a man of peace).

The word *shalom*, although often translated into English as "peace", means far more than just a lack of conflict. The word has overtones of sweet harmony, contentment, and complete satisfaction. It is that sense of abiding peace which can remain even in spite of trouble or conflict. So it is not unreasonable to suggest that the title given to this little book refers to a wonderful musical presentation (the greatest of all songs) that has some relationship to a lifestyle of perfect peace and contentment.

The *Song of Songs* can be read as a love story. It is more than just a random collection of love songs from some unknown period in history or a book about relationships. It is a very down-to-earth matter-of-fact story of a woman who loved – a woman who was married to the most wonderful husband one could ever hope to find. And yet even with this advantage she discovered that happiness in marriage does not come automatically.

Just as there are laws of physics which determine the operation of the physical world in which we live, so also there are laws of relationship. And if we ignore these principles or treat them with contempt then we will never experience the true *shalom* peace and contentment of paradise.

Why should we find this intriguing little love story almost buried amongst a collection of other books that are all considered

---

[6]. M. M. Brayer, *Dictionary Of Pastoral Care and Counselling*, p1159. Chapter entitled "Sexuality, Jewish Theology and Ethics."

to be sacred? After all, we note that there is no specific reference to God anywhere in the Songs. So why should the book be included in any canon of sacred writings?

The answer is simply because, as human beings, we have been designed for relationship. This is the way that the Creator intended it to be.

The family is the basic building block of a healthy human society and the strength of the family is dependent on the quality of the love relationship that should exist between the two people (man and woman) who brought that family into being. Many studies in sociology have confirmed this fact.

In the middle of the 20th century Dr. David Mace began a rescue mission to homeless street children of the East-end slums in the city of London UK. In his efforts to discover why these youngsters chose to leave home and live on the streets he discovered that the problem had a lot to do with the lack of real love between the parents of those children.

In an attempt to address the cause of the problem, rather than just deal with the symptoms, he began the Marriage Enrichment movement. Meanwhile in Spain a Catholic priest doing a similar work with homeless children in that country came to the same conclusion, and he began the Marriage Encounter movement. Attitudes to marriage can and do determine the future of an entire nation or civilisation.

Although we may not know with absolute certainty who wrote The Songs, and when or where that person lived, I hope to demonstrate in the following pages why I believe that the *Song of Songs* was originally written as a book (or possibly as a musical drama) about marriage.

To this end it is possible that the writer composed all of the lyrics herself, and it is also quite probable that she has made use of songs or poetry from other sources. To accept this idea helps to explain many of the problems linguists encounter when they attempt to translate from the original language.

The Search for Paradise

The writing is often assumed to be Hebrew in origin for the lyrics are presented in a style that is typical of Hebrew poetry. However, some of the symbolism and imagery used is more typical of Egyptian love poetry that comes from a period between the fourteenth and twelfth centuries BC

In some of this Egyptian poetry the word "sister" is used for the beloved and "brother" for the lover, and the story is presented in a world of fantasy where the lover can appear both as a shepherd and as a king.[7] This ancient Egyptian poetry describes a world of nature with its profusion of animals, plants, spices, and exotic gardens – a world of joy and contentment where the couple may go for a walk in the garden. It is the world of exquisite beauty where the charm of the beloved makes the heads of all the men turn to catch a glimpse of her.[8] All of these characteristics are also evident in the *Song of Songs*.

But the geography is certainly not Egyptian. Rather it is somewhere in The Promised Land. Mention of the cities of Tirzah and Jerusalem in the one sentence (6:4) would seem to indicate that the author lived somewhere in the vicinity of these two cities, and possibly during the time when Tirzah was capital of the Northern Kingdom (*ca* 900-870BC).

But the Hebrew language is not typical of that used during the ninth or tenth century BC, or during the reign of Solomon. It is more consistent with language that was used about the third century BC, and the songs also contain some words of Greek, Persian, or possibly even Egyptian origin. So this could indicate that the songs were at least edited sometime after Persia and Greece had become world powers. This again suggests some time about the third century BC, rather than the tenth century BC.

But we also need to recognise that the *Song of Songs* was included in the Septuagint, a Greek translation of the Old

---
7. Roland E Murphy *New Jerome Bible Commentary*, p462.
8. John F Craghan C SS R, Commentary on *The Song of Songs and the Book of Wisdom*, (1979) pp4-5.

Testament produced during the third century BC. So we know that the book must have been accepted as part of the canon of sacred Hebrew writings before then. It is also extremely unlikely that the Hebrew language would have been used for folk songs during the third century BC.

By that time in history Hebrew was only used for specific formal or religious purposes and Aramaic was the common language for everyday use. Since the songs were written in Hebrew then either they were written well before the third century BC, or they were intended for some specific religious or relationship teaching.

So we have to accept that all of the available evidence for authorship and for the original date of writing does seem to be rather confusing and contradictory.

However, many of these problems could be explained if we allow for the possibility that the original writer did live during the tenth century BC.[9]

I believe it is quite probable that she was the Egyptian Princess, wife of Solomon, referred to in 1 Kings 3:1. And she has made use of some Egyptian lyrics already known to her. Then at some later date in history a scribe has updated the language of the original manuscript, rather than making a perfect copy.

The reason for doing this could simply have been that the manuscript would then be more readable to the people of his time, in much the same way as our English translations of the Bible have been updated to reflect changes in the English language since the King James Authorised Version was first published in 1611. Please believe me! If you tried to read Wycliffe's original English translation of the bible you would quickly agree that periodic language updates are definitely necessary. Even the language of

---

9. Craig Glickman, *A Song For Lovers* (1976), presents a reasonable argument that the Songs do come from a period in Solomon's life, and have been presented for the purpose of giving instruction about relationships and marriage. *A Song For Lovers* pp 179ff.

the King James authorized version of the year 1611 is a problem for many English-speaking people in the 21st century.

The reason for producing a more readable version of the *Song of Songs* could well have been to make the message more appealing and acceptable to normal working-class people and thus restore within the minds of everyone a greater respect for the relationship of marriage.

There would have been valid reasons for doing this and, regardless of whether we are looking at the tenth century BC or the third century BC, there have always been those who treat marriage with less respect than the Creator had intended.

In the early part of the 20th Century, Carle Zimmerman, Professor of Sociology at Harvard University in the USA did some serious study in an attempt to discover if there was any common cause that brought about the collapse of great civilizations in the past. He found that the common cause was the breakdown of families. A lack of respect for marriage, perverted expressions of sexuality, rising crime rates, and attitudes where the claimed "rights" of minority groups often take precedence over traditional family responsibilities are typical and predictable characteristics of a civilisation or society that has reached the point of selfdestruction.[10]

To summarise Zimmerman's work briefly; it is obvious that when there is a corruption of the concepts of marriage and family, the civilization will destroy itself from within.

To express this a little differently: NO Civilization has ever survived attempts to redefine the concepts of marriage and family.

When the Children of Israel moved into The Promised Land they were surrounded by nations whose people worshipped the gods of fertility. The sexual attitudes and behaviour of the followers of those fertility cults were certainly not designed to inspire any sort of healthy respect for women or for the concepts of marriage and family.

---

10. Carle C Zimmerman, *Family and Civilization*, Harper and Brothers, New York USA, 1947

It was a reaction against the depravity of these fertility cults that caused Greek and Persian philosophers from about the fourth century BC onwards to teach that passion was the cause of evil in this world. Thus, in order to solve the problems of evil, men and women needed to learn to suppress or deny all of their emotions.

These ascetic ideas also had a negative effect on attitudes to marriage and male-female relationships in general. Women were now seen as the seductive temptress who could lead men astray into a life of sensuality and passion. Women should avoid being seen in public, or dress in such a way that their natural beauty was always concealed, and men should avoid contact with them wherever possible.

The ancient Greek philosopher Plato (born in Athens 428 BC) taught that in an ideal state rule should be exercised by what he called "guardians", and to make certain that relationships involving passion would not be put before the good of the State he proposed that these guardians should live together as one large commune with wives and children all shared in common. Sexual activity would be permitted for the purpose of procreation *only*.

Some men even went so far as to teach that young people should never plan to get married or, if they ever did marry, then they should live together as though they were just brother and sister and never consummate their relationship with any sexual act. But I see no effort on their part to explain how the human race could continue if sexual activity between men and women was forbidden.

And so it was that people were constantly faced on the one hand with the blatant sexual immorality of the fertility cults and on the other hand the overreaction of prudish asceticism and its fear of anything to do with sex.

Both of these extremes degrade the status of marriage and also produce attitudes of suspicion regarding members of the opposite sex. So, in a male dominated culture women were then treated with contempt.

These attitudes also stand in contrast to the traditional Hebrew understanding of marriage.

Although Moses warned the Hebrew people that they must never get involved with the sexually immoral fertility cults of the Canaanites, his people were not ascetic prudes. In fact, in opposition to any suggestion of asceticism, Talmudic teaching declares that, "In the world-to-come every person will be called to give account for all the legitimate pleasures one has not partaken".[11]

Ideally, marriage should be a partnership between a man and a woman who have discovered, to their mutual delight, that there are many goals and values in life which they share in common.

Good communication skills and the shared pursuit of these common goals should be significant features of their relationship. It then follows that their physical sexual union as husband and wife (what the Bible refers to as being "one flesh") should be accepted as a natural expression of their already existing emotional and spiritual unity. But, if ever the marriage license is perceived as being just a license to copulate and possibly produce offspring then what should be a precious relationship of mutual encouragement and love is in danger of being dragged into the gutter and reduced to little more than crude animal lust.

So it is quite probable that sometime about the third century BC, in an effort to restore a proper respect for marriage as God intended it should be, Hebrew scribes produced copies of *The Song of Songs* in a language which, although still a "sacred" language, could be easily read and understood by the people of their day.

This suggestion is consistent with remarks made by Theophile Meek in *The Interpreter's Bible*[12] where he tells us that, "these songs are altogether incongruous with the puritanical attitudes of the third century BC, although the present text may come from a date as late as that".

---
11. Quoted by M.M. Brayer, Dictionary of Pastoral Care and Counselling, p1159
12. The Interpreter's Bible, Vol. V, p97

Within the *Song of Songs* we find a strong emphasis on the value of a good relationship, and this stands in contrast to the often impersonal sexual activity that was typical of the fertility cults and of modern pornography. We find a very honourable image of womanhood, a healthy and desirable model for the relationship of marriage, and a scene in which human sexual love is seen as a beautiful God-ordained celebration of a special relationship.

The teaching that can be discovered when we interpret this musical drama as a story of human love would have been significant at the time of original writing and is still very valid even in the twenty-first century.

We also need to remember that, in an attempt to explain the love that God has for his people, the Old Testament prophets often used the illustration of a marriage relationship. Note that this was marriage as in the case of husband and wife – a relationship where there should be some passion, not just a platonic brother-sister relationship. One obvious example of this is the book and teaching of the prophet Hosea.

So, although many interpretations of the *Song of Songs* have emphasised the spiritual aspects of the relationship, we have to acknowledge that the Songs do have some excellent teaching about the physical, emotional and sexual aspects of marriage and human love.

We also need to recognise and remember that when translating from one language "A" to another language "B" there may not be any word in language "B" that can really give the precise meaning of the word used in language "A".

For this reason it is not at all uncommon or surprising when we find that our English translations do not give the full warmth or range of meaning that is implied in the Hebrew text. This is simply because the English language does not have a word that carries the same spectrum or scope of meaning that is implied by that particular word in the Hebrew language.

Interpretation

Because of the confusion that existed regarding the origin of the *Song of Songs* there have, over the centuries, been many different interpretations.

Many Jews interpreted the book as an expression of the love that YHWH[13] has for his people, and hence see it as an allegory of the history of Israel from the time of the Exodus.

Leaders in the early Christian church often interpreted these songs as an allegory of the love of Christ for his bride, the Church. But by the end of the fourth century Theodore of Mopsuetia presented his interpretation that the book celebrates Solomon's marriage to an Egyptian Princess (1 Kings 3:1).

However, this view was condemned by the Church Council of Constantinople (AD553), who insisted that the *Song of Songs* must have a spiritual interpretation and could not be a reference to mere human love. Nevertheless, Theodore's interpretation was upheld by a number of other notable scholars.[14]

Even today, in the twenty-first century, there are still people who would have us believe that the Bible never mentions sex except in a negative way. But, when we examine these songs simply for what they appear to be we discover a very positive acceptance of the beauty and value of sexual love within marriage although the subject is presented here in gentle poetic language. In doing this the writer has treated the subject with a special tenderness that can never be achieved by the use of cold clinical terms or by the crude use of slang. Translations of other ancient

---

13. YHWH is the Hebrew name for God, probably pronounced Yahweh or Jehovah (depending on which school you attended), usually translated as LORD in English Bibles. The Hebrew scribes never included the vowel pointers when they wrote this sacred name and, possibly out of a sense of awesome respect for God, we are told that they never actually spoke the name. So we do not know the proper spelling or pronunciation. I have chosen to write the name using just the four consonants, as did the Hebrew scribes.
14. New Jerome Bible Commentary (1990), section 426m, p523.

books that have a sexual theme, such as *The Kama Sutra* and *The Perfumed Garden*, frequently use crude slang terminology and these works never approach the delicate beauty of the *Song of Songs*.

However, to leave the writing in its symbolic language means that it is often without meaning or understanding for the modern reader who is not familiar with the cultural symbols used by the original writer.

With this in mind I have attempted to explore and explain these symbols and to present them here in words that can be understood in our present day language. For this purpose there is no reasonable alternative than to use matter-of-fact language and clinical terms.

Experienced Marriage Counsellors have identified at least eight behaviour characteristics for couples which are conducive to a long and happy marriage:

> They express their love verbally.
> They are physically affectionate.
> They express their love sexually.
> They express their love with gifts.
> They share in mutual self-disclosure.
> They make time to be alone together.
> They offer each other emotional support.
> They express appreciation and admiration of each other.

Note that all of these characteristics are modelled in this musical drama. So it is evident that one purpose of the *Song of Songs* is to teach us that there should be an unashamed acceptance of verbal and physical expressions of love between a husband and wife, and the writer has achieved this beautifully, without being offensive or crude in any way.

How often, when studying human behavioural psychology do we find that some of the best guidelines for living have been recorded by these ancient Hebrew people about three thousand years ago and this even includes guidelines for lovemaking and sex in marriage. As you study through the text you will find additional examples to those that have been given here.

Whatever interpretations people have attempted to draw from this work there always seem to be some passages that create problems. But remember: these songs were never intended to be a scientific lecture on relationships. They are a form of poetry and, as such, the appeal is often to the aesthetic sense of rhyme and rhythm, rather than a precise argument of logic. And what we have in our English language is just a translation – it is not the original language.

We should therefore not be surprised when we find that there are some passages that seem to yield no precise meaning at all.

Perhaps we need to be constantly reminding ourselves that these songs were originally written something like 3000 years ago, and in a very different culture than we find ourselves living with today. The Songs of Songs is not the product of a 21st Century Western Culture or a modern American or English 'Christian mind – although many of our Bible commentaries obviously are.

Also, we always need to remember that when doing any translation from language "A" to language "B" there is often no word in language "B" that gives precisely the same meaning as the word which was used in language "A". This is one of the reasons why an interpretation of *The Songs* based on the original Hebrew language may expose a more sensitive love story than any commentary based on some English translation.

OUTLINE

Title   1:1

Act 1   1:2 - 2:7   AFFIRMATION

Act 2   2:8 - 3:5   ANTICIPATION - Playful games

Act 3   3:6 - 3:11   IMAGINATION

Act 4   4:1 - 5:1   CELEBRATION

Act 5   5:2 - 6:13   SEPARATION

Act 6   7:1 - 8:4   RESTORATION

Act 7   8:5 - 8:14   REVELATION - Reflections of childhood and concluding remarks.

ACT 1 AFFIRMATION

Song of Songs 1:2 to 2:7 (NIV)

1:1 The song of songs, which is Solomon's.
 2 Let him kiss me with the kisses of his mouth-- for your love is more delightful than wine.
 3 Pleasing is the fragrance of your perfumes; your name is like perfume poured out. No wonder the maidens love you!
 4 Take me away with you--let us hurry! Let the king bring me into his chambers. We rejoice and delight in you ; we will praise your love more than wine. How right they are to adore you!
 5 Dark am I, yet lovely, O daughters of Jerusalem, dark like the tents of Kedar, like the tent curtains of Solomon.
 6 Do not stare at me because I am dark, because I am darkened by the sun. My mother's sons were angry with me and made me take care of the vineyards; my own vineyard I have neglected.
 7 Tell me, you whom I love, where you graze your flock and where you rest your sheep at midday. Why should I be like a veiled woman beside the flocks of your friends?
 8 If you do not know, most beautiful of women, follow the tracks of the sheep and graze your young goats by the tents of the shepherds.
 9 I liken you, my darling, to a mare harnessed to one of the chariots of Pharaoh.
 10 Your cheeks are beautiful with earrings, your neck with strings of jewels.
 11 We will make you earrings of gold, studded with silver.
 12 While the king was at his table, my perfume spread its fragrance.
 13 My lover is to me a sachet of myrrh resting between my breasts.
 14 My lover is to me a cluster of henna blossoms from the vineyards of En Gedi.
 15 How beautiful you are, my darling! Oh, how beautiful! Your eyes are doves.
 16 How handsome you are, my lover! Oh, how charming! And our bed is verdant.
2:1 I am a rose of Sharon, a lily of the valleys.
 2 Like a lily among thorns is my darling among the maidens.
 3 Like an apple tree among the trees of the forest is my lover among the young men. I delight to sit in his shade, and his fruit is sweet to my taste.
 4 He has taken me to the banquet hall, and his banner over me is love.
 5 Strengthen me with raisins, refresh me with apples, for I am faint with love.
 6 His left arm is under my head, and his right arm embraces me.
 7 Daughters of Jerusalem, I charge you by the gazelles and by the does of the field: Do not arouse or awaken love until it so desires.

ACT 1

AFFIRMATION

ACT 1, Scene 1 (Song of Songs 1:2-4a)

Try to imagine for a few moments that you are looking forward to meeting a person whom you love, but you have been separated from them for some time. It could be weeks, it could be days, or it may have just been for a normal working day. As you look forward to meeting this most important person in your life, what are your thoughts? What will be your greeting? What sort of things do you expect to talk about during those first few precious moments together? Would you make smalltalk, possibly about the weather, or about the problems of the world, or the latest newspaper headlines? Or are you bursting to talk about all the exciting things that you have been doing while you were apart, and not with that person?

Or would it be your desire to first renew a sense of intimacy, a reassurance of your mutual love and enthusiasm for your future together? Would you therefore spend those first few moments telling your beloved how much you have looked forward to this reunion, and how you were thinking about them so often whilst you were apart?

Would I be right in guessing that many married couples would react very differently than a lot of courting couples in this situation?

How easily we become preoccupied with the mundane business details of work, or of keeping the household running, or caring for children, and we forget the importance of things like affirmation and encouragement, and the need to keep some romance alive within the relationship.

If we interpret the *Song of Songs* as a stage play or musical drama of some sort we can imagine that Scene One of Act One opens with the woman on the stage. Then, as her lover enters the scene she unashamedly announces to the world in general (or her audience) her feelings about him, and immediately follows this with her first words of greeting to the man himself. Thus:

> 1:2 "Let him kiss me with the kisses of his mouth."

Then, almost as though her lover had heard her comment, she turns and says to him;

> 1:2-3 "For your love is better than wine. Because of the savour of your good ointments your name is like perfume poured out, and for this reason the maidens all adore you." (modified from KJV).

Her first words, when she meets this important man in her life, are to tell him how wonderful she thinks he is. This is an important principle of healthy relationships.

At first glance her opening statement may seem to be just a nice warm greeting for her lover. But when we examine the words she used in the original language we find a profound depth of meaning that may be lost in our English translations.

She expressed a desire to be kissed. But the word she used in expressing this desire can have a meaning far beyond that of just a friendly peck on the cheek. This particular Hebrew word *(nashaq)* is used 35 times in the Old Testament. In many cases it is simply translated as "kiss", but the same word is also used in reference to the authority which Pharaoh bestowed on Joseph when he commissioned him into a position of leadership in the land of Egypt.[15] And in other places we find that the word is used in reference to men who were *"armed* with bows and arrows" (1 Chron, 12:2 and 2 Chron. 17:17 and Psalm 78:9) and also of the living creatures in Ezekiel's vision who *touched* or who *provided mutual support* for one another (Ezekial. 3:13).

The word has connotations of encouragement and of an action to protect, strengthen, fortify, or restore. Joseph's role as leader in Egypt was to protect the nation from being destroyed by the forecast famine.

So in her opening statement the bride may well have been verbalising a desire for some very real expression of emotional support together with love and encouragement, and not just a brief peck on the cheek – or even just a kiss on the lips.

In her statement, "Your *love* is better than wine," the bride has again used what at first reading seems to be an unusual word.

She has used the Hebrew word *dode* or *dowd*. In many other places where we find this word in the Bible it is translated as "uncle".[16] But the word uncle does not seem to make sense in this context. She uses this word thirty-one times in these songs and she is obviously not talking about her uncle.

So let me try to explain: According to the Hebrew-Greek dictionary in my QuickVerse software, the word *dowd* [H1730] is from a word root meaning *to boil*. Hence the word has implications of warmth. Warmth of affection would be quite appropriate in the context of the phrase "your *love* is better than wine".

---

15. Genesis 41:40 "According to thy word shall all my people be ruled . . ." [KJV]
"You shall be in charge . . . all my people are to submit to your orders." [NIV]
16. Leviticus 10:4; 20:20; 25:49; 1 Samuel 10:14-16; 1 Samuel 14:50; 2 Kings 24:17; etc.

And at the same time we need to recognize that the use of the word *dowd* in reference to an uncle should not be too surprising either; because in many societies when a child is born it is the father's brother (an uncle) who is responsible to ensure that the child will be given proper care and adequate provision of human needs.

Even as recently as the 20th century in our English-speaking countries when a new child entered a family it was not uncommon for the parents to nominate someone – often an uncle – as godparent or godfather. The godfather has a responsibility of care. Because of the duty of care involved it would not be inappropriate for a Hebrew-speaking person of Old Testament times to use the word *dowd* in reference to an uncle who is in that caretaker role.

But then we find the same word is also used in Proverbs 7:18 where the adulterous woman says, "Come, let us take our fill of *love* …"

The prophet Ezekiel also used the same word in an allegory where he likens the nation of Israel to a young woman who has grown and reached the age for *love* (Ezek 16:8). Then he says the Babylonians "came into her bed of *love*" (Ezek 23:17).

So it is obvious that, like our English word *love*, the word *dowd* can have a variety of meanings depending on the context, and the writer of these songs has used the word dowd to imply not only caring warmth of affection but also the sexual aspect of marital love. When we look at the context in every case where the word is used in these songs this would be the most logical interpretation.

The writer has also made use of two other words for love: The common Hebrew word for love, *'aheb* or *'ahab* (feminine *'ahabah*) is used eight times.[17] This word has a very similar range of meanings as the English word *love*, and can thus be used in reference to the social, emotional, spiritual, or sexual aspects of a relationship.

---

17. *Song of Songs* 1:3; 1:4; 1:7; 1:16; 3:1; 3:2; 3:3; 3:4.

Another unusual Hebrew word the writer has used nine times in reference to *love* is *ra'yah*. This word is feminine in gender but is not found anywhere else in the Bible. However, when we compare masculine words derived from the same root we find words such as herdsman, shepherd, or pastor. So the expression would seem to refer to a person who cares, or a relationship of caring.

What did the bride mean when she said, "Your *love* is better than wine"?

The root meaning of the word translated here as "wine" is *effervescence*. So when the bride says "Your love is better than wine" she may in fact be saying something like, "The warmth and sincerity of your lovemaking is better than the bubbly or effervescent 'just do it for pleasure' type of lovemaking." The anticipation of life ahead with the secure warmth of genuine affection outshines frivolous celebrating.

Unfortunately we are not given any description of the opening scene for these songs, so we are left to guess. If this is a drama involving one of the wives of Solomon (either fact or fiction) then we could guess that the opening scene is somewhere in the virgins' section of the king's harem. In this case the chorus of onlookers would be the other maidens of the harem who, because of their loyalty to the king, are all supportive of this beautiful woman who is about to move from the status of "maiden" to "wife".

The concept of such a supportive community is not impossible, and we know from the story of Esther that while she was still a maiden in the harem of king Ahasuerus she, "won the favour of everyone who saw her." (Esther 2:15). Yet, understandably, this young bride is feeling somewhat nervous, and perhaps a little insecure, and in need of encouragement.

I know there will be some readers who object to my suggestion that this could be a scene in the king's harem because they are strongly opposed to polygamy. In our Western culture we have been taught to view polygamy with suspicion and contempt, but other social cultures have not always held to this view.

The law against polygamy was first introduced by one of the Roman Emperors and until relatively recent times in many societies that were not subjected to Roman or Western laws a man with more than one wife was not uncommon.

Because the entire system of social welfare in most of those societies, and also in ancient Hebrew culture was based on the family, a single woman of marriageable age, even a widow living on her own, was considered to be an anomaly. There was no widow's pension and in any case the Scriptures say "it is not good for man (or woman) to live alone".

In ancient Hebrew culture a widow was never expected to be left to live alone and forever grieve in her loneliness. There was hope that she would, after an appropriate period of time for grieving, be cared for by someone who could afford to support an additional wife and she would then be fully accepted into a loving, caring, and supportive family.

We see this principle illustrated in the biblical story of Ruth. Although there is no mention of Boaz having another wife – this would not have been a factor worthy of mention in that culture – it would have been highly unlikely for a man of Boaz's age and means to still be unmarried. Yet, in accordance with the Law of Levirate, he happily and generously took on his responsibility to provide a home and potential of children for Ruth, the widowed daughter-in-law of his relative Naomi.

In those cultures where polygamy was normal every woman needed to have a child – preferably a son – to care for her in her old age. There was no age pension and no Aged Care Facilities. A childless widow or spinster faced a formidable future with no-one to care for her in her old age.

If you want another biblical story to illustrate this acceptance of polygamy then consider the situation of Tamar in Genesis chapter 38.

ACT 1 - AFFIRMATION

Tamar had been married to Er, the oldest son of Judah. But we then read that this man was wicked in the sight of the LORD, so the LORD put him to death. Judah therefore instructed his second-born son to "Lie with your brother's wife and fulfil your duty to her as a brother-in-law." This was all in accordance with that ancient custom known as the Law of Levirate where, in the event that a man died and his widow was still childless it was the responsibility of the dead man's brother, or next nearest kinsman, to father a child on behalf of the dead husband.

This law applied regardless of whether or not the chosen male relative was already married. Matters of inheritance, of maintaining the family name, and the woman's right to be the mother of a legitimately conceived child were all considered to be more important than the number of wives that any man might have.

So Onan knew that any child now conceived by Tamar would not be his but would, in legal terms, be deemed to be the child of his brother Er.[18]

Whether or not Onan complained about his obligation to have sexual intercourse with Tamar we do not know, but he certainly did not want her to conceive a child. So, whenever he lay with Tamar he deliberately "spilled his seed on the ground". There were possessions and property involved and Onan, as the oldest surviving son of Judah, was obviously more interested in maintaining his right to inherit that property than he was in taking care of his brother's widow. If Tamar conceived and bore a child then that would mean less of the inheritance for Onan.

---

18. Deuteronomy 25:5-6. Some people see a conflict between this and the commandment of Leviticus 20:21 which forbids a man to marry (literally "to take") his brother's wife. But the law referred to in Leviticus chapter 20 was quite probably intended to prevent the practice found in some other cultures where a married woman was expected to be available as a sexual companion to not only the man she married but to all of his brothers as well. Alternatively, the law may have referred to the situation of divorce rather than widowhood. This would then account for John the Baptist's rebuke of Herod for having married the divorced wife of his brother Philip while Philip was still alive. (Matt 14:3-4; Mark 6:17; Luke 3:19).

Onan's sin was his own selfishness and greed. He failed to treat Tamar with proper respect. Although he made a show of accepting her as a wife he did not really grant her the privileges to which she was entitled. His failure to adequately meet this responsibility was a serious sin, so the LORD put him to death also.

Note that it was Onan's motive in preventing conception, not the method he used, that was condemned as an act of wickedness.

We need to remember that the obligation to care for relatives, especially widows and orphans – which Onan did not do properly – was very important, even if it involved taking another wife.

Another illustration of the concept of social welfare through the relationship of marriage is given by Sheila Draper in her book *Contact*. This story occurred in Melanesian culture but I have often noticed similarities between Melanesian and Hebrew cultures. Norm and Sheila Draper were some of the first Christian missionaries to arrive in the highlands of Dutch New Guinea - what is now Indonesian Papua - and the people in that part of the world were Melanesian.

Sheila describes how, at a time when she was very busy working on a linguistic problem she received an urgent and non-negotiable request to meet the village/tribal chief at some sort of a ceremony.

She described the feast with interesting detail but towards the end of that event the chief stood to his feet to make a speech.

Sheila continues; "I had little idea of what he said but his gesturing towards me, and the frequent kindly looks cast in my direction by the rest of the women indicated that I was the centre of attention. Wrinkling his nose at the sweet potato garden nearby, and making as if to stuff tubers into Senior Wife's string bag, he gave me to understand that because we had no garden land of our own, and had done no gardening since our arrival, I henceforth had the privilege of digging and planting in his family

ACT 1 - AFFIRMATION

gardens - as his seventh wife!! - so that Norm and I would not go hungry.

This was the Chief's way of showing his duty of care for these foreigners who were now accepted as part of the tribal community.

There was not even a hint of jealousy from the other six wives who escorted her back home "to indicate our solidarity in this new arrangement and we parted with considerable goodwill".[19]

Sheila concluded by adding: "Fortunately there seemed to be no reference to any privileges expected of me in return." And that Chief would have known that Sheila and Norm already had two children of their own.

In presenting all that I have in the previous pages I am just trying to emphasise that different cultures do things differently, and the people of Solomon's time certainly had some ideas and customs that were very different than the ones we accept as normal nowadays.

So, what has all this to do with King Solomon? Although there may have been some domestic disputes in his household this great king was known as the "man of peace". This was because, instead of lording it over his neighbouring nations by the use of military force as his father David had done, Solomon married some prominent woman from these countries. He thus entered into a Covenant of Peace with those nations and their leaders would be in breach of the covenant if they ever went to war against the king who had married one of their princesses.

It is simply a fact of history that Solomon had many wives and concubines, (seven hundred princesses and three hundred concubines). But when he was old these wives turned his heart to follow their gods and his heart was not true to the LORD. (1 Kings 11:3-8)

Having many wives is no reason for envy. Just think of the cost involved in providing housing, food and clothing for 1,000 wives

---
19. Sheila Draper, *Contact*, Global Interaction, Melbourne, 2007 pp 151 – 155

and their children! And that's not to mention the obligation he would have had in having to sometimes provide for their relatives as well!!

However, after having tried to explain all that information about marriage and polygamy being an important part of social welfare rules in many societies, I have to admit that there are some reasons to suggest that this scene in the Songs may not be a royal wedding and the scene may possibly not be in a king's harem.

Some writers tell us that in ancient Hebrew weddings the bride and the groom both wore a crown, so it may have been quite appropriate to refer to the groom as "king". Others claim that it was a Syrian custom to refer to the bridegroom as "king" throughout the week of wedding festivities, and the concept of the lover as king was not uncommon in Egyptian love poetry.[20] (But I still think Solomon's Harem is the most likely scene).

Having expressed her very inviting greeting, the bride now adds an even more specific invitation:

1:4a "Take me away with you — let us hurry!"

Then, as if by explanation for those listening to her story, she adds:

1:4b "The king now takes [or carries] me to his chambers."

The scene then changes as the couple depart. We know this, for the bride has just told us so.

ACT 1, Scene 2 (Song of Songs 1:4b - 2:7)

Now addressing her "king", the bride continues to speak,

> 1:4b We rejoice and delight in you; we will praise your love more than wine. How right they are to adore you! [NIV]

---
20. J F Craghan C SS R, *Commentary on The Song of Songs and The Book of Wisdom* (1979).

ACT 1 - AFFIRMATION

1:4b We will rejoice and share this pleasure together; we will praise your love more than wine. How right they are who adore you! [author paraphrase]

This verse is one of those which translators stumble on. Who does the word "we" refer? Some versions of the bible suggest that this phrase is sung by the chorus of onlookers. But the word "your" is masculine singular, so obviously it is the bridegroom or "king" who is the object of the delight not the couple. It is possible that the bride is saying to her lover something like, "We (you and I together) are going to enjoy ourselves, but you are the reason I will be enjoying this." (Hence my suggested paraphrase).

The word translated *"delight"* (Verse 4 in the NIV Bible or *"be glad"* in some translations) is the Hebrew *giyl*, which literally means to spin around under the influence of some strong emotion, such as intense pleasure or joy. And the word translated *"rejoice"* is the Hebrew *samach* which also refers to a spontaneous emotion of intense pleasure, or an unsustainable feeling of ecstasy that is so overwhelming it must be expressed in some sort of physical movement. And the word *"love"* which she used here is again that intriguing word *dowd*. So this bride is definitely expecting an enjoyable and exciting evening!

When we begin to understand the depth of meaning of some of the words that have been used in the original language of these songs it is almost unbelievable when I hear that there are still people who honestly believe that Christians (who supposedly have their origins in Hebrew theology) should never dance, and should never "let their hair down" and enjoy themselves.

By the same token how can anyone believe that a wife should be expected to merely endure her husband's sexual advances, or that she should never take delight in the mutual enjoyment of their "one flesh" relationship?

However, it is also possible to paraphrase verse 4 to read:

1:4 She: "Can we leave here soon? Be my 'king' and take me to your house (bridal chamber or bedroom), where we will rejoice and make love together.

That will be even better than this champagne (effervescent celebrating ?), for our love will be perfect."

[author paraphrase]

She is still expressing her eager anticipation of an exciting evening, but there is a significant change in the last phrase.

So many couples, at the time of their wedding, are convinced that somehow their marriage is going to be the first perfect marriage ever seen on planet earth. And so their first disagreement seems to come as a shock to them.

Those persons who are involved with pre-marriage instruction usually make a considerable effort to try and explain to the engaged couples that whenever two persons from different family backgrounds begin to live together in the same house there will inevitably be some areas of conflict, and some adjustments will need to be made on the part of both individuals involved. Yet many of these young couples do not really seem to believe the things they are told because they so fondly believe the myth that "Our love will be perfect." We find out later that this couple still had to learn that same lesson.

Misunderstandings are inevitable in any relationship. So don't be discouraged when you finally make that same discovery also. You are not abnormal. You are not a failure. You are merely a human being!

Face the conflict, work through it, and you will begin to learn what it really takes to truly love and understand another person.

As this couple now move towards the bridal chamber (or marriage bed) we are told something of the things they talk about together, and it seems that they spend some time outdoors, probably in a garden of some sort. The woman begins first to express doubts about her own physical appearance.

Apparently she doesn't feel all that beautiful – maybe she

ACT 1 - AFFIRMATION

feels unworthy of his love. She explains that one of the reasons for her self-doubt is her suntan.

Yes, I do know that many fair-skinned Australians do not think that way. To them a suntan is (or was) often considered an asset. But this is not so for many people from dark-skinned races. She complains that she is sun-tanned because her brothers made her take care of the family vineyard. Then she adds, ruefully, "My own vineyard I have neglected." And obviously the reference is to her own physical body.

But notice how cleverly this wonderful man takes his beloved's expressions of self-doubt, re-frames them, turns them around, and passes them back as a lovely compliment.

Remember, the headings of *Lover, Friends,* and *Beloved,* that are given in many translations of the *Songs,* are not part of the original text. So this dialogue is probably better understood if we interpret it as typical Hebrew antiphonal singing, where one party makes a comment and the other party responds. Thus:-

1:5 **She:** "I am dark [as in sun-tanned]".

He: "Yet lovely, and these young maidens would all agree with me."

She: "I am dark, like the tents of the Kedar."

He: Beautiful [implied]... "Like the tent curtains of Solomon" [author's comment in brackets]

The bride here acknowledges that she is not perfect, she has imperfections. But in response to her confession she is not rejected or condemned. Instead she finds she is totally accepted.

There is a spiritual lesson here.

As sinners we cannot enter heaven (paradise) while we are stained by our sinful nature. But we come to our heavenly father and plead forgiveness. What hope have we got? Read the scriptures – 1 John 1:8-9 [NIV]:

"If we claim to be without sin, we deceive ourselves and the truth is not in us. But if we confess our sin he is faithful and just and will forgive us our sin and cleanse us from all unrighteousness."

We accept the salvation offered in Christ, and when we genuinely accept him as Lord and Saviour we are then clothed in the righteousness of Christ and therefore are permitted to enter the paradise of heaven. God does not look on our imperfections – He now sees us clothed in the righteousness of Christ. In a similar way the lover declares that he sees his beloved as though she is "clothed" like the tent curtains of Solomon – unblemished beauty!

This husband is full of compliments for his bride. And we have to admit that genuine, unsolicited compliments are wonderful things. They can give an emotional boost that is possibly better than any tonic. But, sadly, in our Western culture some of us have been taught to be suspicious of compliments because we are not sure of the motive behind the words.

It is a great pity that in the political climate that existed in the latter part of the 20th Century many men felt they were no longer permitted to offer compliments to women, even when the praise was thoroughly justified.

Yet I have met a number of women who, when they began to feel that they could safely talk about their real feelings, admitted that they were almost addicted to words of affirmation, praise and approval.

One very beautiful woman I was talking with after a Dick Innes seminar[21] surprised me with her admission that she had an extremely poor sense of self worth. Yet I would have described her as remarkably beautiful, with not even one wisp of hair out of place. So she explained this to me: "When I was just a little

---

21. ACTS International was founded in 1968 in Australia by Richard (Dick) Innes. The organisation has an office in Adelaide, South Australia. They ran some excellent seminars on subjects such as learning to understand yourself and other people.

girl my mother compared me unfavourably with my sister. That really hurt. It *really* did! Ever since then I have done everything I can to make sure that no-one will ever have cause to compare me unfavourably with another person – not *ever* again! What you see is my attempt to cover that feeling of being 'not-good-enough'."

So it may be with this young bride. When she makes remarks about herself such as, "I am dark, like the tents of Qedar," her words may indicate a similar sense of hurt, or shame, from the way she was treated.

A paraphrase of Songs 1:6 could read:

1:6 "My mother's sons treated me harshly and forced me to take care of the vineyards; My own vineyard I have neglected."

To further paraphrase that statement - she is saying, "I was forced work in the sun all day. I had no time to take proper care of my physical body".

We read a lot these days about people whose self-image has been distorted by shame. The problem is often caused by some form of abuse such as bullying or harsh criticism from peers, or from a dysfunctional family, especially during childhood.

We also have to acknowledge the reality of emotional abuse from people in leadership who, in their misguided zeal, sometimes misuse their position of authority. One significant characteristic of abusive communities of any form is that the leaders are more concerned with "appearance management" than they are with a healthy development of the character and personality of the individuals within their care.

By "appearance management" I mean that the leaders (or parents) are more concerned that the people within their care present an *appearance* of being perfect, rather than being concerned about developing the skills and talents and being in touch with the real hopes and dreams of these people. This can lead to an attitude of very stern discipline, where the victim is shamed into exhibiting the right sort of performance, but within herself (or himself) often feels rejected as a failure.

Of course there are times when we need to make our own children, and sometimes other people, aware of areas where they have failed, but we also need to remember to praise and encourage. So we affirm the person for their worth as a human being, not just for the things they have achieved or for how they perform. Although we must never resort to empty flattery it is possible to offer positive, constructive, helpful criticism, together with words of affirmation, instruction and guidance.

This may seem like a parenting issue, but in the context of lovemaking we need to place even more emphasis on the expressions of affirmation and praise.

But to return to this couple in the *Songs;* the bride now says: 1:7 - 8 [NIV].

> She: "Tell me, you whom I love, where you graze your flock and where you rest your sheep at midday? Why should I be like a veiled woman beside the flocks of your friends?"
>
> He: "If you do not know, most beautiful of women, follow the tracks of the sheep and graze your young goats where there are tents for the shepherds."

She asks a simple question about his normal daily work and he responds with a simple answer. But she makes a reference to being, "A veiled woman" in comparison to his many associates and friends.

A veiled woman could imply that she is not really his wife but is just an unmarried attendant who does not want anyone to recognize her, such as a concubine or even a paid prostitute who is not entitled to know anything about the man's personal interests such as hobbies or business life.

One of the subtle dangers that can undermine a marriage relationship is when we have secrets, or large areas of our individual lives that we keep hidden from our spouse. I recognise that there are some people who, because of the very nature of

ACT 1 - AFFIRMATION

their work, have no option but to do this for security reasons. But there may be other areas of our life that we are reluctant to share with our spouse where this restriction does not apply.

We have all learned from the traumas of childhood that we often need to wear an emotional mask, or a veil over our true feelings. But if we really want to develop a healthy, trusting, and truly intimate relationship then we must learn to gradually remove those emotional masks and find some way to communicate all our hopes, dreams, and ambitions to our partner.

Where a man or woman is prepared to discuss such issues with their workmates or friends, but not with their spouse then they are undermining the very foundations of their relationship. The bride is here making an appeal to her husband for this kind of unashamed and open honesty.

The husband responds by again expressing admiration of his bride. Note that at this stage in their dialogue the comments of approval concentrate more on attributes of character, clothing, and adornments. In chapter four he expresses unashamed admiration of her physical body.

1:9-11[NIV]

> **He:** "I liken you, my darling, to a mare harnessed to one of the chariots of Pharaoh.
>
> Your cheeks are beautiful with earrings, your neck with strings of jewels. We will make you earrings of gold, studded with silver."

This man has used compliments we might not normally hear in our Western culture.

When he says, "I liken you, my darling, to a mare harnessed to one of the chariots of Pharaoh" he is certainly not calling his new bride an old nag!

These people would have understood that his expression refers to a most graceful creature in the prime of life.

Horses in the service of Pharaoh would have been the best available, physically perfect in every way, and in training they were brave, obedient, docile, and disciplined. They could be trusted not to wander off if they saw green paddocks along the side of the road, and they would not be distracted or nervous in a crowd. Horses were also considered to be very graceful in their movement. So the husband is saying that his bride is perfect in every way, and he has confidence in her.

Incidentally, there is obviously some poetic licence involved here, for there are authorities who tell us that Pharaoh would have never used mares to draw his chariot, he would have used stallions. But to liken his new bride to a stallion may not have been seen as a compliment, and the remark is obviously intended as a compliment.

The phrase, "Your cheeks are beautiful with earrings" is translated in the Good News Bible and in the Living Bible as a reference to the bride's hairstyle.

That is a legitimate translation of the Hebrew language, and the words could be paraphrased as, "Your hairstyle enhances the natural beauty of your smile."

The mood (or scene?) seems to suddenly change as the bride makes a strange and rather flowery comment.

1:12 – 1:14 [author's paraphrase]

  She: [In soliloquy] Whenever the king was in my presence my perfume spread its fragrance. My lover is like a sachet of myrrh, he shall lie all night close to my breasts [or "in my heart"]. My lover is to me a cluster of henna blossoms from the vineyards of En Gedi.

The writer of *The Songs* has made frequent mention of spices, herbs, and perfumes, and we do well to remember that these lyrics were first written in a social environment where such things were considered to be very important or significant.

There is great power in our sense of smell, and there is also plenty of mention of fragrance throughout other books of the Bible.

Certain aromas can be exciting or stimulating, while other smells can create an atmosphere that is soothing and relaxing. How many of us can identify with some stirring of the emotions when we sense the aroma of a roast meal cooking on a winter's day, or the smell of rain on hot dry ground?

We probably all understand something of the power of fragrance really, because we recognise that the production and sale of perfumes for women is big business in our Western culture. And many modern books dealing with the subject of lovemaking remind us that we need to learn to use healthy expressions of sensuality and to be truly sensuous all five senses (touch, taste, sight, sound, and smell) need to be stimulated. Although music is not specifically mentioned its very presence is implied in the name *Song of Songs*, and the other four senses are all implied or specifically mentioned.

The herbs the bride has mentioned here might be significant: some people see myrrh as a symbol of the bitter-sweet experiences of love, but the herb has a long history of use as a seductive perfume.

In the story of Esther[22] we read that myrrh was used in the preparation of maidens before they were presented for their one-night-with-the-king. Myrrh is also mentioned with specifically sexual or sensual connotations in Proverbs 7:17.

Greek soldiers used myrrh as a medicine to heal wounds; it was fed to Arabian horses to prevent fatigue; Egyptians used it to rejuvenate their skin; and I have read that the herb has been used in the treatment of both asthma and arthritis.

---

22. Refer to the Bible book of Esther 2:12. See also the book Hadassah: One Night with the King by Tommy Tenney (Pub. Bethany House, Minnesota, 2004). I understand that Hadassah is the Hebrew name and Esther is the Greek version of the name used in the Septuagint.

Myrrh also has religious significance. It was one of the ingredients of a special anointing oil used for the consecration of the most holy utensils in the Tabernacle.[23]

Those who like to study the significance of numbers in Scripture may be interested to know that myrrh is mentioned seven times in the *Song of Songs*. Seven is the number that indicates perfection, so the writer may have deliberately used this 7-fold repetition.

The reference to **henna**[24] is intriguing. We are told that the street vendors of Cairo sang, "Oh odours of Paradise, Oh flowers of henna."[25] The small, intenselyscented flowers of this subtropical bush were used to make the seductive perfume known as cyprinum with which Cleopatra scented the sails of her barge on her journey to meet Mark Anthony.

According to George Ryley Scott, in many ancient Egyptian wedding ceremonies each of the guests who accompanied the groom would carry a sprig of henna blossom. Scott also tells us that, as part of the preliminaries in these weddings, the bride would take a lump of henna paste in her hand and receive contributions from her guests, as each of them would place a coin (usually gold) into the paste which she held in her hand.[26]

The Hebrew word *kopher*, which is translated here as "henna", derives from a root meaning "to cover." In Genesis 6:14 we find this word used in reference to the covering of pitch that Noah used on the ark.[27]

But the word may also be translated as *ransom*,[28] or as *redeem*[29] or even as a *bribe*.[30]

---

23. Exodus 30:23.
24. the word *camphire* is used in the King James Authorized translation.
25. Lesley Bremness, *Fragrant Herbal – Enhancing your life with aromatic herbs* (1998), p156.
26. George Ryley Scott, *Curious Customs of Sex and Marriage (1963)*, p117.
27. Genesis 6:14
28. Exodus 30:12; Num. 35:31-32; Job 33:24; 36:18; Prov.6:35; 13:8; 21:18; Isa 43:3.
29. Exodus 21:30; Psalm 49:7
30. 1Samuel 12:3; Amos 5:12

In 1 Samuel 6:18 the word, in its plural form, is translated as *country villages*[31], meaning sheltered or covered places. So the word has connotations of protection, covering, and redemption.

The word henna also has religious significance.

In biblical terms henna is often used as a symbol of redemption, or covenant relationship, and thus its use is appropriate within the context of a wedding.

In the beautiful story of Ruth, the man Boaz who eventually married Ruth, is referred to by Naomi as their "kinsman-redeemer". It is possible, therefore, that the use of henna in Eastern weddings and its mention here in the songs is linked with some cultural belief system where a woman's redemption, or reason for living, could only be fully realised when she became a wife and mother, and it may also refer to the husband's obligation to provide shelter and protection for his wife.

Their dialogue then continues:

1:15 - 1:17

He: Ah, how beautiful you are, my darling! Oh, how beautiful! Your eyes are doves.

She: How handsome you are, my lover! Oh, how charming! And our bed is verdant.

The beams of our house are cedars; our rafters are firs.

[paraphrased]

The reference to doves might lend itself to interpretation. The dove is often considered to be a symbol of peace, innocence, and purity, and we are also told that the eyes are the window of the soul.

In Songs 5:2 and 6:9 the husband again refers to his wife as a dove. So this may be a reference to her character, and the "king" is saying that his bride appears to be both innocent and honest, a

---

31. 1Samuel 6:18

woman who is at peace with herself, and therefore one in whom he can have confidence.

However, the dove was also used as a symbol for Aphrodite, the Greek goddess of sexual love and beauty, possibly equivalent to the Roman goddess Venus.[32]

According to a comment in The Interpreter's Bible, dove birds are known for their warmth of affection when mating. So when he says "Your eyes are doves" he might be suggesting something like, "My darling, you have a sexy gleam in your eye." But I personally prefer the concept of peaceful innocence, and this is consistent with the use of the name Solomon which, when literally translated means *The Peaceful One*.

We should not be too distressed if we find possible references in these lyrics to fertility cult symbols, even though the songs are included in the canon of Holy writings for both the Jewish and the Christian faiths.

Even now in the twenty-first century the symbols of eggs and rabbits (bunnies) are frequently associated with our Easter weekend, yet they are both cult symbols of fertility and new life. Even the evergreen tree, used as a decoration at Christmas time, has some connection with those ancient cults.

Nevertheless, in spite of those pagan connections I personally know of many Christians who buy Easter eggs for their children and have a decorated tree where they place the presents at Christmas time.

Opinions differ as to who sings the words in these few verses, but I believe the way they have been allocated as shown in the quote above does make sense. Once again we see words of acceptance, adoration, affirmation and praise – good dialogue for a loving couple.

Many interpret from these words that the couple are now outside in a garden setting. From what I have read I have learned that many gardens in the East were walled enclosures designed

---
32. Encyclopaedia Britannica (1968) vol 2 page 98

with paths winding among fruit trees and shade trees, fountains and pools with streams of running water, aromatic herbs and blossoms, and places where one could sit and enjoy the whole effect.[33]

So the couple would be in a private garden, not giving a public display. We know from Songs 8:1 that for a couple to be seen even just kissing in public was not acceptable in this culture. Incidentally, the word translated *rafters* appears in later Hebrew writing where it means *furniture*.

Their love-talk dialogue continues:

2:1 - 2:3 [NIV]

She: I am a rose of Sharon, a lily of the valleys.

He: Like a lily among thorns is my darling among the maidens.

She: Like an apple tree among the trees of the forest is my lover among the young men. I delight to sit in his shade, and his fruit is sweet to my taste.

We see here another example of how this wonderful man takes every opportunity to affirm and encourage his bride. She sang, "I am a rose of Sharon, a lily of the valleys."

Translators and commentary writers seem to be uncertain as to precisely what flower the woman is using to describe herself. Some suggest that she is referring to a flesh-coloured flower that appears by the thousands in the warmer regions of the country. In this case the bride might be describing herself as "very common and ordinary – just another one among thousands."

But I prefer to interpret this as a valid response to the lover's frequent words of affirmation and praise. So her comment should read something like, "You make me feel so blessed, like I am *The Rose of Sharon*".

Her husband-to-be then reinforces his words of praise when

---

[33]. The story of Susanna occurred in a garden setting like this. You can read her story in Chapter 13 of the Book of Daniel in some Catholic editions of the Bible (and in the Septuagint bible).

he describes her as a lily among thorns – you are indeed someone very special.

So she now responds with a compliment for him: "Like an apple tree among the trees of the forest is my lover among the young men. I delight to sit in his shade and his fruit is sweet to my taste."

In many cultures trees like the apple, cedar, cypress and palm are frequently used as symbols of love.[34] In saying that her lover is like an apple tree, the bride is admiring his skill in the art of verbal lovemaking. "Your words are sweet, like the fruit of the apple tree. You are someone special, outstanding – so different than all the rest." What is the difference? What are the words of sweetness? This husband is constantly praising his bride.

When I ran a check on the use of the word "fruit" in old and new testaments I discovered that the word is often used in reference to the predictable results of a person's behaviour, character or speech. A well known example is, of course Galatians 5:22 "The *fruit* of the Spirit is love, joy, peace, patience, kindness, goodness faithfulness gentleness and self-control." But there are others.[35]

So when she sang "I delight to sit in his shade and his fruit is sweet to my taste" the bride was saying how much she enjoys hearing him say such nice things about her.

In this first chapter of the Songs we have been introduced to two lovers who are very good at complimenting each other. In fact they seem to take delight in doing so.

Many studies of human behaviour have shown that at the core of the personality is a need to feel significant, or a need for status. Adler described this as the need for what he called "control", Maslow refers to "belongingness needs" and "esteem needs", Crabb refers to the need for "significance" and Robert McGee

---

34. Joseph Dillow, *Solomon On Sex* (1977) p.31.
35. Prov 12:14; Prov 13:2; Jer 6:19; Jer 17:10; Jer 12:19; Hosea 10:11; Amos 6:12; Micah 7:13; Luke 6:42-45; John15:4-5; Rom 7:4-5; Eph 5:9.

has written an entire book on the subject.[36] But apparently the need is not quite the same in both genders.

As a generalisation men need to know they are respected, and women need to know that they are loved, not for what they have achieved or for what they can do, but simply because they are a human being.

Although we may think and react differently, we all crave affirmation, recognition, and acceptance. Failure to meet these needs in a marriage partner may mean that the individual will then seek to have these needs met in other ways. If the husband does not get the encouragement and support he needs from his wife in this area, and if the wife does not get the genuine expressions of affirmation and love she needs from her husband, then there is a danger that each may try to find other ways to meet this basic need of the personality. When a person seeks to do this from sources outside the marriage, even though they may be unaware they are doing so, then the relationship is heading for trouble.

This does not always mean an illicit affair. Many people, both men and women, who are not getting the necessary security and significance from their primary intimate relationship with another human being (that is, within their marriage relationship), will seek to have this basic need met through involvement with their work, or with sport, or their hobby. The unsatisfied need for significance may even be expressed through a lust for possessions, or for power and the control of the lives of other people, or in some strange attempts to become the centre of attention – sometimes through being involved in a series of promiscuous affairs.

All of these things are significant factors in the breakdown of modern marriages. We must learn to give encouragement and avoid negative criticism at all cost. Remember: intimacy

---

36. Robert S. McGee *The Search For Significance* Word Publishing, 1998. (Even Dr Billy Graham recommended that this book "should be read by every Christian".)

and devotion are enhanced when we express mutual praise and appreciation.

Of course this thirst for significance is part of God's design for the human soul. It should lead us to seek a personal relationship with the LORD, but, as the prophet Jeremiah explained (Jer. 2:13) and as I have just tried to describe, a failure to achieve this can lead to addictions in a vain attempt to find satisfaction in life.

ACT 1 Scene 3

The scene now changes again as the bride sings;

2:4-5 [NIV]

She: [in soliloquy] He has taken me to the banquet hall, and his banner over me is love.

Then, addressing her lover, she makes this request:

"Strengthen me with raisin cakes, refresh me with apples; for I am faint with love". [NIV]

We know that the couple have now moved to the bridal suite or bedroom because the woman, as the story-teller, has just told us so.

The words translated *banquet hall* literally mean "house of wine" or possibly "chamber of effervescence". Although the expression is not found anywhere else in the Bible, it has been recognised as a common Oriental reference to the Bridal Chamber.[37]

There are, or have been, societies, such as some of the ancient tribal traditions in parts of Papua New Guinea, where a marriage was celebrated by sharing a meal together. In a social culture where there was no written language then the idea of a public ceremony where there are witnesses to the couple signing their names on a

---
37. Morris Jastrow Jr., The Song of Songs (Philadelphia: J B Lippincott Co., 1921) p170. Quoted by Joseph Dillow Solomon on Sex (1977) p28.

piece of paper was just not a possibility. Missionaries who have worked in these cultures have told me that the normal practice was for the new bride to prepare a meal and when she and her husband both ate some of the food which she had prepared and ate from the same cooking vessel, then they were considered to be formally married.

In the Old Testament there are 285 occasions where the Hebrew noun *berith* (or *beriyth)* has been translated as *covenant.* An associated verb from the same word root means "to eat with". The Apostle Paul touched on the significance of such sharing a meal together when he wrote, "Because there is one loaf we, although we are many individuals, are in effect one body for we all partake of the same loaf." (1 Cor. 10:17).

Paul saw this sharing a meal together as symbolic of their unity. Marriage is a covenant relationship which is often also referred to as a one flesh relationship.[38] In almost all of history the sexual union of husband and wife has been recognised as the official consummation or confirmation of their marriage relationship.

Thus *the House of Wine, the Banquet Hall* and *the Bridal Chamber* all refer to the place where the marriage covenant is formally consummated.

As the scene moves to the banqueting hall (or marriage bed) we hear the bride singing, "His banner over me is love." A banner often represents an unashamed public declaration of intention, plan or purpose. This man is not warm and affectionate to his wife only when they are alone, and then making critical or sarcastic comments about her when in the company of other men. No way! He is not ashamed to declare to the whole world that he loves his wife, and we know from everything else he says about her that "love" means he is prepared to praise her in public.

However, reference to Septuagint, Old Latin, and Syriac manuscripts indicate that this verse may be better translated as a request from the bride to, "Take (or carry) me to the bedroom

---
38. Genesis. 2:20; Matthew. 19:5-6; Mark 10:8; 1 Corinthians. 6:16; Ephesians. 5:31.

and *look upon me with love.*" And the reason she makes this request is simply that she is so overcome with the excitement of sexual arousal that she believes she may even lose control of her actions. She tells us this as she sings, "Strengthen me with raisin cakes, refresh me with apples; for I am faint (feeling dizzy or light headed) with love."

A little earlier she had described her lover as an apple tree among the trees of the forest, and I explained that when she said, "His fruit is sweet to my taste" she was referring to the sweetness of the words he spoke. So now, as she asks him to carry her to the bedroom and "look upon me with love" she adds a gentle hint that she would like him to keep saying nice things about her. Hence, "Refresh me with apples." Words of affirmation and praise should be a natural part of any legitimate lovemaking.

What are we to make of her request to "strengthen me with raisin cakes"? The prophet Hosea uses the same Hebrew word when he tells us that raisin cakes were used in the fertility rites of Canaanite religions.[39] But some translations interpret the items referred to here as "flagons of wine." This is because the Hebrew word used, in both these instances, has connotations of being pressed together or pressed down. Grapes are pressed to extract the juice from which wine is made. But not only are grapes the source of wine, they are also the fruit from which raisins are made. Add to this the idea of something pressed together and we arrive at the interpretation "raisin cakes".

However, in this context, the reference to things that are pressed together could better be understood as a metaphor for embracing, hugging, and physical togetherness. Remember — this is POETRY.

Then, as though by way of explanation of what is now happening, the bride sings;

---

39. Hosea 3:1

ACT 1 - AFFIRMATION

2:6

She [speaking in soliloquy]

His left hand is under my head, and his right hand embraces me.

Many Hebrew scholars agree that the word translated embrace actually means to "stimulate sexually".[40] A similar phrase is found in the Sumuzin Inanna, a love poem of the second millennium BC, which reads, "Your right hand you have placed on my vulva; your left hand strokes my head."

There may be some significance in telling us which hand does what. In most Eastern countries one never offers a gift with the left hand, it is always and only the right hand that is used for this purpose.

2:7 [speaking to her audience]

She: 'Daughters of Jerusalem, please heed this warning!

Do not stir up passion as powerful as this until it can be safely and appropriately satisfied!" [author paraphrase]

The festivity, the perfumes, the conversation and caressing, have all had the effect of bringing this woman to the point where she is almost out of control with the powerful excitement of sexual arousal.

Aware of the emotions that are now surging through her body and almost taking her out of control she expresses a warning to all young people on the dangers of heavy petting with the words, "Daughters of Jerusalem, I charge you by the gazelles and by the does of the field: Do not ever stir up or awaken passion so powerful as this until it can be appropriately and safely satisfied!"

This interpretation (translation) may come as a new idea to some readers, for the verse is often translated to read, "Do not arouse or stir up the sentiment of love until it is pleased to awaken

---

40. Franz Delitzsch, *Commentary on The Song of Songs and Ecclesiastes* (Grand Rapids: Erdmans) quoted by Joseph Dillow Solomon on Sex (1977) pp27 & 32.

of its own accord," and is thus understood to be a declaration to the effect that true love must always be spontaneous.

But perhaps that idea really applies more to infatuation than to love. In my personal experience of life there are times when true love requires positive action that is not so much spontaneous, but is rather a determined decision of the will. Sometimes love requires sacrificial giving, and there are times when true love demands that we be there although, humanly speaking, we would rather be somewhere else.

The belief that true love and sexual passion must be spontaneous may in fact be one of the reasons why some marriages become dull, dry, and boring. In a magazine article where they talk about an eighty-seven year old couple who still have an enjoyable and active love life,[41] sex therapists Joyce and Clifford Penner point out that the mindset which believes that spontaneity must be an essential ingredient of any passionate sexual experience is often a hindrance to the love life of married couples.

Keeping the sensuous and romantic sparkle alive does require some planning. So I am suggesting that, "Do not arouse the sentiment of love until it is pleased to awaken of its own accord," is neither a wise nor a correct interpretation of this verse.

Other interpretations of this verse have been offered; The Good News Bible interprets this as an appeal to not interrupt the couple during love-making, and Kenneth Taylor in the Living Bible interprets this as an appeal to "not awaken my lover; let him sleep."

However, the word used for "love" in this statement is the Hebrew *ahabah*, the feminine form of the word, so the reference would seem to be to the bride (or to her feelings) rather than to her husband, and the context certainly seems to be one of activity associated with sexual passion.

---

41. Keeping The Spark Alive by Dr. Cliff and Joyce Penner, Marriage magazine July/August 1997 (Vol 27 No 4). Published by International Marriage Encounter, MN 55120, USA.

Therefore, to translate this statement as an appeal to not awaken the lover from sleep does not make sense here. But to assume that the reference is to some overpowering feeling of passion experienced by the bride would seem to be more reasonable.

The last word in the sentence (in the Hebrew text) literally means "to be inclined towards", and by extension could mean to feel happy or content with a particular person or situation. Hence I have chosen to interpret the sentence to mean, "Do not stir up the passion of love *until it is appropriate*," or "... until it can be appropriately, legally and safely satisfied."

Sexual passion can be potent stuff, and too many young (unmarried) couples, unaware of and unprepared to deal with the powerful emotions that can be stirred-up, have started a pregnancy that was never intended. There are thousands of young people who have found to their surprise that if you allow yourself to be in a position where sexual passion is "turned on" then all the best intentions in the world can be wildly swept aside.

When this happens it is too late to try saying "No". As someone once said, "Many people walk on this earth, not because their parents wanted a child, but simply because the parents wanted each other." As parents do we honestly communicate to our own children just how powerful (and dangerous in the wrong context) sexual passion can be?

I remember reading a sad testimony, which had been written by a young woman who learned the hard way, and who learned too late. At the age of eighteen she and two of her friends had reason to celebrate, and they chose to go to a night-club to "party." Their plan was to find three likely-looking young men and, by using their own feminine charm, persuade these fellows to pay for any drinks the girls wanted. This all worked out as planned, and they enjoyed their evening, but when the hour became "late" her partner suggested that she come back to his hotel room with him. She agreed to this, her intention being that she would "play along with him" only to a point, and then suggest that he take a shower. Her plan was that while this fellow was under the shower she would grab his remaining money and quietly leave the room never to be seen by him again. But she had failed to understand some important things.

She had underestimated the seductive power of words, especially when persuasive words are associated with certain forms of touching, and she had not yet recognised the almost irresistible power of sexual passion.

As she confessed in her story, by the time that man was under the shower the last thing she wanted to do was leave that room, and the next twenty-four hours were an almost unbelievable experience of previously unknown ecstasy as she and her new "friend" experimented with every sexual activity they could think of.

When she finally did leave to return to her own home he gave her an address and a phone number. Both of these turned out to be false, and she has never seen the man again. She was a virgin before she met this fellow and had intended to stay that way until she was certain she had met the man who would be her husband. She has had no sexual contact with anyone since, but at the time of telling her story she was in a hospital dying of HIV-AIDS. Somebody had failed — badly. But in our experience many parents would be guilty of the same negligence in failing to teach their children just how powerful sexual passion can be.

We must acknowledge that we have been designed and created as emotional and sexual beings, and these two factors are very closely related. As emotional beings we need affirmation and encouragement. We can also be inspired by a sense of adventure. But, sadly, the very techniques that may be used in a positive way to affirm, to inspire, to encourage and to build us up can also be abused, and used to manipulate and put us in a position where we may be exploited.

Gentle words of praise are sweet to our ears, and an appeal to our sense of adventure can inspire us to attempt great and worthwhile things. But such talk can also put us totally off guard, and when used with gentle persuasive touch then sexual passion may be easily ignited. Within the appropriate boundary of marriage such passion may be delightful, but outside this boundary such passion can be dangerous. This is why the bride warns her friends, "Do not stir up passion so powerful as this until it can be completely satisfied in an appropriate time, place, and manner."

Never underestimate the power of words of encouragement and praise, and never underestimate the power of physical touch, for both can be a potent means of communication. For a newborn baby touch is possibly the only form of communication they understand.

The mother who can learn to breast-feed her infant, allowing the child to enjoy a totally unashamed sensation of skin-to-skin contact, communicates to her child a sense of love, security, and acceptance that can never be expressed in words.

Our bodies respond almost instinctively to touch, whether in fear when there is inappropriate touch, or in love with touching that is affirming and appropriate. The nerve endings in our skin can excite us with such a wonderful range of sensations, from the lightness of a feather, or the sensuousness of a gentle breeze, to the warmth of another's hand. Yet it is not just temperature and pressure, for sometimes with physical touching we can recognise that a form of emotional and/or spiritual "power" is being communicated.

Hence the feeling of being skin to skin with someone we love and trust can be one of the most intensely enjoyable sensations we ever experience in the physical world. It is for this reason that many marriage therapists nowadays are recommending that married couples experiment with sleeping together naked. Just to feel the soft warmth of the skin of your partner's body against your own, even when lying back to back, can be very affirming and bring a lovely sense of security. But, for the same reasons, we need to be aware that there are people in this world who will abuse and misuse the power of touch in an inappropriate way, merely to seduce and make use of another person purely for their own satisfaction.

Of course our sense of touch is closely linked to the natural sex drive. We were designed this way, so we need to keep a healthy balance. On the one hand we must not over-react and refuse to touch, for to do so would be to deny a wonderful and powerful God-given means of communication. But we do need to recognise that the combination of touching and sexuality can be abused. The problem is not that we are created as sexual beings.

The problem is not that we are created with a need to be touched.

The problem is with the *motive* of the one who initiates the touching.

Whilst we may rightly condemn the individual who deliberately misuses the seductive power of touch to exploit and manipulate another person for his or her own pleasure, we need to also recognise the powerful dynamic of human emotions, especially in the area of our sexuality. We must acknowledge and understand that many normally conservative unmarried couples, who genuinely respect each other, can easily get carried away. The heat of sexual passion, once ignited, can drive them into activities they had never planned, and for which they have taken no precautions.

In a magazine article entitled *Isn't Sex Supposed to be Fun?* sex therapists Cliff and Joyce Penner[42] explain how a lot of sexual problems in marriage originate because of a contradiction on the part of the couple between their professed beliefs and their actual experience of dating behaviour.

---

42. Cliff and Joyce Penner, Marriage Partnership magazine, Spring 1991. Published by Christianity Today, 465 Gundersen Dve., Carol Stream, Ill 60188 USA.

ACT 1 - AFFIRMATION

As a result many couples come into marriage with tremendous negative feelings of guilt, failure, and confusion regarding their own integrity and their right to enjoy sensual and/or sexual pleasure.

This was demonstrated at one pre-marriage class where Cliff and Joyce Penner were the main teacher couple. A confidential survey involving all the participating couples indicated that all but two of these couples already did have some sexual experience, yet all of them had intended to save themselves for their wedding night.

What was happening was that all of these couples were having what the Penners gently described as "accidents". That is, they were getting sexually involved, but not intentionally. They never planned to have intercourse before the wedding night, and yet they were spending time alone together, such as in one another's apartment. They were thus placing themselves in a position where they were very vulnerable to temptation, and yet were expressing surprise when they found themselves swept away with passion.

Of course, because they had no plans to be sexually active these couples were not taking any precautions against unplanned pregnancies. And yet some of them were having "accidents" as often as twice a week!! Somehow they never seemed to understand the need to avoid spending too much time with just the two of them alone together.

As the Penners point out; after their wedding these couples will still need to learn how to make-love. Even though they have some sexual experience they have not developed the right attitudes.

They will still need to learn to simply give and receive pleasure without any sense of guilt and inhibiting shame. They may still need to learn to unashamedly enjoy naked skin-to-skin contact, simply touching and enjoying the sensation of sharing this together, without the conflict of those old feelings of guilt.

They will still need to learn to invite God into their experience of delight as they enjoy pleasure in the way it was designed to be.

When couples fail to do this they run the risk of not developing a healthy acceptance of their own sexuality, and are then unable to discuss the subject in a positive way. As a result they may never develop a truly satisfying sex life together.

For these people much of their physical expression of love continues to be tainted with feelings of embarrassment and shame, and as a result they cannot talk comfortably together about their own sexual feelings, let alone discuss the subject with their own children. The problem is further compounded when these same children become sexually active during their teenage years simply in an effort to learn about matters that should have been explained to them by their parents. As one unmarried fifteen-year-old mother, who was also the daughter of a teenage mother, said, "My mum is the kind of person who, if you mention sex, she turns red and clams up."

Hearken to the bride's warning and do not stir-up such passion until it can be appropriately satisfied. Our sex drive can be like a wild brumby horse. Left to run wild and undisciplined it can cause a lot of damage, but when it is properly restrained and disciplined it can, like a great race-horse, become a wonderful, powerful, and useful companion, driving us to achieve great things.

ACT 2 ANTICIPATION

Song of Songs 2:8 to 3:5

8 Listen! My lover! Look! Here he comes, leaping across the mountains, bounding over the hills.
9 My lover is like a gazelle or a young stag. Look! There he stands behind our wall, gazing through the windows, peering through the lattice.
10 My lover spoke and said to me, "Arise, my darling, my beautiful one, and come with me.
11 See! The winter is past; the rains are over and gone.
12 Flowers appear on the earth; the season of singing has come, the cooing of doves is heard in our land.
13 The fig tree forms its early fruit; the blossoming vines spread their fragrance. Arise, come, my darling; my beautiful one, come with me."
14 My dove in the clefts of the rock, in the hiding places on the mountainside, show me your face, let me hear your voice; for your voice is sweet, and your face is lovely.
15 Catch for us the foxes, the little foxes that ruin the vineyards, our vineyards that are in bloom.
16 My lover is mine and I am his; he browses among the lilies.
17 Until the day breaks and the shadows flee, turn, my lover, and be like a gazelle or like a young stag on the rugged hills.
3:1 All night long on my bed I looked for the one my heart loves; I looked for him but did not find him.
2 I will get up now and go about the city, through its streets and squares; I will search for the one my heart loves. So I looked for him but did not find him.
3 The watchmen found me as they made their rounds in the city. "Have you seen the one my heart loves?"
4 Scarcely had I passed them when I found the one my heart loves. I held him and would not let him go till I had brought him to my mother's house, to the room of the one who conceived me.   [NIV]
5 She: Daughters of Jerusalem, please heed this warning! Do not stir up passion as powerful as this until it can be safely and appropriately satisfied!" [author paraphrase]

ACT 2

ANTICIPATION

Main theme(s): Springtime, Playfulness.

ACT 2 (2:8-3:5)

Organising the wedding day is one thing. At least many of us had help in getting certain details for the day sorted out and finalised. But what about the wedding night? Who do you ask about this one? Many young brides (and bride-grooms) face this event with some nervousness, and possibly embarrassment. I know my wife wondered who she could ask about the simple procedure of getting undressed in front of her new husband for the first time. But even that question was a difficult one to ask. So she chose a fairly straight-laced aunt whom she believed would not talk about sexual issues and might therefore give the answer she really wanted, and deviously asked, "What happens on the wedding night?" Unfortunately, in response to this question, she was merely referred to another aunt who was more approachable on such matters. So she was still in a quandary, until one of her married friends told her, "I just changed in the bathroom, and came back in my nightwear."

ACT 2 - ANTICIPATION

If we were expecting "fireworks" on our wedding night, then I would only be honest to admit that someone must have dropped them in the water before we tried to light the fuse.

I had no sympathetic and understanding mentor to tell me the things I needed to know. Oh, sure I had read a couple of books, including Kinsey's great volume on *Sexual Behaviour Within the Human Female*, but that was just statistics. It was not a how-to-do-it book. Rather it was just an embarrassing exposure of how sexually active and promiscuous some outwardly prudish people had been in real life. And anyway, although I didn't know it at the time, I needed ideas that Kinsey never even mentioned.

In those days good books about sex within marriage were hard to find. But I had also read Dr David Mace's book *Whom God Hath Joined* and as a result thought that I knew everything I needed to know. How wrong I was! As the weeks grew into months, and then years, I began to discover that I knew nothing – nothing that I really needed to know. Kinsey's book talked about the "average female". But there is no such thing as an "average" person in real life. We are, all of us, a unique individual. The only way that Rose and I could learn to give each other real happiness and pleasure was to talk together. And that meant talking honestly and frankly, without shame or embarrassment about our expectations and about the sort of things we enjoyed. But we had never been taught such skills, nor had we ever seen a role-model of how such things should be discussed.

How does one communicate when both parties are nervous and embarrassed? Well, at least this is an area that has finally been addressed by some writers. In our present era most realistic marriage manuals, or pre-marriage teaching sessions, warn the potential honeymooners to prepare themselves with a sense of humour. You cannot afford to take a wedding night too seriously or you may be disappointed. The nervousness, embarrassment and ignorance of couples in the past has produced many stories, some humorous, some tragic.

When we are faced with any situation where there are feelings of embarrassment we can react in a number of different ways. We may become serious, with the danger that we blame the other person involved for causing the embarrassment, or we may resort to self-criticism, or it may be possible to introduce some element of humour and deal with the situation by not taking things too seriously provided that this is not going to be seen as insensitive or irreverent. A bit of laughter or playfulness can lighten the mood to one of comedy. An otherwise embarrassing incident may then even become the subject of humorous anecdotes in later years.

A healthy playful attitude can also enhance our sense of adventure in dealing with what may be a totally new experience for us, and it gives us a better opportunity to turn the event into a creative time of fun together.

Now, it is one thing to read this sort of advice in a book, but it is another matter again to try and put such ideas into practice in our own life. We keep tripping over our own feelings of awkwardness in a new situation. Most other skills in life we learn by watching, as Dr Comfort has pointed out in his book *More Joy of Sex*.[43]

But in our society today many people would consider such an invasion of privacy with respect to the wedding night to be indecent – although I should point out that this passion for privacy may be a problem of our own making and has not always been the norm in all societies.

Richard Friedenthal[44] recorded the wedding of Martin Luther by explaining how "On the evening of 13th June 1525, according to the custom of the day, [Luther] appeared with his bride before a number of his friends as witnesses. The Pomeranian [Johann] Bugenhagen blessed the couple, who consummated the marriage

---

43. Dr. Alex Comfort, More Joy of Sex (1986), p95 and p168.
44. Richard Friedenthal, *Luther: His Life and Times*, trans. John Nowell (New York: Brace Jovanovich, 1970), p.438. Quoted in Ruth A. Tucker and Walter Liefeld, in *Daughters of the Church* (Grand Rapids: Zondervan Publishing House, 1987), p.180.

ACT 2 - ANTICIPATION

in front of witnesses. [Justus] Jonas reported the next day: 'Luther has taken Katherine von Bora to wife. I was present yesterday and observed the couple on their marriage bed'."

And I have read elsewhere that, at least up until the 18th Century, French court attendants were required to witness the consummation of a royal marriage. Having witnesses to this significant and sacred act in a society where many people were illiterate was every bit as important as it is nowadays to have witnesses to the signing of the Register.

On the 26th day of August 1768 Captain James Cook left England for the South Pacific to observe the passage of the planet Venus across the face of the sun. However, in his journal he also recorded "an observation of Venus of a different kind". Along with a crowd of South-Sea Islanders, he was witness to a young couple's first act of sexual intercourse.

Three senior women from the tribe had been appointed to give the girl instruction if necessary but, the remarkable sea captain noted, she did not seem to be in need of any instruction.

Perhaps, as Anglo-Saxons, we have been very arrogant in assuming that if things are not done in the way that our society considers normal then it must be wrong.

However, in real terms for us, we have to acknowledge that it is far easier to read about some other couple's experience of "game-playing", and then use this as a role-model to build and develop our own ideas.

Unfortunately the stuff we get in films and TV programs these days is often worse than useless, but let's take a look at how this young couple cope with their wedding night in a rather delightful way.

As the scene opens we hear the bride singing as she realises that some significant "barriers" have at last been removed, and she and her husband are now permitted to give full and unashamed expression to their one-flesh relationship. They express their feelings with delight, and talk (or sing) of the joys associated with springtime, and its potential for new life. The "winter" of their separation is now past.

2:8-9 She: [speaking in soliloquy]

> Listen; I hear the voice of my beloved. See how he comes to me, like a playful gazelle or a young stag, leaping across the mountains, skipping across the hills.
>
> There he stands behind the wall, peeping through the window, and with a twinkle in his eye he now gazes through the netting. And now he begins to speak to me, and just listen to what he says! [Author paraphrase]

The bride's song presents a delightful word picture. She describes how her husband is just as excited as she is, but he shows his feelings with nervous action. In this regard she likens him to a young stag leaping over the mountains. Meanwhile she herself experiences an almost trance-like state of bliss, as she anticipates the expected act of consummation.

The reference to a wall may have some connection to Songs 8:9-10 where the wall refers to an invisible barrier, indicating personal discipline and chastity. In Isaiah 5:5, although the context is somewhat different, the wall both protects and separates. But this separation is about to be ended. The wall is no longer a solid wall, it is now represented as a window and then as a lattice. The repetition of the statement using a slightly different idiom in the repetition, as she has done here, is typical of Hebrew poetry.

Actually the word translated as "lattice" is more correctly translated "netting" and, since I have spent some time living in the tropics where we slept under mosquito nets, I assume that the reference is to a mosquito net which surrounds their bed. There is a wonderful sense of fun and games suggested here, and one can imagine the guy playing some kind of a game of "peek-a-boo" as he looks through the netting at his bride.

ACT 2 - ANTICIPATION

This couple have used a light-hearted sense of humour to overcome any possible embarrassment there may otherwise have been. The gazelle is recognised for its form and beauty, and *young stag* is an appropriate simile for youthful vigour. The whole expression suggests playfulness and virility. Incidentally, the idea of "now I'm coming to find you" is also a characteristic of ancient Egyptian love poetry. The bride then concludes her introduction to this scene by drawing attention to what her lover is saying to her:

2:10-15 He [speaking to his bride}

> Rise up, my love, my beautiful one and come with me. For us, it is like the end of winter and the beginning of spring. The birds are singing and so should we. New life is everywhere. Look at all the blossoms and see how the hibernating creatures stir themselves from the earth. The perfume of spring flowers is everywhere. The fig tree has signs of early fruit, the vines are in bloom and it all smells good.
>
> Oh my dove, my precious one, let me explore those hidden places, let me see the beauty of your body.
>
> Let me look at you. Let me hear your voice, for your voice is music to my ears, and you are so lovely to look upon.
>
> We must not allow those little foxes of fear and inhibition to sneak in and spoil things when our love is only just beginning to bloom. [Author paraphrase]

With gentle poetic language the lover encourages and affirms his bride. It is a pity that our culture does not role model this sort of lovemaking more often. He offers an invitation with the words, "Rise up my darling, come with me." A similar invitation is given again in 4:8 and 7:11.

The invitation is always in the context of lovemaking, and always follows on from some expression of praise of the beloved's beauty.

The "winter" of their separation is now ended and, with his gentle persuasion, the bridegroom describes how the first signs of spring are beginning to appear. "Flowers appear on the earth; the season of singing has come, the cooing of doves is heard in our land."

The word *singing* which he uses here is a specific technical word referring to ritual songs, especially those associated with the Hebrew festivals of Succoth and Matzoth – autumn and springtime. This couple are about to consummate a precious covenant-relationship which has spiritual and religious significance, and it may be significant that he has used a special word here.

However, these songs are full of double entendre – expressions of double meaning – words that have both religious as well as sexual innuendo. So the lover-bridegroom could quite conceivably be using poetic language to also describe some of the changes that are occurring within the body of his bride as the normal result of sexual arousal.

He then continues; "My dove in the cleft of the rock, in the hiding places on the mountainside, show me your face, let me hear your voice; for your voice is sweet, and your face is lovely." [NRSV]

Many interpreters see this as simply another example of the hide-and-seek theme of Egyptian love poetry, but it could also quite definitely be understood as the groom's request, or words of encouragement, when the bride hesitates because she still feels shy and uncertain. So the dialogue can be understood as comments made by the groom (lover) as he seeks permission to touch and caress her entire body, as in my paraphrase: "Oh my dove, my precious one, let me explore those hidden places. Let me see the beauty of your body."

Many English translations of these verses mention "The cleft in the rock", as with the NIV, "*My dove in the clefts of the rock, in*

ACT 2 - ANTICIPATION

the hiding places on the mountainside, show me your face and let me hear your voice."

The cleft means what it says – an opening. The rock can mean a strong-hold, or the word can mean a place that is not normally visible or easily accessible. *Hiding places* or secret places can refer to something that is covered. *Mountainside* means "an inaccessible place". *Let me see your face* can be translated as, "Let me look at you (ie: at your body)". The word translated *face* can also refer to a beautiful shape or a pleasing scene.

So we can interpret this as the lover asking permission to look, to touch, and to explore those areas of her body which have previously been forbidden to him. He then asks, "Let me hear your voice; for your voice is sweet." In other words, "Speak to me darling. Are you still awake? I do love it when you murmur sounds of pleasure and approval."

It is uncertain who sings the next line, "Catch for us the little foxes that spoil the vine." Some translations attribute this to the bridegroom, some to the bride. The "little foxes" are proverbial symbols of destroyers – as in Nehemiah 4:3 and Ezekiel 13:4. These little creatures would slip into the vineyard at night-time and chew at the base of the vines, thus ring-barking and effectively destroying the vines.

So it may be in a love relationship. The niggly little things, if left unresolved, can eventually undermine and destroy the relationship.

For intimacy to grow we must have good communication. He has asked to hear her voice, and she obliges;

2:16-17 [in soliloquy]

> She : My beloved is mine and I am his. He is browsing among the lilies.

Then, addressing her beloved, she says,

> Until the dawn comes and the shadows flee away, come to me, my beloved, and be like a gazelle or a young stag on the

'mountain of spices' [or 'mound of bether']."
[Author paraphrase]

The bride first addresses some remarks to her (imaginary?) audience with the words, "My beloved is mine, and I am his." In so doing she reaffirms her understanding that for sexual intimacy to be truly beautiful it requires the mutual commitment of both parties to the relationship.

Then, as a means of explaining what is now happening, she tells us that her lover is *browsing among the lilies*.

In Songs 5:13 the word lilies is used to describe the lips of the lover, and many interpreters believe it is very likely that the reference here is to some pink or red flower, such as the lotus.

The term *lotus* may refer to any one of several different plants, but especially to a species of flower known as *Nymphaea Lotus* that are native to Southeast Asia and West tropical regions of Africa.

The word *Nymphae minora* (Latin for smaller lips) refers to the inner lips at the entrance to the vagina of the human female. So this probably gives us a significant clue as to where the lover is "browsing".

The phrase "He browses among the lilies" is obviously a reference to the lover's stimulation of the sexual parts of her physical body (*pubic mound, pudenda,* or *mound of venus*) and she is certainly enjoying whatever it is they are doing. So she now offers a very explicit invitation with the words, "Until the day breaks, turn, my lover, and (let us) be active like a gazelle or a young stag on the mound (mountain) of Bether."

"Bether" is simply a transliteration of the word used in the Hebrew text, and the word derives from a root meaning "to cut, separate, or divide", or "to thrust through". In the present context *separation* could imply "vulva", being either that part of the body where it separates into two legs, or, more explicitly, that part where the labia separate to enable entrance into the vagina.

ACT 2 - ANTICIPATION

The mountain [mound] of bether would thus be a reference by the bride to her own pubic mound. The young stag and the gazelle are suggestive of the playful enthusiasm of youth. And then again the reference to a gazelle on the hills might be seen as a poetic description of the spinal and/or pelvic movements of a couple during coition.

The smooth flowing movement of young stag bounding around on the mountains could be a beautifully poetic description of the spinal movement of a human couple in the act of coition.

So her request, "turn, my lover, and (let us) be like a gazelle or a young stag on the mound of Bether", is fairly obviously a specific invitation to her husband to now complete their love-play with full sexual connection.

The mountain of myrrh, the hill of incense, and the *spice-laden mountain(s)* mentioned in The Songs are all expressions used in reference to the woman's Mound of Venus (pubic mound).

Kenneth Taylor, in *The Living Bible*, has implied a definite connection of thought between the mountain of bether and the mountain of myrrh by translating this phrase in 2:17 as the *mountain of spices.* Some other authorities translate this phrase (in 2:17) as *the mound of the cleft* (as with the NRSV), and the thesaurus offers words such as opening, cleavage, fissure or crevice, as alternatives for cleft.

The root word from which *Bether* is derived is/was also used in the descriptions of various ceremonies where a covenant was established between God and mankind. In Genesis 15:10 we read that Abraham was told to take certain animals, cut them in two down the middle, and then separate the two halves. The prophet Jeremiah also uses the same word in reference to a similar ceremony associated with a covenant relationship, and Jeremiah specifically adds that the men involved were to "pass between the two separated halves" (Refer Jer. 34:18-19). The word *Bether,* therefore, does have connections with the formal establishment of a covenant relationship, and the Jerusalem Bible translates the phrase (in 2:17) as *the mound* [or mountain] *of the covenant*.

The acts of separating and passing through (or passing between) were obviously important features of the covenant ceremonies we read about in the Old Testament. So also, the act of sexual intercourse, where the penis of the man separates and passes between the labia of the woman is not just a biological act necessary for reproduction: it is an expression of a most sacred covenant relationship. Throughout the Bible, and all Hebrew teaching, marriage is considered to be a covenant relationship and, like all covenants, the survival of the contract is dependant on the integrity, trustworthiness and faithfulness of the persons involved.

In many societies the covenant of marriage between a man and a woman is celebrated [or consummated] with sexual intercourse, so the phrase *mountain [mound] of the covenant* does convey significant symbolism.

One important feature in God's design of human beings is that the virgin female has been designed with a thin membrane (hymen) across the entrance to her vagina. The tearing of the hymen has traditionally been as a result of the woman's first experience of sexual intercourse, although nowadays, with such an active or athletic lifestyle, many young women have torn the hymen before this event.

The symbolism of this can be likened to the tearing of the curtain in the temple as described in the *Gospel According to Matthew*[45]. The significance of the torn curtain in the Temple is that mankind has now been granted access into the Holy of Holies, into the most intimate, personal, covenant relationship with God.

In this regard consider the similarities to this explanation of the new covenant as found in the *Letter to the Hebrews*:

---

45. Matthew 27:51

ACT 2 - ANTICIPATION

> Therefore, since we have confidence to enter the Most Holy Place .... by the way opened to us through the curtain ... let us draw near with a sincere heart in full assurance of faith . ... and let us consider how to stir-up one another to love and good works, not neglecting to meet together, as is the habit of some, but encouraging one another.
>
> Hebrews 10:19-25 [author paraphrase]

The permission to enter into the Holy of Holies which the writer has referred to in the letter to the Hebrews and the act of sexual intercourse between a wife and her husband are both related to the ratification of a covenant relationship. The covenant is formally validated by the act of going "beyond the curtain" and entering into the most holy place.

However, as any Hebrew mind would have clearly understood, the one who enters must first have permission and legal authority to do so because unlawful entry, in either case, would incur severe condemnation and possibly even the penalty of death. So there is good reason to believe that the words which the writer of the Songs has used for this fairly explicit invitation have been carefully chosen, and in this way she has indicated her understanding that sexual intercourse is not just an intensely pleasurable activity, it is also a sacred celebration of a special relationship.

In his book entitled *Manhood*, Steve Biddulph[46] suggests that, although we may justifiably object to pornography, we actually do need some form of wholesome erotica. We need some way to convey to our children what may be going on inside the hearts and minds of two people who are contemplating marriage.

Sex education in its present form, in most schools, merely teaches the plumbing and geography of the human body, together with some of the basic facts about venereal diseases and, in some cases, the gymnastics and various possible positions that may be used for sexual intercourse.

---
46. Steve Buddulph *Manhood* (1995), p 64 ff.

Available evidence indicates that this approach only encourages experimentation but does not deal with the real issues involved in a relationship of genuine love. This is nothing like an adequate sex education.

Even the controversial Dr. Alex Comfort admits that, "In one respect we now realise that the moralists were right, in scope if not in approach, and that sex cannot be taught to children apart from an awareness of human relationships." [47] He then adds this significant comment: "There is no field in which information is more avidly sought. ... [But] to go beyond the mechanical ... involves us in ... counselling." Unfortunately, the sad reality is that talking about the emotional aspects of a sexual relationship is an all but impossible task for many people (including parents) who, for any reason, have feelings of guilt or shame about their own sexuality.

Many other writers have also acknowledged that, while teaching simple facts about "the birds and the bees" may be adequate for young children, this is grossly inadequate when trying to talk with teenagers or young adults about the subject of human sexuality. And yet it seems that for many people in the mid-to-late twentieth century the "birds and bees" sort of teaching was the limit of any sex and relationships education that they were ever given, if any. So it is no wonder that we have produced a culture that seems to understand sex as a rather crude, degrading, animal-like behaviour.

Steve Biddulph admits that proper "love education" is really a lot more challenging. As he says, we need some way to convey to our children what is really going on inside the minds of two people in love. But where do we find acceptable resources for this sort of sex education in our present-day English-speaking Western culture?

Dr Alex Comfort may have attempted to meet this need with his *Joy of Sex* books although he claims that he originally wrote

---

47. Dr. Alex Comfort The Anxiety Makers (1968), p22.

the first of those books for his medical students as they seemed to be so appallingly ignorant about problems associated with human sexual activity. So his books are not really designed for use as sex education material and certainly not for teenagers.

But I have read that his more recent editions of The Joy of Sex he does focus a lot more on the need to develop a good emotional relationship in order for a married couple to enjoy a mutually pleasurable sex life.

As I have already stated, I believe it might be possible that the *Song of Songs* was originally written in order to provide a resource that could be used to meet this need for sex and relationships education.

See how this woman tries to describe her thoughts and feelings as she anticipates the celebration of the sexual part of her marriage. Now almost in a swoon from sheer excitement she tells us how she so often dreamed about this night. Thus, returning to her soliloquy, she continues:

3:1-4

> **She:** As I lay on my bed night after night I dreamed of the one I love; In my dreams I was looking for him, but could never find him.
>
> I went wandering through the city. Through its streets and alleys I looked for the one I love. I looked but could not find him.
>
> The watchmen patrolling the city confronted me. I asked them, "Have you seen my lover?" As soon as I had left them I found him. I held him and would not let him go until I had brought him to my mother's house, and into the room where I was conceived.   [Author paraphrase]

In her song the woman is telling us about a recurring dream that she experienced as she looked forward to this moment. Perhaps a more dramatic paraphrase of her words could read,

"This is what I dreamed of for so long. How many nights have I dreamed of being in bed with my lover. How I longed for him. But of course he was never there. I even dreamed of wandering the streets looking for him."

Like many modern brides she was probably counting the sleeps as she looked forward to this night of celebration.

It may be significant that the two verbs "to seek" and "to find" both occur four times in these four verses, and the phrase *the one my heart loves* (or *my lover*) also occurs four times in these four verses.

Those who are interested in the study of the significance of numbers, as used in the Bible tell us that the number four is symbolic of creation, or of this physical world in which we live. So the original writer may have deliberately used this fourfold repetition to emphasise her reference to the new creation of springtime. Be that as it may, we are obviously meant to understand just how much this bride adores her husband and how much she has been looking forward to this celebration.

Who are these "watchmen of the city" who confront this woman and sometimes treat her rather unkindly? Later she complains that these men actually beat her and left her feeling naked, bruised, and ashamed (Songs 5:7). Is she referring to those self-appointed guardians of public morality who, in the eyes of many people, are often seen as kill-joys who make us feel guilty about even thinking of such things as sensual pleasure?

Such people exist in our society today. They were very much in evidence at the time of Christ and for several centuries prior to that time. So it would seem safe to assume that they existed during the time of King Solomon.

Or is this woman referring to some struggle she has with feelings of shame. This could possibly be the result of the way she was treated as a child. Those of us who have had the privilege of living and working in different countries and different cultures will be aware that attitudes and behaviour can vary significantly from one culture to another and even from one family to another. What is accepted as normal in one group may be treated as shocking or shameful in another.

According to our history books there have at times been some extremely outspoken ascetic leaders who seem to have considered it sinful to even enjoy the normal sensual pleasures of being human and alive on planet earth. But we have been created with our five senses, and surely our creator God intended us to *use* and appreciate these. (And I did say to *use*, I did *not* say "abuse"). Most of us are born with the sense of sight, and we have the right to enjoy the aesthetic beauty of the natural scenery in God's creation, with all its harmony of colour, shape, and movement. We have been given a sense of hearing, and many of us enjoy beautiful music with its harmony of rhythm and tone. We have also been created with our senses of taste and smell. Because of this we can enjoy good food (or identify when the food has gone bad), and our sense of taste also enhances the feeling of refreshment when we take a cool drink if we are hot and thirsty. And of course we have been created with a sense of touch, and there is an innate need in all humans to not only feel totally accepted, but also (in appropriate circumstances) to enjoy the pleasures of simply being touched, held, and hugged.

So do these watchmen, who suddenly appear in her dreams, represent some distorted expression of conscience within a woman who has been made to feel ashamed that she is feminine, and that she has a longing to be held, to be hugged and cherished by someone in a relationship of mutual love, trust, security, and passion?

If this is the case then these watchmen made the woman feel embarrassed about the subject of her dreaming. Some of us could identify with a reaction such as this: "I am just a working girl – and an imperfect one at that – what right have I got to be dreaming about my wedding night? C'mon girl; there's another day of *work* tomorrow! Get to sleep."

The bride has already indicated that she has problems with low self esteem and feelings of shame for at one stage she said to her lover, "Don't look down on me because of my suntan. My brothers treated me harshly and made me responsible for the care of the vineyard. I had no time to care for myself."(1:6).

By contrast, we are happy to note, her husband and the group of supportive friends all offer her loving encouragement, convince her of her worth and beauty as a person, and reassure her that her longing-for-love is perfectly acceptable.

Yet it seems that even now she is confused between those past dreams and present reality. She has told us how, in her dreams, she pleaded with those watchmen of the city to allow her to be with her beloved, but then suddenly she realises that he is here and this is no longer just a dream.

She reaches out, touches warm flesh and joyfully sings, "I held him and would not let him go." She finds this exciting! And, as the thrill surges through her body, this scene closes as she again gives voice to her heart-felt warning, which seems to be a significant theme of *The Songs*, "Young People of Jerusalem, whatever you do, don't play with fire! Do not stir up passion like this until it can be properly satisfied!" (3:5). This warning appears three times in the Songs (2:7; 3:5 and 8:4). I am inclined to believe that *The Song of Songs* was originally written with the intention of being a form of sex and relationships education, and, as I have already indicated in comments at the end of Act 1 this warning is possibly the most significant message the writer wanted to convey, not just to the young women (or daughters) of Jerusalem but to all teenagers for years to come.

Something to Think About

One of the most powerful motivators that affect the choices we make in life is the belief that life should be worth living – we desire a reason for living, or "something, or someone, to live for".

ACT 2 - ANTICIPATION

This of course is one of the reasons why we can find so many parallels between the relationship of the two lovers in this story and the spiritual relationship that should exist between God and His people. We have been designed for relationship.

Thus the writer of these songs reminds us of some important principles of healthy relationships:

Do you recall the deeper meaning of that word kiss which the bride used in her first utterance of Act 1? That word had overtones of not just encouragement and support but also of an action to protect, and the word could even be used of *soldiers equipped with weapons*. Do we perhaps have a similar connection of thought in our English language between words like *enamour* (to inspire with love) and *armour* (protective clothing used in the days of sword-fighting) or *armourer* (one who prepares or cares for weapons)? Certainly within a relationship of true love there should be some assurance of protection and support, as well as **encourage**-ment and affirmation.

In addition to this sense of protection, when we are, as we say, "in love" there should be a sense wherein we feel like a new person. There is that growing awareness that in the past there had always been a part of our life that was incomplete, but somehow this relationship of love has provided that missing piece and we now feel complete, whole, or even "healed", restored, or redeemed.

There is a definite connection between being in a healthy relationship and living with a sense of wholeness, and this is evident not just in the *Song of Songs* but also in other books of the Bible. Many of us may not have recognised this simply because the full impact of the meaning of the words used in the original language is not always carried over into our English translations.

One of the words in our English bible that is frequently misunderstood is translated into English as *"perfect"*. The Apostle Paul wrote, "Be perfect, be of good comfort, … live in peace." (2 Cor. 13:11). The writer of the letter to the Hebrews wrote, "Now [may] the God of peace … make you perfect." (Heb. 13:20-21).

And Peter also sent a similar message when he wrote, "The God of all grace [will] … make you perfect." (1 Peter 5:10).

This was not a clamouring for impossible perfectionism. In every case the exhortation refers to *the completion of a work of creation* – a growing towards wholeness and maturity. The word translated as perfect is, in the original language, *katartizo* which means "to complete thoroughly" or depending on the context, "to repair and restore". It is the same word that is used where we read that James and John were *repairing* (or mending) their fishing-nets. Those New Testament writers were encouraging the pursuit not just of holiness but also of wholeness. And perhaps we need to recognise that there is a connection between wholeness and holiness.

In this regard, those who seek a spiritual interpretation of the Songs have good reason to see parallels between the Christ (or the Messiah) and the lover in the *Song of Songs*.

When we interpret the *Song of Songs* as a story of two lovers rather than an obscure allegory of some sort or just a random collection of love songs, then we can see a beautiful example of how this sense of wholeness develops within the bride as she describes her experience of being loved by a faithful, considerate and loving husband. We also see that genuine and sincere expressions of acceptance, adoration, affirmation and appreciation, are fundamental to the growth of a healthy love relationship.

When we are looking forward to some special event the excitement and anticipation of what may be ahead can add a great deal to the joy of the celebration itself. This is born out in Acts Three and Four where the bride attempts to share with us some of her hopes and dreams as she was looking forward to the celebration of this relationship with her husband.

ACT 3 IMAGINATION

Song of Songs 3:6-11

6 Who is this coming up from the desert like a column of smoke, perfumed with myrrh and incense made from all the spices of the merchant?

7 Look! It is Solomon's carriage, escorted by sixty warriors, the noblest of Israel,

8 all of them wearing the sword, all experienced in battle, each with his sword at his side, prepared for the terrors of the night.

9 King Solomon made for himself the carriage; he made it of wood from Lebanon.

10 Its posts he made of silver, its base of gold. Its seat was upholstered with purple, its interior lovingly inlaid by the daughters of Jerusalem.

11 Come out, you daughters of Zion, and look at King Solomon wearing the crown, the crown with which his mother crowned him on the day of his wedding, the day his heart rejoiced. [NIV]

ACT 3

IMAGINATION

Significant theme: An overture to intimacy.

Act Two ended with the bride in a dream or trance state, and Act 3 continues in this dream state. Yet this section seems to create problems for almost all interpretations of the *Songs*. The scene which she now describes is of a procession approaching the city. The scene could be consistent with the king fantasy typical of Egyptian love poetry. But remember also that the name *Solomon* ("the peaceful one") is related to the Hebrew *Shalom* meaning peace and contentment, so some writers have suggested that the thought here could possibly be, "peace and contentment are coming at last."

However, another possible interpretation is that the name Solomon should read *Shelem*, the name of a fertility god[48] (the two names are very similar in Hebrew). In which case the writer may have deliberately used a common scene of a cultic procession in order to add emphasis to the word-picture she is trying to create. And by so doing, the writer has given warning of a "change of pace".

---
48. The Interpreter's Bible Vol 5 pp 119 to 120

ACT 3 - IMAGINATION

If this were a video presentation of instruction for husbands and wives, or for pre-marriage instruction, then this is where, according to our modern Australian, British, or American censorship classifications, we move from the 'PG' rating to the 'R' rated presentations.

It is possible that the writer has used the scene from a well recognised and commonly understood procession in order to indicate the explicit sexual nature of the scene that is to follow. But, as will be explained shortly, this is no reason to be offended by the celebration scene in Act Four.

The expression "coming up from the desert" occurs twice in the Songs (3:6 and 8:5) and in each case follows on from the bride's appeal to the young people of Jerusalem to not stir up sexual passion until such a powerful emotion can be appropriately satisfied. So in each case this would seem to be the opening theme for a new scene.

Who is this coming up ... can also be legitimately translated *What is this ...*, and, strangely, the feminine form of the verb *coming up* has been used. According to my bible dictionary the word translated *smoke* can be understood figuratively to mean "anger", but perhaps it could also mean "passionate desire"

Frankincense (or incense) is often used as a symbol of prayer, which in turn can be an expression of desire, and, as already explained, the perfumes myrrh and incense are also used elsewhere in the *Songs* and in other books of the Bible within a context of sexual passion or action.

Overall there seems to be confusing information when we start digging into the words used in this part of the *Songs*, but this is fairly typical of the whole book. Dreams are strange things, and often make no logical sense.

But we do need to remember that this is poetry, probably set to music. If we were to do a study of some of the works of Gilbert and Sullivan or Rodgers and Hammerstein we would almost certainly find some songs that seem to make little or no sense, especially if we had not been able to actually observe the production on stage or screen and get some comprehension of the context. With Gilbert and Sullivan in particular we often had to understand the political background as well as the cultural context in order to understand what some of their songs were really hinting at. So we should not be surprised to find equally baffling problems in trying to understand some of the lyrics in the *Song of Songs*.

In his appeal for better quality erotica (ie. acceptable information about sexual love and/or stories with a sexual theme), Steve Biddulph[49] said we need something that will tell us more of what is going on inside the hearts and minds of two people in love.

Well, I am suggesting that the writer of these songs might have just presented us with the two dreams in *Songs* chapter three for this very reason.

The Songs, Sex, and Pornography

When our daughter was in High School her English teacher told the class that the *Song of Songs* was nothing more than ancient pornography. Then a few weeks later he wrote a letter to the local newspaper recommending that teenagers should engage in sexual activity with a number of different partners as this would be their best means of sex education. He was opposed to teaching this subject from books or spoken lessons.

So we do need to deal with this subject before we go any further

It is obvious from that school teacher's comment and from many other sources that there are many misguided people who believe that any material which deals with the subject of sex is pornographic, and this includes any attempt at sex education and also the *Song of Songs*.

49. See footnote 46 on page 71.

Such a simplistic understanding of the sexual aspect of marriage can lead to a very unhealthy attitude to marriage and to God's creation.

So what do you think people mean when they use this highly emotive but poorly defined word? How would you define the word *pornography?*

One Judge in a Court of Law was heard to say, "I can't define the word, but I certainly know pornography when I see it." That is not a definition!! If he had a mindset that was very anti-sex then he could quite probably classify any attempt at sex education as pornographic.

The word *pornography* is derived from two words of the ancient Greek language in which the New Testament was first written: *porné* and *graphos*.

The Greek noun *porné* means *prostitute* or *cult prostitute* and the word *graphos* refers to writing or drawing – from which we get our English word graphics. The associated verb (or "doing" word, for those of you who have forgotten your lessons in the English language) is *porneia*. So the original meaning of the word *pornography* would be: *"the graphic description* (in words or pictures) *of sex-cult activity."*

The *porné* were a significant part of the fertility cults who inhabited the biblical land of Canaan, and there were still plenty of them in the city of Corinth during New Testament times. The followers of these fertility cults believed there was some form of sympathetic magic connecting human sexual activity with the new life in nature which is observed every Spring.

So in order to ensure good crops and an abundant harvest the devotees of these cults engaged in rituals where the entire adult population were expected to be involved in an uninhibited public celebration of sexual activity. [There is more information about this in the Appendix - Is Eros Evil?].

So was that High School English teacher advocating that teenagers should involve themselves in a pornographic lifestyle as a means of sex education, but should avoid reading what I consider is a remarkably beautiful love story?

In the original Greek version of the New Testament the word *porneia* is used 26 times and is always in reference to sexual activity **outside the relationship of marriage**. So a story that describes a married couple legitimately performing their sacred marriage rite should not be classed as pornography.

At the foot of this page is a list of the verses where this word occurs in the New Testament so you can check it out for yourself.[50]

By its very nature pornography treats the concepts of marriage, commitment and faithfulness with contempt. Porn encourages promiscuity and sexual activity that has nothing to do with the life-long relationship of marriage. In many cases it tends to be a crude very selfish and even violent activity that puts undue emphasis on physical performance and physical attributes, such as the size of the man's penis and the size of the woman's breasts – usually all grossly larger than normal.

By contrast, true love is defined and described more by attitudes.[51] In the *Songs* we are presented with a beautiful description of a love that is exclusive, faithful, pure and secure. Faithfulness and the quality of relationship are significant features of *The Songs*.

Genesis 1:28 clearly states that humans were created male and female and sexual intercourse is necessary for the purpose of reproduction. Until very recent years, performance of the sacred marriage rite (the act of sexual intercourse)[52] was an essential part of the legal consummation of any marriage. Without that act the couple were not legally married. So to classify the *Songs* as pornography is not justified.

---

50. Matt 15:19; Matt 19:19; Mark 7:21; John 8:41; Acts 15:20; Acts 15:29; Acts 21:25; Rom 1:29; 1Cor 5:1; 1Cor 6:13; 1Cor 7:2; 2 Cor 12:21; Gal 5:19 Eph 5:3; Col 3:5; 1Thess 4:3; Rev 2:21; Rev 9:21; Rev 14:8; Rev 17:2; Rev 17:4 Rev 18:3; Rev 19:2
51. See bible passages such as 1 Corinthians 13; Ephesians 5:1-7 & Eph 5:25-33; Philippians 2:6-11
52. See comments regarding the wedding of Martin and Catherine Luther on page 62.

However, having said all of that, I know there are still some people who would insist that the *Song of Songs* is pornographic simply because it includes a description of two naked people.

The fear of nakedness is a **culturally learned reaction**, so we need to take a look at what some other social cultures and also what the bible says about nakedness.

In his book *The Mastery of Sex*, Dr. Weatherhead has a section on Clothing and Nakedness. His opening statement to that section is:

> "If a beautiful woman came on to a stage completely naked and posed there, her hands clasped behind her head, as I have often seen beautiful Armenian women do on the banks of the Diala river after their ceremonial bathing, there would be nothing indecent in the situation.[53]

I personally agree with Dr. Weatherhead. My opinion is that if a man or a woman considers a scene of naked people to be pornographic even when there is nothing deliberately crude or sexual about the scene then I would suggest that the problem is in the mind of the beholder – that is, in the mind of one who is looking. And yet I suspect there would be many folk in the 21st Century who would not agree or would even be shocked at such a statement.

However, Dr. Weatherhead did continue with a significant comment:

> "But, **if** that woman made a single gesture of a certain kind, or if a single member of the audience giggled [sniggered] then the whole situation would become indecent."[54]

He justifies his comment about the audience giggling or sniggering when he explains how a friend of his was, on one occasion, in a sculpture gallery. He was a man with a great taste

---

53. Dr Leslie D Weatherhead, *The Mastery of Sex* pg 151.
54. Ibid pg 152

for true art and in his own small way a connoisseur of sculpture. The gallery was full of beautiful figures of Greek men and women, many of them naked. The doctor's friend was going from one statue to the next rejoicing at the consummate skill of the great masters who had created these magnificent works of art. While he was there a party of tourists entered the gallery, both men and women.

Some of the party gaped at the figures with half-guilty looks, then one of the party made a vulgar remark in reference to the scene of nakedness. Some of the women blushed scarlet and with half-suppressed giggles the party left the gallery.

Dr. Weatherhead's friend said he had felt hot with shame that a place of such beautiful art had been made a place of obscenity because of some people's "beastly minds".

Dr. Weatherhead's comment on those "beastly minds" was:

> Those "beastly minds" to the psychologist are not merely deplorable, they are to him what loathsome scales on the skin are to a physician: symptoms of an inner disharmony that call for treatment rather than abuse. And one of the tasks of religion and psychology in this generation is to promote a true attitude to sex and rescue it from being thought unclean.[55]

He then mentions his own experience when he was an officer in the Mess of a British regiment whose duty included looking after forty thousand Armenian refugees. Those women he mentioned earlier were simply drying themselves in the sun after their ceremonial bathing.

Although they were standing there totally naked many of them would not make any attempt at concealment, not even so much as turn around to face away from the men, even while a whole regiment was marching past.

Because non-sexual nakedness was accepted as normal in their culture there was nothing immodest, pornographic, or suggestive

---
55. Ibid pg 154

in the behaviour of those women. So those women saw no reason to hide themselves.

From my own personal experience and observation of other social cultures where I have worked or visited – places where for countless generations women never covered their breasts and in some cases total non-sexual nudity was acceptable – I am convinced that prudery does not produce sexual purity! All it has achieved is a dangerous curiosity about the human body and a guaranteed lucrative market for the publishers of pornography.

The problem is that many teenagers (especially boys) who have not been given a healthy or adequate sex education and are thus desperate for some sort of information or "what does the body of an adult human female look like?", turn to pornography and thereby learn a very unhealthy concept of human sexuality and sexual behaviour. Laws that make it illegal for anyone under the age of 18 to even see a picture of a naked human body are foolish, especially when those pictures are part of a healthy sex education.

Perhaps Proverbs 27:7 sums this up well. A paraphrase of the proverb reads: *For a person who is well fed, even honey has no appeal, but a starving man will eat rubbish.*

When typical teenagers (boys especially) who have not been given a healthy understanding of human sexuality find what they think might be a source of information about that mysterious subject they usually read it with glee. But if that "information" is pornographic then harmful rubbish will be absorbed into their thinking processes = a serious problem!

The only reasonable prevention for this problem is to ensure that the child has been given appropriate information about basic human biology including sexuality and opportunities to see what the naked body of a person of the opposite sex looks like. And this needs to be done soon after birth, at least during the first four or five years of life before they start school and certainly before the hormones of puberty kick in.

If it is of any help to readers who are looking for ideas of how this can be done I am game to admit that in our family the two boys were often in the bath together (saves on water when you're dependant on rainwater tanks). When our daughter joined the family, and as soon as she was old enough to sit safely in the bath (age about 12months) she shared the bath with her two brothers. Questions, when asked were answered appropriately.

To quote from Dr Weatherhead's book:

> "The child must have his questions answered when he asks them: they must be answered truthfully and the child should not be told more than he asks. The child who is taught this way will know that he can always go to his informant (parents in this case) when he wants more knowledge and knows that he will get a true (honest) answer." [56]

I have known of other families, in places where there was a shortage of water, where mum, dad and children – including teenagers – would all be in the bathroom together taking turn-about to spend a brief time under the shower – enough to get wet – then step aside and use a wet face-washer (flannel) to do the necessary soaping bit. When other family members had all got themselves wet all over then the one who started first steps under the shower to rinse-off and the others would all follow in turn.

Yes, I know Dr Joyce Brothers claimed that children who see parents or siblings when they are naked will suffer serious emotional trauma. But I have never seen even one case-history to prove that, and I know there are hundreds of families where occasional non-sexual nudity is not uncommon and there was no evidence of the problems that Dr Brothers predicted.

---

56. From Dr Weatherhead's book The Mastery of Sex pg 165, Use of the pronoun "he" is gender inclusive (means "he" or "she" as appropriate.)

The Biblical Acceptance of "Naked"

We must recognise that there is a big difference between the acceptance of nakedness in what may be considered an appropriate situation, and some form of crude, exhibitionist, or provocative behaviour that has overtones of sexual abuse, promiscuity, incest, or other immoral activity.

The ancient Hebrews obviously recognised this distinction for we find that within the books of the Old Testament at least three different Hebrew words are used to describe the concept of "naked".

The word *'arowm* (meaning simply "without clothes") is used in Genesis 2:25 where we read that, in the original paradise of Eden, Adam and Eve were both naked and not ashamed. However, in the next chapter (Genesis 3:7-11) a slightly different word *('eyrom)* is used in reference to their nakedness because their condition is now confused with feelings of vulnerability, fear, and failure.

This word *('eyrom)* is used by prophets who are warning the people of Israel that if they do not remain faithful to their God then He will allow them to be defeated in war and they will become slaves to their enemies and serve them in "hunger, thirst, and *nakedness" ('eyrom)*.[57] Captives in war were often stripped and marched away naked, probably for the specific purpose of adding to their feeling of humiliation. It is for this reason that the word "naked" has connotations of shame.

The word *'arowm* (simple *unashamedly naked*, as with Adam and Eve in the garden before the fall) is also used in reference to the naked all-night prayer session with Samuel[58], and of the prophet Isaiah when he walked around *"naked* and barefoot"[59] for three years. The same word is also used by Job and the writer

---
57. In the Hebrew text, the word *'eyrom* is used in Deuteronomy 28:46, and Ezekiel 23:29.
58. 1 Samuel 19:24
59. Isaiah chapter 20

of Ecclesiastes where they both make the observation that we are all born naked.[60]

However, there is yet another but more sinister word, *'ervah*. This word usually refers specifically to the *pudenda* (external sex organs) but is often translated into English as *"nakedness"* or, in some versions, by the use of the English word *"shame"*.

The word *'ervah* is used in situations where there is exposing or flaunting of the naked body in a crude and suggestive manner where there are connotation of unlawful sexual activity, such as incest, adultery, crude exhibitionism, prostitution, or other indecent behaviour.

That is where "naked" does become pornographic.

The prophet Ezekiel rebuked his people, "because you exposed your *nakedness* (Heb. *'ervah*) in promiscuity with many lovers"[61], and declares that the nation has "carried on her prostitution and flaunted her *nakedness.*"[62]

The prophet Jeremiah declares that "Jerusalem has sinned and become unclean ... her *nakedness* (*'ervah*) has been exposed."[63] By this he means that the sexual promiscuity of these folk has now become well known.

The shame of nakedness in all of these contexts was not with the physical human body that God designed. It was always with immoral behaviour and the associated sexual promiscuity.

When Moses warned his people, "your camp must be holy so that YHWH [the LORD] will not see anything *indecent* (Heb. *'ervah*) amongst you," (Deuteronomy 23:14.) he was not condemning the people for removing their clothes in order to take a bath or wash their bodies. This was simply a statement that there must not be any crude or pornographic exhibitionism, or any other type of sexual misbehaviour such as incest or adultery, within the community.

---

60. Job 1:21, and Ecclesiastes 5:15
61. Ezekiel 16:36
62. Ezekiel 23:18
63. Lamentations 1:8.

Those who quote Leviticus chapters 18:6-17 in condemnation of any lifestyle that permits some measure of nakedness even within the home overlook the real teaching of those particular commands. In a social culture where it was not at all uncommon to see other family members with no clothes on, those laws expressly forbid *gazing in a lustful manner* at the sex organs (pudenda = Heb. *'ervah*) of any close relative. That law forbids lustful looking where there is intention of using a victim, as some may have gazed upon captives in war who had been stripped naked and are being marched away to be sold into slavery.

Modern translations of Leviticus have interpreted these verses as looking with the specific intention of sexual intercourse. Hence the New Living Translation of the Bible translates Leviticus 18:6 as; "You must never have *sexual intercourse* with a close relative." But this tends to sidestep the real issue which is the condemnation of lecherous looking where the pornography is in the mind of the beholder. Jesus of Nazareth merely used a logical interpretation to this law when he said that *any* man who looks at *any* woman with lust is already guilty of adultery because of what is going on in his thinking.[64] Note that the lustful looking is every bit as evil as the doing!!

It seems that we may have conceded defeat to the influence of a very warped culture which presents a perverted and degrading image of the human body and sexual lovemaking.

But writers like Dr. Leslie Weatherhead, Sheila Kitzinger, Dr. John White, and Steve Biddulph assert that the proper response is not to concede defeat in these areas and treat the naked body as a shameful thing but rather to present a more powerful image – a positive, realistic and attractive image of morality and chastity. This is turn means that we must adopt a wholesome acceptance of the physical body and the way our bodies have been designed, and of the way they work – including all the sexual parts.

---

64. Matthew 5:27-28. See also 2 Peter 2: 14-20

Do some of those people who are afraid of nakedness really believe that Michelangelo's artwork, including the ceiling of the Sistine Chapel, is mere pornography? Does this mean that God, as Creator, was giving his approval to pornography when we read in the creation story that, "The man and the woman were both naked and were not ashamed"?

And how should we interpret that strange experience recorded of King Saul where even he was so overcome by some recognition of God's power that, apparently along with several others, he "stripped off his clothes also, and prophesied before Samuel . . . and lay down naked [*'arowm*] all that day and all that night" (1Sam.19:24); or God's instruction to Isaiah that he was to walk naked [*'arowm*] and barefoot for three years (Isa.20:3); or Ezekiel who used the description of the changes in a woman's body as she goes through the bodily changes of puberty as a sermon illustration (Ezek. 16:7)? Even a child in that culture who was old enough to read would have very likely been aware of the bodily changes the Prophet Ezekiel was describing.

And what are we to make of these very reliable records concerning baptism in the early Christian church?

Those people did not equate nakedness with pornography, nor did they assume that nudity in mixed company would automatically lead to sexual activity.

In The Apostolic Tradition, Hippolytus of Rome (ca AD170-236) explains how the normal procedures for baptism involved unashamed nudity. Excerpts from the translation of his works read:

> The Neophytes shall put off their clothes. And they shall baptise the little children first. ... And next they shall baptise the grown men; and last the women, who shall all have loosed their hair and laid aside the gold ornaments which they were wearing. Let no one go down into the water having any alien object with them. ... And let them stand in the water naked. And let a deacon likewise go down into the water.

The Songs, Sex, and Pornography

Then, at the conclusion of these proceedings we read,
> And so each one drying himself with a towel they shall now put on their clothes. [65]

From Rome to Jerusalem, and a century or more later, Cyril of Jerusalem (AD315 - 386) tells us that the normal procedure was for the candidates to *"enter the inner room of the baptistery and divest themselves completely of all their garments"*.[66] He is also quoted as saying in one of his baptismal sermons, *"You are now stripped and naked, in this also imitating Christ on His cross. ... And you bear the likeness of the first-formed Adam, who was naked in the garden."* [67]

It was only after leaving the water that candidates were re-clothed, each with a single white garment. In this we see a beautiful symbolism of putting off or washing away the old nature and putting on the righteousness of Christ.

Note that these services included men, women, and children. A fifth Century mosaic in Santa Maria in Cosmedin, Ravenna, is one of many works of art from the early church that illustrate nude baptism. So we know that during the first four or five centuries of the Christian church the practice was very normal, certainly not uncommon.

This was not pornography. These people obviously did not look upon one another with sexual lust, nor did they see each other as mere things to be used for their own selfish pleasure. Not only would they have failed to see any sexual connotation about nakedness in this context, they would have shown mutual respect for each other, recognising that everyone involved in

---

65. Rev. Gregory Dix (Ed), *The Treatise on the Apostolic Tradition of St. Hippolytus of Rome*, (Ridgefield, Connecticut: Moorhouse Publishing) pp 33-38. [Of course the word "himself" is gender inclusive - includes women and also girls and boys.]
66. Encyclopaedia Britannica (1962) Vol. 3 p83, Baptism in the Early Church.
67. Henry Bettenson (Ed), The Later Christian Fathers: A Selection From the Writings of the Fathers from Cyril of Jerusalem to Leo The Great, (London: Oxford University Press) p43.

these services was an individual person and fellow heir of the kingdom of heaven. They had no cause to fear that anyone would take advantage of them, or that they would be the subject of crude comment. They would have remembered the law of Leviticus 18:6 and also Jesus condemnation of lustful looking, and they would have had appropriate respect for the relationship of marriage. Within their fellowships there was an atmosphere of *agapé* love and in such an atmosphere it is safe to allow oneself to be vulnerable.

Of course the heated New Testament debate about circumcision now begins to make more sense when we realise that such "evidence" would be obvious to everyone whenever a man or boy was baptised, or whenever they went to bathe in the public bath houses, which many people did at least once a week. Whether or not these bath houses required specific times for women and different times for men depended (from what I have read) on the whim of the Emperor. So, as with the baptismal services, there could have been times when boys, girls, men and women would have possibly seen people of all ages and both genders nude in one of these bath houses. Even the ascetic Augustine mentioned visiting these places with his father as though it was the most normal thing for any teenage boy to do.

It is probably for this reason that when Paul asked Timothy to accompany him on one of his missionary journeys he first requested that Timothy, whose father was a Greek, should be circumcised. (Acts 16:1-3) Paul obviously did not want to run the risk of a religious riot whenever they went for their daily ablutions.

Remember that these people lived at a time and place when slavery was common. We are told that slaves were sometimes sold naked in the market place and, if they wore anything at all while working, it was often little more than a loincloth. Prisoners of war were usually stripped of everything, including their clothing, and then marched away naked to be sold in some slave market.

It is for this reason that nakedness sometimes had connotations of shame. But there was no shame associated with nudity for baptism, or with bathing in the public bath-houses, and, of course, no suggestion of shame when the nakedness was within the context of a healthy marriage relationship.

Children in those societies would have grown-up simply accepting the physical differences between male and female and between child and adult without any suggestion that this knowledge might be considered sexually stimulating. They did not have to endure the problems of post-Freudian philosophies which seem to automatically associate nudity with sexual misconduct. Instead they worked from a different belief system, and therefore had far healthier minds and attitudes than what seems to be considered normal by many people in our society today.

So I believe it is quite legitimate to say that the original writer of the *Song of Songs* would have been highly offended if she ever heard anyone say that her literary masterpiece is pornographic.

But, I hear some people say, that was two or three thousand years ago. Can you give us something more recent than that?

Yes I can: One of the first things I learned when I started doing research on this subject was a remarkable difference in censorship of movie films between the USA and Scandinavian countries.

Many films from the USA were heavily censored or even banned in countries such as Scandinavia because there was too much violence and they did not want their children to start thinking that violence is an acceptable way of dealing with conflict or disagreement.

But the Scandinavians had no problem with casual non-sexual nudity. It was part of their lifestyle. An entire family – Mum, Dad and all the children and possibly friends and other people could all be naked together in the Sauna. Many movie films from this part of the world had scenes where people were naked but not involved in explicitly sexual or pornographic behaviour. The Americans could not cope with this, and to cut out the nude scenes in the movie would lose much of the overall story, so many films from Scandinavian counties were not acceptable in USA cinemas.

I even heard of one preacher in Australia who told his congregation that brochures advertising women's nightwear and underwear were pornographic. He was putting sexual connotations on pictures that were never intended to be seen that way, and effectively telling his congregation that it was normal to do that. Talk about spreading a mental **dis**-ease!!

The law of Leviticus 18:6 forbids lustful looking, but it does not forbid admiring with awe and wonder some of the beauties of God's creation.

In Leviticus chapter 20 we find what some people might think are rather harsh laws, such as Lev 20:10 "If a man commits adultery with another man's wife . . . Both the adulterer and the adulteress must be put to death." That sounds rather harsh. But we must realise that if paradise is going to be paradise for anyone it must be paradise for everyone.

If we allow even just one deliberate lawbreaker into our community of "paradise" it ceases to be paradise for anyone. You never know when the bad guy might come to take advantage of you as his next victim. So the bad guy must be identified and removed from the community.

Moses had no means of establishing a gaol (jail) when the Israelites were in the wilderness for 40 years. So the only solution was to put the lawbreakers to death. Most of us do something similar if our physical body gets infected with a disease of some sort. One of the first things we often do is to apply some kind of antibiotic to kill any harmful germs. So Moses was just doing what was necessary in an attempt to maintain a standard of behaviour that would be acceptable in the paradise of the Promised Land.

And we know from Holy Scripture that deliberate lawbreakers will not be permitted to enter the paradise of Heaven. [68]

In contrast to the healthy acceptance of God's design of the human body which is evident throughout all of the bible and has obviously been accepted as normal in some other social groups on planet earth, many people in our present western society have made such an absurd mystery about the naked human body that their young people cannot discern the important difference which should exist between the sinful lust to posses and the simple pleasure of a scene which should have an aesthetic beauty of its own. In a morally healthy society the sight of a naked body in a non-sexual setting should produce no different reaction than the sight of a hand, a foot or a face.

The publishers of pornography in our modern world have exploited this ignorance and mystery and created for themselves a market that is worth millions of dollars every year. The evil in their productions is not so much that they describe human sexual anatomy or sexual behaviour but that they do so in a degrading manner. The problems are not just due to a lack of clothing. Yes, pornography does encourage lustful looking, but the basic problem is a lack of respect – a lack of respect for other people, a lack of respect for the Creator, and a lack of respect for the relationship of marriage.

It is because of a healthy and wholesome acceptance of the way God designed and created our physical bodies, and the way He intended things to work that the writer of *The Songs* has been able to present the celebration scene of chapter 4 with a sense of delightful purity. There is nothing in the least bit crude or smutty in this presentation of a couple celebrating their sacred marriage rite.

Apart from the warnings about stirring-up passion in an inappropriate time or manner the writer of *The Songs* has not

---

68. Check these references: 1 Corinthians 6:9-11; Galatians 5:19-21; Revelation 21:8; Revelation 22:15.

made any suggestion that sex, for a married couple, should be seen as something evil or sinful. Rather she seems to have made a point of presenting sexual lovemaking as a beautiful and sacred celebration of a special relationship. Likewise there is no problem describing a scene with a naked couple, simply because this is part of God's design, and in the right context the subject should not be indecent.

So pornography should not be determined by the lack of clothing but by the lack of respect for God's creation and a lack of respect for the God-ordained covenant relationship of marriage. It should be the *context* and *motive* of any nudity or sexual activity that determines whether or not a publication is described or classified as pornographic.

Therefore consider this statement as a definition of pornography:

> **Pornography is any material, (image, video, book, magazine, etc.) that degrades the covenant relationship of marriage, encourages sexual promiscuity, and reduces sexual intercourse to a purely physical act where people are merely treated as sex objects – or sex toys.**

Think about that definition carefully. Whilst it certainly exonerates the artwork of Michelangelo and similar artists, it condemns many of our modern magazines – even those produced for women and for teenagers – because they condone and even encourage sexual promiscuity.

The silence of our moral guardians (watchmen of the city?) in regard to such magazines may be significant when we now see many magazines actively encouraging promiscuity, sodomy, and involvement with the occult.

Bible writers have always been outspoken in warning about the dangers of these activities. But the fear of nakedness has also been used as a very effective distracter. While many parents have been almost obsessed with trying to prevent their children ever seeing an image of a naked human body, the minds of those same children have been filled with nightmarish scenes from horror movies, or violence in the name of video-games, drama, documentaries, or news-bulletins.

Too often the role-models they have been given present the hero as an aggressive and violent person. Not a good element for a happy marriage or healthy family. Meanwhile the belief system which claims that nude is always crude tends to create confusion in the minds of our children.

At one extreme there develops a shameful fear of the physical body, at the other extreme we find an unhealthy and perverted curiosity. Neither of these two attitudes can give a good foundation for a happy marriage either.

In conclusion then, perhaps it would be fair to say that the subject of human sexuality may be a bit like carbon.

For many people, when you ask them to describe the element carbon, what comes to mind is a fine black powder that leaves a smutty mess on everything it touches. But carbon is an *essential* element of the world in which we live. It is present in some form in every living thing – animal and vegetable!

But, better than that, how many people recognise that a beautiful sparkling diamond is nothing more than a crystal of pure carbon. Hold a clear diamond up to the light and one can see a range of different colours as pure sunlight is refracted through the various faces of that wonderful crystal.

When I mention an interpretation of *The Songs* which presents a story of human (sexual) love some people are not favourably impressed because to them such an interpretation must be pornographic.

But when we can see this as a story of a couple whose relationship reflects something of pure *agapé* love then we have to acknowledge that this story is a gem – it is a beautiful sparkling jewel. As we examine the story through different facets we find a wonderful range of warmth and colour as we see different aspects of the qualities that make up their expression of pure, honest and healthy love.

In his letter to the young Pastor Titus the Apostle Paul wrote, "To the pure all things are pure."[69] When we have learned to praise God for the beauty of His creation and simply accept things for the way He has designed them, then we should be able to appreciate the scene of a married couple celebrating their Marriage Rite such as we find described here in the *Song of Songs* and simply be glad of its beauty.

The Confusion Between Love and Lust

While the lust to possess, or the lust to use and to control the life of some other person may be typical of many cults it has no place in a relationship of genuine love. Hence exploitation of any sort was forbidden in Levitical law and was frequently condemned by the Hebrew prophets as well as by Christ Jesus.

Unfortunately the lust to possess has become so accepted as "normal" within our Western culture that it has polluted our understanding of the word "love". In the English language we use the word "love" in relation to every kind of affection, from totally sacrificial compassion, where one is prepared to die in defence of the loved-one, through to the utterly selfish lust to possess and use for one's own pleasure alone. But other languages have shown more discernment.

We know that the ancient Greeks had a number of different words for love. We are told that they used the word *eros* to express the idea of sexual love. However Plato used this word in reference to the love of God. But the word is not used anywhere in the Bible. Instead, Christians adopted the Greek word *agapé* and gave it a distinctively Christian sense. Even the Septuagint (Greek) translation of the *Song of Songs* uses the word *agapé* for "love".

---
69. Titus 1:15

Anders Nygren, an authority on the ancient Greek language, tells us that, "The Christian idea of love ... involves a revolution in ethical outlook [that is] without parallel in the history of ethics." He tells us that *eros*, although nowadays thought of exclusively as sexual love, was not originally used in this sense only. He explains that *eros* is acquisitive desire, whereas *agapé* is sacrificial giving. *Eros* is egocentric; *agapé* is unselfish. *Eros* is the desire to get and possess ...; *agapé* is freedom in giving. ... *Eros* is determined by the [inherent] quality, beauty and worth of its object [and thus] recognises value in its object, [whereas] *agapé* loves and creates value in its object.[70]

These people did not necessarily use the word *eros* only in reference to sexual love. When they spoke of sexual passion they used the word *epithumia* [arising from, or out-of heat]. It was some of the leaders in the Early Christian Church who, in their quest for an experience or expression of the totally pure and sacrificial quality of *agapé* love, recognised that within sexual love there often is a very powerful desire for self-gratification. Probably quite correctly they referred to this as *eros*, and therefore taught that sexual love is always tainted with some measure of selfishness. For this reason they believed that sexual love is always tainted with sin.

It is unfortunate that we now use the word *eros* almost exclusively in reference to sexual love because, ideally, the love between a husband and wife should really be more in the category of *agapé*, while at the same time *eros* affects far more in life than just the sex drive.

The man who says, "I just love my new car" is really referring to a form of *eros* love. The woman who says, "I would just love to own a house like that" is really referring to a form of *eros* love. Of course the teenage boy who tries to seduce his girlfriend with the tired old line, "If you really loved me you would have sex

---

70. Quoted by Selwyn Hughes, Every Day With Jesus daily Bible study notes, 24th Oct., 1996.

with me" is most certainly motivated by *eros*. If he really loved his girlfriend he would never make any demands that might threaten her sense of personal worth, security, or acceptance.

A significant factor of pure *agapé* love is the motivation to give, or to serve, rather than the lust to get, or to use. Within a relationship of *agapé* love it is safe to allow oneself to be vulnerable. Learning to feel safe in what could otherwise be a position of vulnerability can be an important step in establishing foundations of trust. This is why the unashamed acceptance of nakedness within a marriage relationship should be seen as beneficial and healthy. It was also because of mutual trust that Christians in the Early Church were able to accept total nudity in their baptismal services without fear of being used, abused, ridiculed, molested, or rejected.

The celebration scene in Act 4 is of a legitimate married couple performing what is a legally required act for the consummation of their marriage relationship. So to condemn the *Song of Songs* as pornography is not justified.

Far from being offensive, the scenes that are presented to us in the next few chapters of the *Songs* should inspire all of us to enrich our own marriage relationships by improving our skills in the verbal and physical expressions of love. We are talking here about making love, and for a married couple that should not be pornography.

Sex, Prayer and Intimacy

There is, of course, a spiritual parallel to all that has been said here regarding lovemaking and relationships.

In Hebrew writing the verb *'to know'* is often used in reference to sexual intercourse, and the same word is also used throughout the Bible to describe an individual's personal relationship with God.[71]

---

[71]. At least seventeen times in the Old Testament alone: Genesis 4:1; 4:17; 4:25; 19:5;

Prayer and sexual intercourse are both related to the experience of knowing a person and developing intimate communication with that person. Both can also be a means of rejoicing. Did you notice that the two Hebrew words for rejoice (*samach* and *giyl*) each imply the expression of intense joy through almost involuntary physical movement. Both words are used in reference to worship, and both words are also used in reference to sexual intercourse. Although the emphasis really needs to be on the amount of time we spend in unashamedly transparent (or nakedly honest) communion together, rather than on the brief moments when we communicate our mutual acceptance and love in "tongues of ecstasy", in both cases this interaction should be characterised by excitement and joy.[72]

Put in simple terms, if we wish to develop an intimate relationship with someone then we need to get to know and understand that person by spending time with them. By contrast, a literal translation of Proverbs 9:13 tells us that the foolish woman who makes herself available for promiscuous sex does not know (anything or anyone). Sex for her has nothing to do with a long-term personal relationship.

So the idea that the *Song of Songs* provides good teaching about the relationship between a husband and wife expressed through mutual affirmation and sexual union is totally compatible with the interpretation of the spiritual relationship between God and mankind based on worship and prayer. The two views do not contradict. Likewise, a marriage that is totally devoid of physical contact can be about a barren and pointless as a spiritual journey where there is no praise, prayer or worship.

19:8; 24:16; 38:36; Numbers 31:17-18; 31:35; Judges 11:39; 19:22; 19:25; 21:11-12; 1Samuel 1:19; 1 Kings 1:4; and also Matthew 1:25; and Luke 1:34. In the Old Testament the Hebrew word is yada'. This word has a wide range of meanings including; to know, to see, to understand, to discern or ascertain by observation or experience.

72. NOTE: References relating to the phrase "to know" are taken from the transliterated Hebrew and Greek texts. The actual words **to know** do not appear in many modern English translations of the Bible because the English translations often make use of more appropriate English words.

ACT 4 CELEBRATION

Song of Songs 4:1 to 5:1

This is basically the NIV text but the indicators "He says" and "She says" have been added.

He says:

4:1 How beautiful you are, my darling! How very beautiful!
   You have eyes like those of a dove.
   Your hair flows - like a flock of goats descending from Mount Gilead.
2 Beautiful teeth - like a flock of sheep just shorn, coming up from the washing. Each has its twin; not one of them is alone.
3 Beautiful red lips - like a scarlet ribbon - your mouth is lovely.
   Your rosy cheeks have a beautiful glow - like the halves of a pomegranate.
4 Your neck is like the tower of David, built with elegance ; on it hang a thousand shields, all of them shields of warriors.
5 Your two breasts are beautiful - like twin fawns of a gazelle that browse among the lilies.
6 Until the day breaks and the shadows flee, I will go to the mountain of myrrh and to the hill of incense.
7 You are absolutely beautiful my darling; Perfection in every way.
8 Come with me from Lebanon, my bride, come with me from Lebanon. Descend from the crest of Amana, from the top of Senir, the summit of Hermon, from the lions' dens and the mountain haunts of the leopards.
9 You have truly won my heart, my sister, my bride; One glance from your eyes and I am yours,. And I love that necklace you are wearing.
10 How delightful is your love, my sister, my bride! How much more pleasing is your love than wine, and the fragrance of your perfume than any spice!
11 Your lips drop sweetness as the honeycomb, my bride; milk and honey are under your tongue. The fragrance of your garments is like that of Lebanon.
12 You are a garden locked up, my sister, my bride; you are a spring enclosed, a sealed fountain.

She says:

13 Your plants are an orchard of pomegranates with choice fruits, with henna and nard.
14 Nard and saffron, calamus and cinnamon, with every kind of incense tree, with myrrh and aloes and all the finest spices.
15 You are a garden fountain, a well of flowing water streaming down from Lebanon
16 Awake, north wind, and come, south wind! Blow on my garden, that its fragrance may spread abroad. Let my lover come into his garden and taste its choice fruits.

He says:

5:1 I have come into my garden, my sister, my bride; I have gathered my myrrh with my spice. I have eaten my honeycomb and my honey; I have drunk my wine and my milk.

Unknown speaker:

Eat, O friends, and drink; drink your fill, O lovers.

[Author Paraphrase]

ACT 4

CELEBRATION

Significant words: My spouse.
Significant theme: Garden of spices.

Sexual intercourse to some people is merely a physical act
that is so loaded with degradation and shame
they cannot even talk about it.

But to others
it is a delicious and beautiful God-ordained expression
of the emotional and spiritual unity and love
that should exist
between a wife and her husband.

The Song of Songs presents the latter view.

Having briefly turned away from the bedroom scene while we were presented with the dreams of Act 3, which were obviously intended to suggest great feelings of excitement and anticipation on the part of the bride, our focus is now returned to the bridal chamber and to specific words and actions. We also notice from here on that the lovemaking becomes more explicit. This is the logical lead-up to the consummation or celebration of their special covenant relationship. The lover sings praises of her physical beauty. In so doing he expresses praise for seven different aspects of her loveliness. Seven is the number that indicates perfection. So, even in the number of compliments mentioned here, the writer has reinforced the husband's expressions of praise regarding the beauty and perfection of his bride.

Remember, she needs this reassurance, for back in 1:5-6 she was fearful that her husband would be all too aware of her imperfections. Even the most beautiful of women may feel some insecurity on her wedding night, but the perfect husband is sensitive to his wife's need for reassurance, and he recognises the need to make her feel secure in his love.

Of course there is a Christian Gospel parallel here; as the words of one well-known chorus puts it: *"I, though so unworthy, still am a child of His care, for His word teaches me that His love reaches me – everywhere."*

To return to the honeymooning couple:

Previously the 'lover' sang of the beauty of her character and clothing, but now he focuses more specifically of the beauty of her body. How then can anyone conclude that the physical body is a shameful thing? God declared the Garden of Eden scene with the naked Adam and Eve to be very good, and the concept is reiterated here. Not only does this chapter express approval of the beauty of the naked body (in the right context) but, as we will soon discover, it expresses God's approval of sexual lovemaking (in the right context).

ACT 4 - CELEBRATION

4:1-7 [He continues to speak words of praise and encouragement to his bride]

He: How beautiful you are, my darling, how very beautiful.

Your eyes behind your veil have the peace and beauty of a dove.

Your hair - like the flowing movement of a flock of goats coming down the slopes of Gilead,

Your teeth - perfect, like a flock of shorn ewes that have come from the washing, all of which are twins, not one of them is alone.

Your lips are like a crimson thread, and your mouth is lovely;

Your cheeks are like halves of a pomegranate behind your veil.

Your neck is like the tower of David, built in courses; on it hang a thousand bucklers, all of them shields of warriors.

Your breasts are beautiful - like two fawns, twins of a gazelle feeding among the lilies.

Until the day breaks and the shadows flee, I will go to the mountain of myrrh and the hill of frankincense.

You are absolutely beautiful my darling, perfect in every way.

[Author paraphrase]

Describing the beloved's hair as being like a flock of goats may seem a strange idea, but the Good News Bible translates the verse beautifully as, "Your hair dances, like a flock of goats bounding down the hills". The emphasis in the original language is on the wave-like flowing.

This couple obviously enjoy the open air and the beauties of nature, for this is evident in the imagery used to reassure the bride of her own natural beauty.

We know that this woman has a beautiful smile of even white teeth and lovely red lips because the lover has just said:

> Your teeth are like a flock of sheep .... Each has its twin; not one of them is alone. Your lips are like a scarlet thread, and your mouth is lovely. [4:2-3 NIV]

Rather than ewes that have just been shorn the lover is more likely alluding to washed sheep ready for shearing. The Hebrew language implies this, and newly shorn sheep are sometimes not very beautiful.

The lover likens the cheeks of his beloved to pomegranates. This is a fruit about the size of an orange which, when ripe, has a reddish-maroon skin that is smooth and hard on the outside. Inside is a mass of red pulp-covered seeds, and sometimes a quantity of acidic juice. Because of the mass of seeds inside, the fruit was often used as a symbol of fertility. For Moses it was one of the chief attributes of the Promised Land and Solomon used the pomegranate as a significant ornament in the Temple. The simile here is obviously referring to the rosy blush on the bride's cheeks. Thus, "Your temples behind your veil," may be better translated as blushing cheeks framed by beautiful hair, as Kenneth Taylor has done in *The Living Bible*.

The language used to describe her breasts is beautifully poetic with its "two fawns, twins of a gazelle, that feed among the lilies" (4:5).

The word picture implies that the bride is now leaning over and probably astride of her husband as he lays back on the bed. Then, as she lowers her upper body closer to him, her breasts pointing down, the shape reminds him of the nose of a friendly young fawn – twin fawns actually, because there are two. He enjoys the sensuality of soft warm flesh as these "twin fawns" brush against his cheeks or as he kisses and caresses the nipples with his lips - hence "feeding among the lilies."

As the lover uses his lips to stimulate the nipples of her breasts it is very believable when we read that his hands move lovingly down her body towards that sacred mound of *Bether* (mound of the covenant). The words describes the action: "I will go to the mountain of myrrh – to the hill of incense." (4:6).

As indicated earlier, the mound of *Bether* is a specific reference to the beloved's pubic mound. *The mountain of myrrh* and *the hill of incense* refer to the same place. This is another example of synthetic parallelism, very typical of Hebrew poetry.

In her book *Mountain of Spices*, Hannah Hurnard[73] compares the spices mentioned in the *Songs* with the nine fruits of the Spirit mentioned in Paul's letter to the Galatians (Gal 5:22-23), and in so doing suggests that incense is symbolic of faith, and myrrh is symbolic of meekness.

If we understand meekness as surrender then this becomes very meaningful. According to sex therapist Margo Anand,[74] the word *surrender* has significant roots. The word *render* has the meaning "to melt", and *sur* implies "super" or "higher". Hence the true meaning of surrender is "to melt or blend into that which is higher than yourself."

True surrender (in this context) is a conscious decision of the will. It means opening your heart to the other person in complete trust. And trust of course is closely related to faith.

We are not talking about any sort of power struggle here. Remember, this is an act of love. So surrender here has nothing whatever to do with an admission of defeat, but rather it is a delicious melting together of two persons.

Surrender, in this context, as with the real meaning of the word meekness, does not mean defeat in some argument. Rather it refers to the harmonious pursuit of a common goal. It is where each person becomes sensitive to the needs and desires of the other – is aware of the other's level of excitement and responds

---

73. Hurnard, Hannah, *Mountain of Spices*. (1983-90) UK: Kingsway.
74. Margo Anand, The Art of Sexual Ecstasy (1990) Aquarian Press,, London UK

with joy and enthusiasm accepting the other's pleasure with delight instead of envy. Any attitude of aggression, any demand for submission which degrades, or for performance that cannot be given with gladness, is not love, it is abuse. In this respect the act of sexual intercourse between husband and wife can be seen as an illustration of the "meekness" with which a Christian should respond or surrender to the will of God.

The act of sexual intercourse is a form of "melting together" and an act of surrender for both persons involved. The female partner in particular does make herself vulnerable. As an act of trust, she "opens herself" – including her physical body – and allows her husband to enter her, both physically and emotionally. The female partner is trusting in faith that her lover will enter her as an act of love, not as an act of exploitation or violence. Hence, to refer to the woman's genital area as the "mountain of myrrh" and the "hill of incense" is, once again, very beautiful symbolism.

This couple seem to be in no great hurry. This is a special event for both of them and they obviously intend to enjoy the journey "until the day breaks and the shadows flee." Remember, the bride used these words when she first invited her lover to give some attention to the "mound of Bether" (2:17), but now he is the one who reassures her that they will not rush ahead. Instead he intends to hold back and savour the pleasure. Oh that more husbands had understood this before the wedding night.

Making love is not something one does in a five-minute coffee break! Nor should the first sexual experience for a married couple be attempted somewhere around midnight after a long day, which for many newly-weds has been both physically and emotionally exhausting.

We need to re-think our wedding day routines. This couple had time to relax, to walk and talk together in the garden, to take time to savour this special occasion. This is definitely one situation where the proverb *pleasure is found along the way, not [just] at the end of the road* would seem to be very appropriate.

ACT 4 - CELEBRATION

Note also that there is no suggestion of shame in describing a naked couple simply enjoying each other. There is no need to be ashamed in this context! Shame has its origins in fear. But where there is mutual love, trust, and understanding, there should be no cause for fear or shame.

The distorted doctrines that taught people to be ashamed of their physical body have no place in this part of Scripture. Those legalistic and ascetic ideas which presented such unhealthy attitudes regarding the human body have their origins in pagan philosophies rather than biblical or Hebrew teaching. Those attitudes developed in cultures that were morally depraved, and the people had every reason to be ashamed of their *behaviour*. But why insult the God of love, the creator himself, by declaring the physical body, which He designed, to be indecent?

It is worth noting at this point that even commendable actions, such as praying or giving to charity can become offensive when these acts are done in public merely to gain attention and for one's own honour and glory.

So Jesus of Nazareth taught:

> Take care! Do not do your good deeds in public, to be admired by others When you give a gift don't shout about it as the hypocrites do – blowing trumpets in the synagogues and streets to call attention to their acts of charity! When you do a kindness to someone, do it in secret and don't boast about it.

And ...

> When you pray, don't be like the hypocrites who pretend piety by praying publicly on street corners and in the synagogues where everyone can see them. ... When you pray, go away by yourself all alone, and shut the door behind you. When you pray in secret your Father, who knows your secrets, will reward you.
> Matthew 6:1-6 [TLB]

Prayer and lovemaking are both a means (and method) of private and intimate communication between two persons. Within the right context, and with a proper motive, there is nothing offensive about either of them. But they would be indecent if the driving motive is a crude or exhibitionist display.

This couple in the *Song of Songs* are not flaunting themselves in a crude display of exhibitionism. Their nakedness is merely an expression of their total openness and wholehearted acceptance of each other.

There is nothing immodest about nakedness in this context. There is no suggestion of shame or embarrassment as the husband continues to sing in praise about the beauty of his bride.

Those who insist that the *Song of Songs* should really only be interpreted as an allegory of some sort point out that no human being ever meets the standards of beauty which these two lovers use to describe each other.

While there may be some truth in this, those critics have overlooked an important law of human relationships which is that we should always emphasise the points worthy of praise. Secondly, if you want to choose a role model, why not choose a model of perfection? Too many young people nowadays are presented with unhealthy and untidy role models. It simply makes sense to present good role models, the epitome of perfection, such as we see presented in these beautiful songs.

Now, having hopefully reassured his wife of her own natural beauty, and that she is admired, adored and totally accepted, the husband turns his attention to emotional reassurance. He is sensitive to her possible feelings of nervous apprehension about this experience, which will be totally new for her. He sings,

> **4:8-12** Come with me from Lebanon, my bride, come with me from Lebanon. Descend from the crest of Amana, from the top of Senir, the summit of Hermon, from the lions' dens and the mountain haunts of the leopards.

ACT 4 - CELEBRATION

> You have stolen my heart, my sister, my bride; you have stolen my heart with one glance of your eyes, with one jewel of your necklace.
>
> How delightful is your love, my sister, my bride! How much more pleasing is your love than wine, and the fragrance of your perfume than any spice! Your lips drop sweetness as the honeycomb, my bride; milk and honey are under your tongue. The fragrance of your garments is like that of Lebanon. You are a garden locked up, my sister, my bride; you are a spring enclosed, a sealed fountain.   [NIV]

Remember: this is poetry. So we should expect some elaborate poetic expressions.

In asking her to "descend from the crest of Amana, from the top of Senir, from the summit of Hermon" he is appealing to his bride to leave behind any possible lofty attitudes that might inhibit her whole-hearted enjoyment of their first experience of sexual union together.

The dens of lions and mountain leopards were fearful places. He is thus encouraging her to leave her fears behind. The husband is anxious that his new bride will find this a totally satisfying experience, so he expresses his desire that she will be able to put aside all her fears and anxiety and simply enjoy this new adventure they are about to experience together.

The phrase *with me* in the original Hebrew implies "with me and no-one else".

Incidentally, in the Hebrew text this is the first time he has used the word *kallah* (meaning *wife* or *spouse*, as with the KJV) in reference to his beloved, and this is significant since this is now almost the moment of consummation.

The lover (now definitely husband) has given an excellent role model in the use of verbal foreplay and we need to remember that good foreplay must stir-up desire not only within the physical body, but also within the mind and the emotions.

A person cannot give-in to sensual pleasure with sufficient enthusiasm while half of that person's heart or mind is still bound by fears and inhibitions, or feelings of inappropriate guilt and shame. Hence, in order to enjoy truly satisfying sexual communion, the need for emotional turn-ons may actually be greater than the need for physical stimulation.[75]

All reputable modern sex therapists emphasise that foreplay involves far more than just physical touch. Foreplay may include almost anything that stimulates the senses or that can be described as sensual and, at least at this stage of a relationship, should involve a fair bit of talking.

We have just observed a good role model of verbal foreplay using sensuous talk. But there is also the non-verbal interaction, such as the twinkle in the eye, the right sort of smile, the gentle loving touch as fingers brush through the hair or elsewhere, enjoying beautiful music together, or enjoying the beauty of a sunset together.

This couple in the *Song of Songs* have shown us how to just relax and enjoy the togetherness. There is no urgent rush to come together physically.

Masters and Johnson have also emphasised this with their *Sensate Focus* program where couples are encouraged to learn (or re-learn) the art of simply relaxing and just enjoying the pleasure of being together – where they can reach out and touch each other but with no specific demand for sexual performance.[76]

He says, "You have stolen my heart with one glance of your eyes," (4:9). This phrase could also be paraphrased as something like, "Just to see your smile makes my heart feel good." The word translated eyes can also mean "outward appearance" or "countenance".

---

75. Considerable attention is given to this matter by Dr. Daniel Brown in the book *An Analysis of Human Sexual Response* (1967) particularly in the chapter entitled 'Female Orgasm and Sexual Inadequacy'.
76. "Sensate Focus" was the main feature of the educational video *Sex Pleasuring* (1976).

Within a spiritual context, the introduction to communion or to a time of prayer is often described as "Adoration and Praise". In the context of sexual union (or communion) we may need to be reminded that similar principles apply. Be generous with your words of adoration and praise.

The woman is obviously not just a passive partner in the lovemaking scene either, for when she says, "Your love is sweeter than wine," the word she uses is again that intriguing word *dode (dowd)*. In other words, "The warmth of your lovemaking is so-o-o enjoyable and reassuring."

The expression *My sister my spouse* (which occurs four times in this section) is also common in other ancient love songs in reference to a beloved companion. The twofold expression is used to reinforce the feelings of love and devotion. And it is not only her physical form that is so attractive, but every thing about her is beautiful.

The expression, "Your lips drop sweetness as the honeycomb, my bride; milk and honey are under your tongue." (4:11 NIV) could be paraphrased to read, "Every word that drops from your lips is pure sweetness to me." Milk and honey were described as some of the main attributes of the Promised Land, and could be understood as symbols of fertility but, in this context, is more likely to be a reference to sweet and pleasant words.

When he says, "The fragrance of your garments is like that of Lebanon," the husband has used a word that refers to clothing in general, so we cannot be certain exactly what sort of garment he is talking about. Although nakedness would seem to be the logical "dress" for the actual act of coition, some form of revealing clothing is usually far more alluring and effective for the purpose of seduction. Stark naked tends to be just that – stark! It offers very little sense of adventure, or discovery.[77]

---

77. The technique is described by Sheila Kitzinger in her book *A Woman's Experience of Sex*.

With his attention now focused on the "mountain of myrrh" the lover describes this part of his beloved's body as a garden. He sings, "A garden locked up is my sister, my bride, a garden locked, a fountain sealed." (4:12 RSV). The garden obviously refers to the bride's genitals or pubic mound and the whole idea is full of poetic and symbolic beauty.

The Hebrew word *gan* (or *gannah* in its feminine form) is literally translated "a fenced or hidden place" and, to the Hebrew mind especially, the reference to a garden would have implied the beauty and perfection of the Garden of Eden. Thus to describe the wife's genitals as a garden is to say the place is beautiful, and a source of refreshment but also a place where new life can develop when seeds have been planted. There is nothing distasteful, obscene, or offensive about it.

To enter here is like entering paradise. "Locked-up, enclosed, sealed", are poetic references to her virginity.

The bride then responds by expressing some very flowery and poetic words in praise of her husband, and one could get the impression that the air in this scene is pretty heavy with the smell of perfumes. However, the specific herbs and spices, and the words she uses, may again be very significant. She says,

> **4:13-15** "Your contribution is an orchard of pomegranates with choice fruits, with henna and nard, nard and saffron, calamus and cinnamon, with every kind of incense tree, with myrrh and aloes and all the finest spices. You are a garden fountain, a well of flowing water streaming down from Lebanon."
>
> [author paraphrase]

She mentions a garden of spices, but again there is far more "spice" in her poetry than first meets the eye.

When we look at the actual Hebrew words used in this section of her song it seems that the words have been carefully chosen for their double meanings. I had been warned that some of this writing may be very bold in its description of the human body, but frankly was still surprised to discover just how honest this woman really is.

Certainly these people were no prudes! We will see shortly just how unashamedly the bride is hinting at some very explicit references to her husband's sexual equipment, but this is done in beautiful poetic language and without any suggestion of vulgarity.

But first let us take a brief look at the reported characteristics of some of these spices:

To an Eastern mind in particular many of these spices would be related not only to religious worship but also to sensuous lovemaking. Now I realise that the next 3 or 4 paragraphs may seem to be heavy going for some readers, but I do ask that you persevere and read it. It will all make a lot more sense when you get to the end.

I have already mentioned that **henna** has connections with Cleopatra's famous seductive perfume *cyprinum*. **Saffron** has a long history both as a perfume and also as an aphrodisiac.

Saffron and **henna** were both constituents of a paste which Arabian brides used to soften their skin and to give a seductive aroma.

In the book *Fragrant Herbal* (1998), Lesley Bremness tells us that **cinnamon** has a reputation for inspiring lively desire and, when used in moderation, is considered to be a male aphrodisiac.

The smell of **nard** (or spikenard – what we now call **lavender**) is said to aid relaxation. **Incense** (or **frankincense**) is normally in the form of sticks which, when burned, give off a scent that helps to calm the nerves but is also supposed to aid inspiration. For this reason incense is often used in places of meditation and prayer. **Myrrh** has a rich balsamic odour similar to frankincense but with a slightly sweeter, sharper edge and may also be used as an aid to meditation and prayer. However, we also know from Proverbs 7:17 that prostitutes used the spices myrrh, cinnamon, and aloes to create a seductive aroma. Myrrh and aloes are also mentioned as fragrances in Psalm 45:8, which is recognised as a wedding song.

But wait. Yes, there is more. You may remember that I mentioned how, in this part of her song, the bride may be hinting at some very explicit references to her husband's sexual equipment. Consider these points:- The Hebrew word for *cinnamon* comes from a root meaning to erect (as in upright rolls of cinnamon bark). The word *calamus* means a reed (as erect), or some resemblance of a rod or shaft, and the word *trees* is from a Hebrew word that implies firmness. The word translated as plants actually means a missile of attack (ie: a spear), or can also mean a shoot of growth. The word **orchard** *(pardec)* is a Persian word that may also be translated as park or forest. The Hebrew word for **pomegranate** derives from a word that basically means rise up. And the pomegranate fruit is often used as a symbol of fertility.

The word **choice** comes from a word-root meaning to be eminent. The word itself is used to indicate that an object or person is distinguished or precious. The word translated **fruits** can mean either fruit, or something fruitful. The word translated **fountain** is sometimes used figuratively as a source of satisfaction, and **waters** is the Hebrew word *mayim* which is a common euphemism for semen. So the expression living waters may suggest life giving fluid.

The country of Lebanon was noted for its magnificent forests, especially the cedars of Lebanon, which are mentioned elsewhere in the Bible as symbols of natural wealth and beauty. But there are also ranges of mountains in the interior of Lebanon and the River of Adonis flows from these mountains. Adonis was the Syrian god of fertility and vegetation, and in the spring of each year he was the object of a special pilgrimage. So the phrase "streams from Lebanon" may have some connection in thought to wealth and beauty but within this context some allusion to Adonis, and thus to fertility, would seem to be very probable.

ACT 4 - CELEBRATION

So, what do you make of all that? Some would say that the bride is speaking of this man's upright character, wealth, and strength of personality. It is possible that we could paraphrase this to read something like, "My beloved is outstanding, more distinguished than any other tree in forest. The one who redeems me is of great worth. He stands tall, firm, and erect, a fruitful and honourable man who satisfies all my needs." But, in this context, would you also agree that she may be using some very clever double entendre?

She speaks of some distinguished and precious thing that can be a source of great satisfaction. Would you agree that perhaps she could be referring to her husband's hard and erect penis? And she certainly does not seem to be offended by the sight. On the contrary she seems to be expressing some delightful anticipation about this thing she is describing in such poetic and spicy language.

As already indicated, the verse "You are a garden fountain, a well of living water, like the streams flowing from the Lebanon mountains," may be a reference to "life giving fluid", and to her husband as a source of satisfaction for her. However, some versions have translated this verse to read, "I am a garden fountain ..." If the reference is to the bride herself then she could be alluding to the flow of lubricating fluid from her own vagina, an indication that she is now very definitely sexually aroused.

This interpretation would make sense as a prelude to her invitation, which follows immediately after these words, for her husband to enter his garden and enjoy the pleasurable experience.

It is surely significant to note that, although this woman is a virgin, she is not sexually ignorant or naive. She obviously has a very good idea of what to expect, and is not ashamed to talk about such things. It is foolishness to believe that ignorance and innocence are the same. I would love to know what these people did, in practical terms, about sex education for I feel sure we could all learn some very useful ideas that may be helpful even for our present generation.

A January 1995 edition of Readers' Digest contained an article entitled 'Sex Secrets Men Wish Wives Knew',[78] written by Barbara de Angelis who, as a Therapist, claims to have counselled thousands of couples.

She says, "I have gained valuable knowledge about why men act as they do, particularly when it comes to sexual lovemaking. Now I want to share the secrets I have learned." I read this article because my wife brought it to my attention with a comment that said something like, "This woman knows what she is talking about."

Barbara de Angelis makes the important observation that for men, sexual rejection is often interpreted as total rejection. For men, sex is a fundamental way of offering themselves emotionally and physically. When a husband makes a sexual overture to his wife, he is doing more than just asking for sex. He is subconsciously saying, "Please accept me." If the wife simply turns him down without an adequate and acceptable explanation, he does not understand, "Not now." What he understands the woman to mean is, "I don't want you. You are not desirable." Although it may be most unreasonable there are men who accept, "I have a headache" as a total rejection of them as a person.

This may be an area where we all need to work on improving our communication skills. If you say, "Not interested" to your husband's sexual invitation or request then you may need to explain why. You may have a very good reason, but do not be embarrassed to say so and a truly loving husband will (must) accept your refusal. Nevertheless, you may need to explain that you are not rejecting your husband as a person. Reassure him that you still love him and accept him as a person, as a man.

---

78. The Readers Digest article was condensed from *Secrets About Men Every Woman Should Know*, Barbara de Angelis (NY: Bantam Doubleday Dell Publishing Grp 1990)

ACT 4 - CELEBRATION

Remember, if a woman continually declares that sexual intercourse with her husband is somehow disgusting or offensive, then the man might begin to feel totally rejected by his wife and this feeling of rejection will often flow over into other areas of the man's life. He may then go to almost ridiculous extremes in an effort to achieve some feeling of significance and esteem through his work or his sport or from relationships with other people and it is possible you could lose him.

Steve Biddulph[79] also recognises that many men believe that rejection of a sexual overture means total rejection of them as a person, and he exhorts men to reject this erroneous thinking. But it is stamped deep into the male psyche.

In fact, it is probably true to say that when a wife makes an effort to keep herself physically attractive and also express genuine delight in the orgasms which she is able to share with her husband then she communicates a message of acceptance and love that is far more powerful than words alone could ever convey.

Regardless of how we achieve it, a healthy respect for oneself and for other members of society must always be an important part of any Relationships Education we pass on to our children. Somehow we need to inspire in our children a healthy acceptance of who they are and what they are in accordance with God's sexual design, and also an understanding of what that means in terms of healthy human relationships.

This bride obviously has a healthy acceptance of her own sexuality, and she is not afraid of, or embarrassed by, her husband's obvious sexuality. Mutual acceptance and respect in this regard is clearly implied throughout the *Songs*. It is significant that this bride here praises her husband's sexual apparatus, and in so doing she has expressed her total acceptance of him as a human being. She is obviously not offended by the sight of his "symbol of manhood".

---

79. *Manhood*, 1995, p68

If you want to find paradise in your marriage then forget the crude humour you learned at school, and accept the sex organs as something God designed and created. Treat them with honour, reverence, and respect. I have already noted, in the comments regarding the mound of *bether*, that this woman considered the reproductive organs to be sacred and holy, and the act of sexual union as something similar to entering the Most Holy Place in the temple.

And even in our present science-oriented culture we have to acknow-ledge that the operation of both the male and the female sex organs indicates an awesome and wonderful design. The mechanics, the hydraulics (ie: the means by which the penis becomes erect and the labia become soft, warm, and moist), and the electronics (ie: the nerve system, and how these organs respond to messages from the brain) all indicate an ingenious design. But please do not hear me saying that we should worship the penis, or some phallic symbol, as did adherents to the followers of the god Baal, and other ancient fertility cults. No way! We worship the Creator of all things, but we treat his creation with the awe, reverence and respect it deserves.

Remember that, according to the Genesis account, it was God Himself who designed and created Adam and Eve as sexual beings, and that was before there was any mention of sin entering the world. Legitimate sensual and sexual pleasure is not the devil's idea; it is merely his intention to corrupt and spoil God's wonderful design.

How many couples have experimented to find just what is the most sensitive part on the body of their partner, or really know what sort of hugging, stroking, or touching he or she prefers?

This wife is not ignorant of these matters, and it would not be at all unreasonable to believe that her verbal expressions of praise were accompanied by appropriate physical touching. Similarly, it is only reasonable to assume that, as the husband sang praises of his wife as a "garden ... a fountain of satisfaction", he also was engaged in appropriate physical touching of her "mountain of spices".

However one interprets these few verses, it is obvious that this couple have demonstrated a totally unashamed and uninhibited acceptance of each other's body, and they have both expressed a deep appreciation of the fact that they are sexual creatures, as God designed us to be. Oh that we could teach our young people to have the same sort of respect for themselves, and a similar unashamed acceptance of their own body, including all the reproductive organs, as something wholesome and designed by God – something to be treated with honour and respect.

We pause in wonder as we study the operation of the human eye, and so many other functions of the human body. Let's treat the reproductive organs with the same sense of reverence and respect, and grant them the honour they deserve.

At this point the bride now verbalises her passionate desire for her husband to enter her and consummate this special relationship of marriage with full genital coupling. Typical of her poetic language, she says:

> 4:16 "Awake, north wind, and come, south wind!
> Blow on my garden, that its fragrance may spread abroad.
> Let my lover come into his garden and taste its choice fruits
> [NIV]

Note that it is the woman who takes the initiative to invite her husband to enter.

There is, of course, a spiritual parallel to this in that it is the responsibility of any believer to ask the Lord to enter into his or her own heart. God, as redeemer, does not gate-crash anybody's life. Note also that the wife described her vagina as his garden. The teaching which Paul gives to the Christians in Corinth is consistent with this, for Paul tells us that the wife does not have total authority over her own body, because the husband is also part-owner; likewise the husband does not have total authority over his own body, the wife has some claim of ownership.[80]

And note that Paul also added, "...do not deprive one another except perhaps by agreement for a set time, to devote yourselves to prayer, and then come together again, so that Satan may not tempt you because of your lack of self-control." Paul thereby makes a statement that he sees the sexual bonding of husband and wife as a normal and acceptable celebration of their one-flesh relationship, and the activity is not necessarily only for the conception of offspring. But I would warn any men reading this – do not take that as permission to demand anything! Be sensitive to her feelings and state of health.!!

The husband responds by declaring that he has done exactly what his beloved had asked of him, with the words;

> 5:1 "I have come into my garden, my sister, my bride; I have gathered my myrrh with my spice. I have eaten my honeycomb and my honey; I have drunk my wine and my milk." [NIV]

The Hebrew word translated here as "drunk" (drunk my wine . . .) has a connotation of banqueting. Could the husband be using this as poetic way of describing a most enjoyable and satisfying celebration he has been able to share with his (now) wife?

The reference to spices with milk and honey might refer of the blending of their body fluids with the climax of their lovemaking, and the reference to wine might imply satisfaction.

The expression of delight associated with the moment of entry is another area where we find a striking similarity between the sexual and the spiritual.

---

80. 1 Corinthians 7:4

ACT 4 - CELEBRATION

From what I have read and heard, many couples believe that orgasm is the goal of all sexual coupling. But from his experience in counselling Dr. Rollo May warns that this is not the way it should be. He writes:

> The moment of greatest significance in lovemaking, as judged by what people remember of the experience, and what patients dream about, is not the moment of orgasm. It is, rather, the moment of entrance, the moment of penetration of the penis of the man into the [warm, moist and inviting] vagina of the woman.
>
> This is the moment that shakes us, that has within it the great wonder, tremendous and tremulous ... This is the moment when the person's reactions to their lovemaking experience are most original, most individual, most truly their own. This, and not the orgasm, is the moment of union.[81]

Some of the women who contributed to The Hite Report expressed reactions consistent with this view, in that it is often the moment of entry that brings with it an almost overwhelming wave of emotional feeling. One woman wrote,

> Penetration leads to a great and large feeling. It is difficult to describe – my body is electric all over, and I desire physical and spiritual union with [she named her husband]. Sometimes I am praying to God, ... and it is ecstatic joy.[82]

The moment of entry is also where we find a parallel between the sexual and the spiritual, although this may often be lost on people from non-conformist churches.

There have been times when I have walked through the entrance door into some large cathedral and been almost overcome by a sense of awe. This is a sacred and holy place. It is

---

81. Dr. Rollo May, *Love and Will*. Quoted by Frank Sutherland in *Beyond The Sexual Revolution*, p77.
82. The Hite Report, p201

a precious privilege just to enter here, as it were to enter, in some special way, into the presence of God.

By contrast, with the less formal nonconformists, too often people rush in just as the service is about to start, or if they arrive early they still rush in and immediately start to busy themselves with organising equipment for whatever task is ahead of them for the day.

It is possible that those people miss something of the sense of awe at being in a sacred place of worship, although their activity does not necessarily mean there is no sense of anticipation. With some of our Pentecostal friends there may even be an expectation that at some stage during the service someone will offer to pray specifically for them.

They will gladly accept this invitation, perhaps hoping that in some wonderful way they will then be touched by the Spirit and experience something like a spiritual orgasm. Or perhaps they hope to achieve this through their own fervent "worship". But I wonder if somehow they miss out on something of the depth of feeling that can only come when we enter a sacred place with an appropriate sense of awe.

To continue with some "wisdom" from Dr. Rollo May:

Although women obviously enjoy orgasm, and some are capable of more than one in a session of lovemaking, for them this is part of the overall package of feeling totally appreciated and accepted by a faithful, caring, and understanding partner.

When women complain that the act of lovemaking is over too quickly it may be because the physical union is not seen as part of a long-term ongoing expression of affirmation and total acceptance. For them the emphasis needs to be not just on the physical but also on the emotional and spiritual unity. By contrast, the concept of frantically thrusting and grinding away in a desperate attempt to achieve climax is typical of the boring, predictable, and unimaginative pornographic movies produced for male consumers. It is not a characteristic of good lovemaking!!

ACT 4 - CELEBRATION

Of course there is a spiritual parallel to this. Those Christians who tend to over-emphasise signs, wonders, and manifestations often fail to recognise that different people with different personalities have different ways of expressing their intimacy with the LORD. It is not that these people do not know the LORD, or have not experienced the Joy of The LORD.

It is just that they have different ways of expressing their joy in a precious and personal relationship.

And so Act 4 closes with an expression of absolute approval of the newly-wed couple's mutual pleasure;

> "Eat, O friends. Enjoy your banquet and satiate yourselves with lovemaking!" (5:1b paraphrased)

Note the words, "Enjoy (savour), ... satiate ..."

Commentators differ widely regarding the identity of the one who speaks these words. Some believe this is sung by the choir, and thereby the bride's group of supportive friends have affirmed her right to enjoy sexual pleasure. However, others prefer to interpret that it is God Himself who expresses His full approval of everything that has taken place throughout this scene.

This interpretation may be important. Anyone who has been involved with married couples discussing their sexual problems, or who has read some of the books describing the sexual frustration and associated fantasies that have been reported by many women, will be aware that there are a number of them who are troubled by their "inner parent" condemning their "inner child" for simply enjoying the fun and pleasures of sex.

Shere Hite[83] reports that more than 95% of the women who responded to her questionnaires indicated that they had been brought up to believe that sex was "bad", or at the very least was a subject that must never be mentioned. Some of these women reported that they overcome this problem by fantasising during

---
83. The Hite Report, p39

their lovemaking, and for some of them this fantasy involved making love in front of an approving audience.

Those who have actually been involved in acting that required simulated sexual intercourse on stage have reported that audience approval had a powerful effect in releasing their own inhibitions about sexual activity. And even during the 1990's at our Marriage Enrichment seminars we had people who thanked us, sometimes with tears of gratitude, for having simply shown them that it is not only permissible but also possible for a husband and wife to talk honestly and frankly about sexual matters without being overcome by feelings of embarrassment or shame.

Many people seem to have problems adjusting from the "sex is forbidden" concept of childhood and pre-marriage days, to the "do it and enjoy it" concept of marriage. The writer of these songs has hinted at this with her references to "the watchmen of the city". If it is some help to imagine that God is watching and declaring His approval of your husband-wife expressions of sexual love, then we would say, "Why not?" My wife and I would not be the first to admit that we have stopped during sexual lovemaking and while still coupled together given thanks to God for the way that He designed and created our physical bodies. I am convinced that God designed sex not just for procreation, but also for intimate communication and emotional bonding between a wife and her husband.

As we consider all that this woman has communicated to her readers in Act 4 we have to agree that she has described a beautiful scene of sexual lovemaking, but in doing so she has avoided the use of crude slang or explicit sexual terms. This adds to the beauty of her prose, because slang terminology and explicit sexual language both tend to lack the warmth and emotion that is needed for such an emotionallycharged subject. Have you noticed that throughout these songs the couple always express their desire and their interest in sexual matters by using rather beautiful poetic terms and symbols for what could otherwise be embarrassing language.

The Ecstacy of Relationship

Our enjoyment of *legitimate* sensual pleasure is obviously meant to be an important part of the Creator's basic design provided that this is experienced within the context of a healthy relationship.

Doing enjoyable things together, or sharing emotional experiences together, can be a very effective means of drawing people into a closer bond of friendship. Hence the moonlight swim, or walking together in a park or in a beautiful garden, or sitting together and listening to beautiful music, are all examples of togetherness activities which a couple in a healthy relationship should enjoy doing together. Where the act of sexual union is undertaken with mutual desire and mutual pleasure then the sharing together of these powerful and intensely pleasurable feelings can have a very positive effect on the growth of real intimacy. But, with all of these activities, the experience only becomes really meaningful when it is related to the other person with whom it is shared, rather than our own personal pleasure.

In his book *A Celebration of Sex,* Dr Rosenau emphasises the importance of a good spiritual and emotional relationship in order to develop a satisfying sex life. While he quite frankly agrees that making love has great potential to excite as well as to unite, it is the relationship that gives it context and meaning. As he says,

> Without an intimate relationship we find that sex becomes just another activity. Going on a roller coaster ride can also be exciting, but we wouldn't want to do that several times a month for the next 20 years or maybe even for the rest of our lives. So

it is with sex: without the relationship the activity tends to lose its dynamic appeal.[84]

When we engage in sexual activity purely to satisfy our own "need" for sensual pleasure, it is like getting ourselves stuck in a dead-end street. Eventually the activity loses its appeal and we find we are looking for new ideas to restore the original thrill and sense of adventure. Certainly there are hundreds of books and magazines that present us with ideas and suggestions of how to do this, but it stands to reason that the honeymoon has got to end sometime. Eventually the inevitable unresolved conflicts outweigh the excitement of the sex appeal, and the relationship runs into trouble. There is even a danger that some marriages may become just another business contract, and the business involved in many cases seems to be little more than operating a child-minding centre together with a boarding house.

What do we do to revitalise the excitement when the first thrill of discovery wears thin and the activity becomes monotonous? Then there is the danger of seeking a new sense of adventure with a new and different partner. Even some ancient Hebrews acknowledged this problem.

They admitted that if it were not for the sex drive, which Hebrews described as *yetzer ha-ra* (the evil inclination), then no man would ever build a house, marry a wife, or raise a family.[85] Sexual desire has been given to us to provide that motivation, but it must be held in balance with the sacrificial component of *agapé* – the love that seeks a relationship, rather than purely selfish gratification.

This is not just a Christian opinion. Many other writers acknowledge the same truth. In her book *The Art of Sexual Ecstasy*, Margo Anand, a Tantric sex therapist, expresses a very

---

84. Dr. Douglas Rosenau, *A Celebration of Sex* (1994), pp23-34.
85. Quoted by I H Fishbein, *Dictionary of Pastoral Care and Counselling* (1990), p679.

similar viewpoint.[86] Yet Ms Anand is certainly not writing from a Christian perspective. On the contrary, many would describe her book as New Age. But even from her point of view she tells us that the desire to unite sexually with another human being is a reflection of an underlying spiritual need to experience wholeness and complete intimacy. And she also points out that when deprived of its sacred dimension sexual energy will eventually be directed against itself, which in turn results in disrespect and may thus lead to sexual violence rather than building an atmosphere of love.

Margo Anand also warns her readers that the reduction of sex to a purely physical act will promote an externalised view of intercourse in which lovemaking is perceived as a mere performance. So, as with the Christian writers, this Tantric Sex-therapist also confirms that sexual lovemaking is not simply a question of physical stimulation. Rather it is a matter of delicate harmonisation between two persons in a relationship that requires trust, openness, creativity, and many other mental, emotional, and spiritual qualities. She also very strongly affirms that a good sexual encounter requires a deep level of communication between the two individuals involved. It is only when we finally achieve such heart-to-heart connection with each other that communication becomes communion, and lovemaking can then carry you to an experience of real ecstasy.[87]

The *Song of Songs* has also emphasised the ecstasy of a relationship, as opposed to the mere physical pleasure that can be achieved through sexual activity on its own. In reading through both of the books mentioned above (*A Celebration of Sex* and *The Art of Sexual Ecstasy*) I was frequently finding ideas presented by both of these writers that are very much in agreement with the role models we find in the *Songs*.

---

86. Margo Anand, The Art of Sexual Ecstasy (1992), pp32 ff.
87. Margo Anand, The Art of Sexual Ecstasy (1992), p60.

For real intimacy to be achieved we must first prove that we can *always* be trusted to treat our partner with such love and respect that s/he will know with absolute confidence that it is safe to reveal to us the true hidden person of the heart. When this level of trust has been firmly established and we have learned that we can safely reveal to our partner all of our emotions, – fears and insecurities as well as feelings of joy and excitement – only when we know with *absolute confidence* that it is safe to invite that person into the most sacred depths of our being, and that they can be trusted to minister to us with understanding, tenderness and strength to heal those uncertainties, fears, and insecurities – only then do we have real intimacy. Such a level of intimacy requires mutual respect and mutual appreciation, and leads to the growth of a healthy sense of self-worth.

When the physical act of sexual union becomes an expression of this emotional and spiritual intimacy only then do we begin to approach real ecstasy. When both of us, as marriage partners, have together achieved this level of understanding then we have become "one-flesh" and are permitted to truly enjoy each other's pleasure (as the bride expressed it, *"Come into my garden and taste [enjoy] the sweet delights"* 4:16).

ACT 5   SEPARATION

Song of Songs 5:2 to 6:13

2 I slept but my heart was awake. Listen! My lover is knocking: "Open to me, my sister, my darling, my dove, my flawless one. My head is drenched with dew, my hair with the dampness of the night."

3 I have taken off my robe-- must I put it on again? I have washed my feet-- must I soil them again?

4 My lover thrust his hand through the latch-opening; my heart began to pound for him.

5 I arose to open for my lover, and my hands dripped with myrrh, my fingers with flowing myrrh, on the handles of the lock.

6 I opened for my lover, but my lover had left; he was gone. My heart sank at his departure. I looked for him but did not find him. I called him but he did not answer.

7 The watchmen found me as they made their rounds in the city. They beat me, they bruised me; they took away my cloak, those watchmen of the walls!

8 O daughters of Jerusalem, I charge you-- if you find my lover, what will you tell him? Tell him I am faint with love.

9 How is your beloved better than others, most beautiful of women? How is your beloved better than others, that you charge us so?

10 - 16 My lover is radiant and ruddy, outstanding among ten thousand. His head is purest gold; his hair is wavy and black as a raven. His eyes are like doves by the water streams, washed in milk, mounted like jewels. His cheeks are like beds of spice yielding perfume. His lips are like lilies dripping with myrrh. His arms are rods of gold set with chrysolite. His body is like polished ivory decorated with sapphires. His legs are pillars of marble set on bases of pure gold. His appearance is like Lebanon, His arms are rods of gold set with chrysolite. His body is like polished ivory decorated with sapphires. His legs are pillars of marble set on bases of pure gold. His appearance is like Lebanon, choice as its cedars.

His mouth is sweetness itself; he is altogether lovely. This is my lover, this is my friend, O daughters of Jerusalem.

6:1 Where has your lover gone, most beautiful of women? Which way did your lover turn, that we may look for him with you?

2 My lover has gone down to his garden, to the beds of spices, to browse in the gardens and to gather lilies.

3 I am my lover's and my lover is mine; he browses among the lilies.

4 You are beautiful, my darling, as Tirzah, lovely as Jerusalem, majestic as troops with banners.

5 Turn your eyes from me; they overwhelm me. Your hair is like a flock of goats descending from Gilead.

6 Your teeth are like a flock of sheep coming up from the washing. Each has its twin, not one of them is alone.

7 Your temples behind your veil are like the halves of a pomegranate.

8 Sixty queens there may be, and eighty concubines, and virgins beyond number;

9 but my dove, my perfect one, is unique, the only daughter of her mother, the favorite of the one who bore her. The maidens saw her and called her blessed; the queens and concubines praised her. 9 but my dove, my perfect one, is unique, the only daughter of her mother, the favorite of the one who bore her. The maidens saw her and called her blessed; the queens and concubines praised her.

10 Who is this that appears like the dawn, fair as the moon, bright as the sun, majestic as the stars in procession?

11 I went down to the grove of nut trees to look at the new growth in the valley, to see if the vines had budded or the pomegranates were in bloom.

12 Before I realized it, my desire set me among the royal chariots of my people.

13 Come back, come back, O Shulammite; come back, come back, that we may gaze on you! Why would you gaze on the Shulammite as on the dance of Mahanaim?   [NIV]

ACT 5

SEPARATION

Significant theme: When the passion of first love has faded.

Fairy tales read, ".. and they lived happily ever after". It does not happen like that in real life, and the writer makes an effort here to warn us that there will be problems. Happiness in a marriage relationship is not automatic. There will be misunderstandings and disappointments, and we need to learn some skills that will help us deal with our conflict issues.

So the chronology of this section does not have to be important, for its primary purpose seems to be to teach some important lessons about maintaining the intimacy and "romantic sparkle" in a marriage relation-ship, and there are timeless truths and lessons to be learned.

One of the major problems in marriages today is that we get our priorities confused. If many business men (and we can read that as business women also) put as little effort into building their business as they do into building a relationship with their spouse then their business would be a failure.

So it is valid for all of us as married couples to ask ourselves and to ask each other, "What are our real priorities?" Which is more important, children or career? Building a business or building a relationship?

Is "paradise" for us defined as having a happy family, or having a lot of possessions, or being in a job where I can feel that I am needed?

Christians are certainly not exempt from this confusion, as Ed Silvoso says in his video presentation *How to Have Intimacy in Marriage*,[88] many people in ministry are "committing adultery" with their job.

When work pressures begin to be more important than the marriage relationship and there is insufficient time for the couple to enjoy just being alone together there can be a dangerous tendency for one or both partners to feel rejected and resentful. Instead of welcoming the presence of her husband when he comes home the wife may unconsciously react by rejecting him. The same situation can apply in reverse when it is the wife who is working long hours and her work responsibilities are taking her away from what should be family togetherness time. In these subtle little ways the preciousness of intimacy can be lost.

We are introduced to the song in Act 5 with this description of a dream which I have paraphrased in contemporary language:

She [As she describes her dream - or was it a nightmare?]

> 5:2-8 One night, as I was sleeping, my heart was awakened in a dream. I heard the voice of my beloved calling and he was asking, "Open to me, my sister, my darling, my dove, my flawless one. I have been out in the night and am covered with dew."
>
> But I replied, "I have undressed for the night. Why should I get dressed again? And I have already washed my feet, and do not wish to get them dirty again."

---

88. Video (63 mins) distributed by Institute of Basic Life Principles, USA (1992).

ACT 5 - SEPARATION

Then my beloved simply put his hand to the entrance, [and opened the door] my emotions were stirred with excitement.

I jumped up to open for him and my hands dripped with myrrh, my fingers with liquid myrrh as I moved to open for him.

I began to realise how much I really longed for him, but he had already withdrawn from me, and appeared to be asleep, wrapped in his blanket.

My desire was now running wild, and I really wanted him.

I spoke his name, but there was no reply. My thoughts really bothered me and I began to feel rather foolish and guilty.

Then in my dream I was running down a street where those moral guardians of the city found me.

They hit me, and wounded me. Those moral guardians stripped my veil from me, and I felt so foolish and vulnerable standing there in the street, and feeling very foolish and naked.

So I beg you, my friends, if you can get any response from my beloved, tell him that I am overcome with a passionate desire to be reunited with him.   [author paraphrase]

In some translations (TLB, GNB) this section is quite clearly stated as the woman's dream, for she sings, "I dreamt my lover knocked." In other versions (AV, NIV, NRSV, etc.) we read, "I slept, but my heart was awake." Possibly she is referring to one of those occasions when we lie in bed only half asleep, and our mind switches between the real world and the dream state. Remember also, that the heart was considered to be the seat of moral decision-making in Hebrew thought.

She then continues, "Listen, my lover is knocking." [NIV]. We are not told what this man has been doing, or why he is so late home, but the reference to his head covered in dew would suggest this is sometime in the very early hours of the morning. Possibly he has been working long hours in the gardens, but in any case he has been working well past midnight.

As he signals his arrival, the greeting he uses indicates that whatever the reason for his late homecoming his wife has not been forgotten. We know this because he uses a four-fold expression of love for her, and it seems that he had hoped she might come and greet him at the door. Now, for some people, this can be a very controversial topic. I have learned that some career-oriented women would scorn the idea of going to the door to greet their husband.

Many books about love and marriage remind us of the importance of saying those three little words, "I love you". But these words become empty and meaningless if they are not backed up by appropriate attitudes and behaviour.

We heard of one man who, when he left for work each morning, would always kiss his wife goodbye and say, "I love you." But then after he had left the house and she went to the bathroom she would find his toothpaste and shaving gear left untidily around the hand-basin. His towel, and sometimes his clothes from the day before, were often found on the floor instead of placed in the laundry basket. His attitude of apparently expecting his wife to play the role of domestic servant negated his parting words of love.

In another case the husband would often come home from work and find his wife, who did not work outside the home, slouched at the table and reading some romance novel while the breakfast dishes were still unwashed in the kitchen sink. He also complained that she was now nearly thirty kilograms over weight. Yet she would often come and whisper in his ear, "I love you darling." But, in the understanding of this man, if his wife really loved him then she would show her respect and her love for him by taking some pride in her own appearance. And, according to his belief system, when seen with him in public she should always stand tall, thus indicating that she was proud to be seen with this man who was, after all, the man she had chosen to marry. Her spoken words of affection fell on deaf ears because her body language was seen as a constant denial of the things she said. This man did not look forward to coming home from work, and felt that as a husband he was obviously a complete failure. Any romantic ideas he might have had were now trashed by the depressing sight that met him as he stepped through the door into his own home.

Early in 1997 Rose (my wife) was present at a ladies fellowship meeting when she was handed a sheet of paper entitled *Tips to look after your husband*. The ten ideas she read on that page were extracted from a 1950 school textbook on Home Economics. They included not only recommendations about planning meals at least a day in advance, but also suggested that the wife should make an effort to prepare herself for her husband's home-coming. The wife should take at least a fifteen minute rest, so the book said, and put a ribbon in her hair so that she will appear bright and fresh to welcome her work-weary husband. Rose told me that all the other women present at that meeting treated these ideas with contempt. "Is that supposed to be a joke?" was one woman's scornful comment.

In contrast to the reaction expressed by those ladies, and the apparent disinterest shown by this woman in the *Song of Songs,* Martin Luther is reported to have said that it should be the responsibility of every wife to make her husband glad he came home. Or maybe it was his wife who said that? Nevertheless it seems a fairly revolutionary idea in a culture where truly religious people were being taught that they should remain unmarried.

In the 1970's Marabel Morgan even suggested that a thoughtful wife could brighten up her husband's day by meeting him at the door wearing little more than a smile and baby-doll pyjamas, as she did for her husband once, much to the delight of both her husband and their children.

She knew that her husband had been expecting a stressful day at work and she simply wanted to help him to unwind, to relax, and to enjoy the evening with his family. Of course this meant leaving the pressures and problems of his work outside the house, so she had planned this very unorthodox welcome home for him. But the idea was so successful that afterwards she frequently used variations on the same theme. Of course in a marriage where both partners work outside the home there may be pressures and stresses that will make some of her ideas unworkable. But does our materialistic culture, with the two income family, a big house, nice car, boat, caravan, etc., guarantee happiness?

No! It is harmony that creates a happy home and an emotionally healthy family. And we don't buy that with money. When both partners in a marriage are committed to their career, who is going to create a home, a haven, where a family with children can grow and develop, in an emotionally healthy environment?

In emphasising the need to provide some sort of a welcome-home greeting for your marriage partner, Mrs Morgan even suggests that the tone for the entire evening may be set during the first four minutes you spend together at the end of your working day. However, this wife had obviously lived centuries before Marabel Morgan and could never have been able to read any of her books, nor attended any of her classes, and she responded to the greeting of her husband's home-coming with indifference.

How many individuals reading these words can identify with this scene? "He has ignored me all evening. Why should I make him welcome now?" "He is more interested in his work than he is in me."

And how many husbands complain that their wife is more interested in her career or her hobby than she is in her marriage or her family? What are our real priorities in life? What do we really believe is the pathway to paradise? A financial fortune, or a supportive and loving family?

ACT 5 - SEPARATION

Worshippers of materialism are not the only people who may treat their family responsibilities lightly. Shame-damaged people, who seem to be scared of the real intimacies of marriage, will often escape from the threat of intimacy by focusing on their work. They may be guilty of "committing adultery" with their ministry, and their spouse and family miss out on love.

Rose and I have often heard tearful women say something like, "My dad always had time for other people's kids, but he never had time for me." This was particularly so where the father had been involved in some form of social welfare work or ministry. We have a responsibility to make our homes a place where all family members feel welcome, loved, and safe.

For Marabel Morgan this even included mum and dad, and their two children.[89] So the little gestures, such as a wave from the door when we leave, and a special welcome when we return home, may be very important.

But some of us men may be guilty of taking those little gestures for granted. There was a time when, for several months, I was a full-time student and Rose went out to work to earn money and put bread on the table while I stayed at home to listen to recorded lectures, read textbooks, and write assignments. Each morning I would race through the necessary housework, then get on with my study program for the rest of the day. After several weeks Rose gently pointed out to me that when it was I who was leaving for work she would always wave me goodbye and make some point of greeting me when I returned home. I had simply failed to realise the importance of these little gestures, which were a non-verbal way of saying, "I miss you when you are not here, and I look forward to meeting you when you come home each night."

Such behaviour is an important non-verbal expression of love, and some of us may have to make a disciplined effort until these become a habit.

---
89. Marabel Morgan, *The Total Woman* (1979) p94

Husbands and wives who take each other for granted are playing a dangerous and foolish game. Remember that many people in the business world spend the day with other individuals who are making a real effort to appear attractive, helpful, and co-operative, and then these folk come home and find a partner who treats them with indifference. Is it any wonder that we hear so many stories of business people who end up in bed with their secretary? What is more important to you? Your pride? Your career? Or your marriage and family, and your relationship with your spouse? Do you really believe that you will find "paradise" through involvement in your career at the cost of destroying your marriage, and possibly losing the respect of your own children?

So perhaps some of us can identify with the strange conflict of emotions described in this woman's dreams.

We do not know what sort of a day this man had at work, as the wife had never asked. All we know is that when he came home he gave his wife a verbal greeting of something like, "Darling I love you." but she responded with a disappointing lack of interest. So she makes her excuses, apparently stays where she is, in bed, while he lets himself in at the door, and yet almost in the next breath this woman starts telling us how she is almost panting with desire, wanting her husband to come and spend time with her.

Rather than criticise her, at least we should commend her for her honesty in telling us how easily these things can happen. As I have already tried to explain, it is these little misunderstandings, so insignificant at the time, which can be the beginning of a breakdown in the intimacy of any relationship.

Christians seeking for a spiritual interpretation of this section should immediately recognise a similarity to the scene described in the book of Revelation where we read of the church in Laodicea. The criticism of this church was that these people had become smug and self-satisfied. They were so preoccupied with their feelings of wealth and their own little programs and

ACT 5 - SEPARATION

attitudes of self-righteousness that the LORD had effectively been left out of their lives, and for this reason He threatens to reject them (to "spew them out, like vomit") if they do not return to the enthusiasm of their first love. Then, after this rebuke, we read the well known verse, "Behold, I stand at the door and knock" (Revelation 3:20).

Note well that this challenge was not given to a bunch of pagans. It was addressed to a group of people who professed to love The LORD. But these people had become so complacent, self-sufficient and pleased with themselves that they were no longer in intimate fellowship with the one they claimed to worship. In this verse the LORD himself demonstrates his love by expressing his desire for the restoration of an intimate relationship with these self-righteous people.

To return to the incident in the *Songs*, notice how the main emphasis here really seems to be on the wife's self-satisfied complacency. The husband had expressed his love, and his interest in a warm welcome from his wife, but he was rebuffed. However it seems he is a gentleman and he does not demand attention or force the issue.

Perhaps at this point we can learn an important lesson. The loving husband does not make demands. He merely expresses his love and his desire, but when he receives no real encouragement he simply leaves his wife to continue her rest, and does not make a pest of himself. So he simply withdrew, apparently wrapped himself in his blanket, and went straight to sleep.

On the other hand however, as Steve Biddulph[90] tells us, the practice of not confronting an issue where there is obviously some misunderstanding is a typical reaction of many husbands. And it is a reaction women sometimes do not appreciate. They (ie: women) seem to be more prepared to discuss issues where emotional feelings are involved, whereas men tend to withdraw, in confusion.

---
90. Steve Biddulph, *Manhood*, (1995)

Of course these statements are generalisations. But sometimes we do need to be more sensitive to the difference between persevering (a desirable reaction), or making a pest of ourselves (which is **not** a desirable reaction). This is often another one of those areas where we have expectations that are never put into words, and are never adequately discussed between husband and wife. Because we are not all mindreaders, and because every individual person is different, this is a common cause of unresolved conflict within marriage.

Perhaps in this case the husband could have been just a little more persistent, and he might have been pleasantly surprised, because she now tells us something of her own feelings. She says, "My heart began to pound for him". The Hebrew language actually tells us that this is emotion which touches the very core of her being. She is now really wanting some attention from him, but it seems that he is not listening. She whispers his name, but gets no response, and explains to those who are listening to her story that, "He had withdrawn himself". The word translated "withdrawn" is from a root meaning "to turn" or "to enwrap". So this could suggest he is curled up, wrapped in a blanket. Now the tables are turned. She is now the one who is very interested, but the husband is now sound asleep — or maybe just pretending to be so (?).

How many married people treat their partner this way? They take each other for granted, but still expect to be given preferential treatment at all times. And if you want a spiritual analogy, how many people treat their relationship with the Lord in the same way. Like the Church in Laodicea (Revelation Ch.3), they busy themselves with their own little programs, while their Redeemer is virtually ignored. Then, when they suddenly want something, they expect to be honoured and blessed, like a wonderful and truly faithful friend.

If we truly desire a relationship of real intimacy with someone we love then we need to learn to accept, admire, adapt to, and appreciate this person. The man in this story obviously had responsibilities which required his attention and meant he was sometimes late home. If the man here is in fact King Solomon himself (as some scholars believe), then such responsibilities would be very normal. And the further anyone moves upward in business management the more these issues intrude into family life. When we act in love we must learn to accept the reality of the situation, and adapt ourselves to it. We have already seen how this man put into practice the principles of admiration and appreciation of his wife, but it seems that "Mrs Solomon" had temporarily forgotten this.

This writer has wanted to teach us something, and to illustrate her point she presented this scene as a dream. Typical of a dream, we now have a sudden change of scene to the streets of the city where she is immediately confronted by these "watchmen", and because she now feels guilty for the way she has just responded, all those feelings of shame and condemnation from her childhood come crowding back into her memory. She feels condemned, accused, and guilty. So she describes her feelings as some form of harsh punishment. "They beat me; they bruised me; they took away my veil." And she is left feeling "naked and vulnerable." It is interesting that naked and vulnerable or not clothed with true righteousness is also the accusation made against the Church in Laodicea (Revelation 3:18).

Have you ever faced such emotions? Can you identify with her awful feeling of embarrassment – here I am, filled with passionate desire, and feeling rejected. Yes, emotionally bruised and vulnerable. I wonder if she is now thinking, "How did my husband feel when I said, in effect, 'Not tonight. I am simply not interested in going to the door to greet you'?"

In her song the woman expresses her feelings by asking her friends, "If you find my lover (ie: if you are able to get some response from him in some way) tell him that I am overcome with passionate desire for him."

This musical program has presented us with what may seem to some people to have been a fairly mild misunderstanding on the part of these two lovers. But I would suspect that there are many people in the world who are grieving over a separation and who could identify with this woman's pleading as she cries to the wind, "If there is somebody who can talk to my beloved will you please tell him that I still love him." And we could easily reverse the genders – there will be many men with aching hearts who would be so glad if someone could convince their estranged wife with the message, "Darling, I really do still love you." Big and painful separations can have such small beginnings.

The group of friends or those listening to her story, now challenge the woman to explain why her husband is so special.

The Young Women of Jerusalem:

5:9 "How is your beloved better than others, most beautiful of women?

What is so special about him that you ask us to help you find him?

One of the many beneficial exercises couples were often encouraged to do at a Marriage Enrichment weekend was to write down all the positive attributes of their relationship and all the things they like about their partner. This was obviously not a new idea. These ancient Hebrews seemed to recognise the value of such an exercise for these women challenge "the Shulammite" with the question, in effect, "Why is he so special?" And here is one wife who responds with a most definite assertion, "He is wonderful!"

In our modern society, where it seems almost fashionable to emphasise the negatives, it is good to be reminded of the importance of looking for the positives. This is a lesson we need to learn for the good of any relationship, and our marriage relationship in particular.

ACT 5 - SEPARATION

The woman then responds to the challenge from her friends with these words:-

She: [responding to the challenge from her friends]

5:10-16 My beloved is all radiant and ruddy, outstanding among ten thousand. His head is the purest gold; his hair is wavy, and black as a raven. His eyes are like doves beside springs of water, bathed in milk, fitly set. His cheeks are like beds of spices, yielding fragrance. His lips are lilies, distilling liquid myrrh.

His arms are rounded gold, set with jewels. His body is ivory work, encrusted with sapphires. His legs are alabaster columns, set upon bases of gold. His appearance is like Lebanon, choice as the cedars. His speech is most sweet, and he is altogether desir-able. This is my beloved and this is my friend, O daughters of Jerusalem.   [author paraphrase]

Unlike the descriptions of 4:1-7 and 6:4-9 the wife speaks here in the third person, and thus she is responding to the friends who challenged her with the question. Remember; this is poetry so we don't take the words too literally. But she certainly seems to be telling her friends, and perhaps reassuring herself, that this man to whom she is married is really someone very special, and therefore it is worth her making a special effort to keep their relationship "alive".

The reference to *gold* in 5:11 "His head is finest gold" is not a reference to colour, but to integrity and purity, and in 5:15, "His legs are alabaster columns, set upon bases of gold" the reference would be to nobility of form and posture.

The expression, "His mouth is sweetness" (5:16 NIV) does not need to refer to just the physical mouth but also to what emanates from the mouth (as with NRSV). In other words, "The very words he speaks are pure sweetness. He is altogether lovely. This is my lover. This is my friend."

Notice that she refers to her husband as her friend. It is a sad and grievous thing to find married couples who do not consider each other as best friends. What a sad and sick world it is where couples, motivated by "sexual chemistry" simply leap into bed together, or leap into marriage, without first taking the time to establish a healthy and sound friendship that will last a lifetime.

The advantage of being friends with our spouse was demonstrated from research conducted by a Dr David Weeks of the Royal Edinburgh Hospital. He conducted a survey of 3,500 people who look up to fourteen years younger than their real age and, according to his report, found that the quality of their marriage relationship had slowed down the ageing process for these people. Dr Weeks claimed that it was not the quality or quantity of their sex life, but all of these people regarded their spouse as their best friend.[91]

Why were marriages of yesteryear more stable than they are today? Well one of the reasons is probably that in many cases our forebears courted and then married someone who was a friend before they became lovers.

The Young Women of Jerusalem:

6:1 "Where has your lover gone, most beautiful of women?
Which way did your lover turn, that we may look for him with you?" [NIV]

The friends ask, "Where did he go?" or possibly, "When did he walk away?" (so that we may seek him with you).

This response from her friends demonstrates a good counselling technique and also a model of how a support group ought to work. Unlike Job's friends, who confronted the poor man with accusations and condemnation, the group of friends in the *Song of Songs* have been there to listen, to offer words of encouragement and support, and also to express affirmation and approval of appropriate behaviour. A good support group

---
91. Reported in the *Ballarat Courier*, 3rd January 1996, p20

should also be there to offer words of wise counsel when asked or required, and often such counsel amounts to simply asking the right questions at the right time. This is a good principle of counselling – gentle and supportive concern while at the same time helping the counselee to acknowledge and face up to their real situation.

Hence they ask, "When did your husband leave you?" or possibly, "Where has he gone?" In other words, "Has he really left you, or do you just have a wrong perception of the situation?" And she responds:

She

6:2-3 "My lover has gone down to his garden, to the beds of spices, to browse in the gardens and to gather lilies.

I am my lover's and my lover is mine; he is browsing among the lilies." [NIV]

Typical of a dream that flows from one scene to another because of some connection of thought, she responds to her friends' question by suggesting that her husband has gone down to the garden (possibly to work?).

But to this couple gardens have romantic connotations and there is possibly a deliberate double meaning in the words she has used here.

We could interpret her statement "he is browsing among the lilies" to indicate that the husband has in fact made some response, at this point in time, and placed a hand on her "garden of spices" as he gave her a sleepy cuddle. This would then be understood as a very gentle, non verbal, expression of reassurance that he is not really ignoring her entirely.

We have already learned that the reference to lilies may be a poetic allusion to the woman's labia (the lips of her vagina). The word translated "browsing" actually means "becoming acquainted with", and the word "gather" implies a task normally done with the hand. So she responds to this gesture with a verbal affirmation of their mutual commitment, using the refrain, "I belong to my lover, and my lover is mine." And he begins to murmur words of praise.

He [speaking to his wife]

6:4-10 "My darling, you are as pretty as the lovely land of Tirzah.

> Yes, beautiful as Jerusalem. You have indeed captured my heart, and when you look at me like that I just melt."
>
> [author paraphrase]
>
> "The waves of your hair are beautiful, like a flock of goats winding down the slopes of Gilead. Your teeth are white and even – like very pregnant ewes coming up from the washing, each with a perfectly matched twin. And your cheeks, hiding beneath your hair, have a healthy glow like two halves of a ripe pomegranate. Let the king have his sixty queens, eighty concubines, and young women without number, but I love only one, and she is as lovely as a dove. The only daughter of your mother – your mother's precious child. The women of Jerusalem were delighted when they saw you, and even the women from the palace praise you. 'Who is this,' they ask, 'arising as the dawn, fair as the moon, pure as the sun, so utterly captivating'?"   [author paraphrase]

Verses 8-9 of the script quoted above are from the Good News Bible. This translation obviously implies a relationship between one man and his one wife, both of whom are known to people from the palace, but who are not necessarily the king and queen. This could be some aspect of the Royalty fantasy which is typical of Egyptian love songs.

However, many other translations of the *Songs* tell us that in her dream the woman hears her husband say something like:

ACT 5 - SEPARATION

He

6:8-9 "Sixty queens there may be, and eighty concubines, and virgins beyond number; but my dove, my perfect one, is unique.

"The only daughter of her mother, the favourite of the one who bore her. The maidens saw her and they called her blessed;

"even the queens and concubines praised her."   [NIV]

This statement would seem to make sense if these songs had been written by Solomon's wife who was the daughter of Pharaoh.[92]

In any case, even supposing this woman now imagines herself to be in the king's harem she does not feel threatened by the presence of "sixty queens, eighty concubines, and innumerable young maidens". She has thus gained a measure of trust, confidence, and self assurance, and does not feel threatened by the green eyed monster of jealousy.

As someone once said, "Any woman who puts love into her love-making does not need to fear competition." We will discover shortly just how much enthusiasm this beautiful woman can put into her lovemaking, but just for now she continues to tell us more of her thoughts, actions, and desires relating to this event:

She [in soliloquy]

6:11-12 "I went down into the grove of nut trees to look at the new growth in the valley, to see if the vines had budded or the pomegranates were in bloom.

"Before I realised it, I was lost to the thrill of my desire —

I wanted to make love with my husband even more desperately than the chariot rider wants to win his race when

---
92. 1 Kings 3:1 and 1 Kings 11:1

the crowd cheers him on."
[author paraphrase but very similar to NIV]

As her thoughts and dreams have wandered from gardens to the delightful and beautiful design of the human body this woman is becoming aware that her own "private garden" is sending her some messages. Her thoughts go down to "the garden of nuts, to see [consider] the fruits of the valley, [and] to see if the vine has flourished, and the pomegranates budded."

The word *nuts* or *nut trees* is another of those foreign words, probably Persian. But when we see this in the context of the paragraph which follows then it could be understood as a reference to male genitals.

The word translated *valley* means a narrow valley in which a stream runs, or a shaft, such as a mine shaft. The word *flourished* means "to bloom, to blossom, or to spread out" (specifically as a bird extending its wings), and the word *budded* can also mean "to blossom".

I do trust that my readers have enough respect for the awesome wonder of God's creation in the human body to accept the suggestion that we have here some beautifully poetic language describing the changes in a woman's genitals as she becomes sexually aroused. Those married couples who have taken the trouble to carefully study the geography of each others genitalia (as the modern marriage manuals all recommend) may recognise the hidden meanings in this poetic language.

The pomegranate produces a bright pink or red flower with a single layer of petals which form a trumpet shape. Hence the reference to pomegranate blossom in this context could be understood as a poetic description of the entrance to a vagina when it is in a state of sexual arousal. Remember, these people were very matter-of-fact. They were certainly not unduly prudish!

This wife would have been unashamedly aware of how the human body responds to sexual arousal. We make a big mistake when we accept the lie that sexual ignorance means sexual innocence. Their unashamed acceptance of such knowledge should never be read to imply promiscuous behaviour.

She then makes some strange comment to the effect that, "My desire set me among the royal chariots of my people."

Most commentary writers seem to be puzzled by this strange verse. The NIV translators have added a footnote to the effect that the meaning of this verse in Hebrew is uncertain, and T J Meek, in his exegesis for *The Interpreter's Bible*, explains that the confusion pre-dates even the Septuagint, Old Latin, and Vulgate translations of the Bible.

It is possible that in this verse the writer is trying to tell us something of the uninhibited and passionate desire that is now affecting her behaviour. Having acknowledged just how "turned on" she is, this wife now feels like doing something really crazy and "way out" in order to express herself.

Is it possible that, due to some outrageous sense of wild adventure, this woman wanted to go for a ride in a chariot, simply to give expression to those powerful feelings? Or perhaps you would prefer the interpretation of The Good News Bible which translates this verse as:

> 6:12 "I am trembling; [with excitement] you have made me as eager for lovemaking as a chariot driver is for battle,"

Or maybe the paraphrase quoted earlier as,

> 6:12 "Before I realised it, I was lost to the thrill of my desire – I wanted to make love with my husband even more urgently than the chariot rider wants to win his race when the crowd cheers him on."

As the dream fades away, and as the wife moves to get out of her bed, we hear the choir of friends singing:

> 6:13 Friends: "Come back, come back, O Shulammite; come back, come back, that we may gaze on you!"

[And she responds]

She: "Why would you gaze on the Shulammite as on the dance of Mahanaim?"

The words quoted here as "come back, come back" can also be translated "turn, turn" or as "dance, dance", and the next scene is obviously a dance routine, which is described variously as the "dance of Mahanaim" or the "dance of two armies".

Many commentary writers seem to have a problem understanding the significance of this title. But if the word is *Mahanaim*, as in the NIV translation, then surely the reference here is to separation (ie: two groups or two camps), for the place *Mahanaim* seems to have significance with regard to separation and family conflict.

Jacob gave the name Mahanaim to the place where he met with an angel on the night before he was to be reunited with his brother Esau, and Jacob was apparently apprehensive of how his brother would respond to the meeting (Genesis ch. 32).

This same place (or same word) was also significant for David, the father of Solomon, during the conflict with his own father-in-law King Saul (2 Samuel 2:8-29) and again later with his son Absalom (2 Sam 17:24-27; 19:32; and 1Kings 2:8). Now the wife in this story is obviously anxious to bring about an end to the separation which she feels has occurred between herself and her husband, and within this context her dancing is obviously intended to restore a sense of intimacy to the relationship.

However, according to comment in *The Interpreter's Bible* Vol. V, p134, it is also possible that the original writer may have used the plural form of the word (Heb. *machaneh* = armies) rather than the dual form (*mahanaim* = two camps). For this reason T.J. Meek suggests that the "dance of Mahanaim" should be more correctly translated as *"war dance"*.

ACT 5 - SEPARATION

So this performance should not be understood as a wife who feels neglected making a plaintive appeal to her husband to take some notice of her, but should rather be seen as some form of celebration. The idea is not too far removed from the American practice of having a cheer squad who put on a brief victory dance each time their team scores a touchdown. Or perhaps we could imagine something like the All Blacks rugby team running on to the field and performing a *haka* before the game begins. Such a performance has its origins in a war dance, but nowadays may simply be a hearty method of inspiring team morale, a challenge to the opposing team, or just an entertaining way of saying, "We plan to win this one."

We learn another important lesson from the wife's reaction here. She may have been feeling a little insecure, or threatened, because she thought her husband was more interested in his work than in her as a person. But she does not simply withdraw further into her own shell, as some people have done, and protest to her friends about the insensitivity of men.

No. She needs to remind this man that he is married, and for this reason he has a commitment to his wife as well as to his work. And she intends to communicate this to him, not by nagging or by negative criticism, but in a manner that will inspire a pleasant response, or even an enthusiastic response. To this end she intends to use all the natural gifts God has given her, and present herself in a way that will definitely grab the man's attention, and remind him that really she is more interesting, and just as important to him as is his work. She also knows the power of her feminine sexuality. So this is not a dance of defeat. This is a celebration of certain victory!

Assessing the Value of a Relationship

When we are faced with a decision regarding initiating a relationship with another person, or restoring a relationship which for some reason has broken down, there are four points we need to consider:-
1. What will this relationship cost me?
2. What is this person worth? Or, what sort of character is this person with whom I am thinking of establishing this relationship?
3. What blessings or benefits will I gain from this relationship?
4. Do I have some obligation to start a friendship with this person?

Consider the situation we have just observed in Act 5:

1. What was it going to cost the Shulammite?
Very little. Nothing more than a slight inconvenience. (5:3).
2. What sort of person was the other party? What was he worth?
He was wonderful. We could not put a price on him. He was beyond compare. (5:10-16).
3. What were the benefits to be gained from this relationship?
An improvement in her own sense of dignity and self worth, which is beyond measure. (6:4-10).

By comparison, let us consider these points in relation to the testimony concerning the eighteen-year-old girl and her two friends who wanted to celebrate? Do you remember how they went to a night-club to "party", and in order to avoid paying for the evening themselves they formed a short term relationship with three men?

1. What did it cost this young woman?
   It eventually cost even her own life.
2. What was the fellow worth? What sort of person was he?
   Well, both of the people involved in that sad but true story went into this very brief relationship with the intention of "using" or exploiting the other.

   Her motives were not very honourable, but neither were his, and he was HIV positive, but evidently did not warn the woman of this fact. He left her with a false address, a phoney telephone number and a deadly disease. What was he worth, as a chaperone for the evening? Well, what do you think he was worth ...?
3. What were the benefits to be gained for this woman?
   A hangover? A headache? A disease no-one ever wants. Oh, yes, she did get an evening of "entertainment". But what is the motivation that drives people to believe that this sort of entertainment is so desirable?

Sure, they have a little alcohol and this supposedly helps free up a few inhibitions, but that can be dangerous. There are many people who can have an hilarious time even while they are cold sober, and their advantage is that they can continue to enjoy the memory of the event years later. Would you agree that perhaps the basic motivation is often a desperate need or desire to feel accepted by a particular group, and thus feel that we are a person of significance?

Maybe there are better ways to satisfy our basic need for significance?

I do not mean to be critical of the unfortunate young woman in that story. I don't doubt that she was normally a very sensible and rational human being, but when sexual passion takes control the voice of reason can barely be heard. As Dr Paul Tournier once said, "We are controlled by feelings, not by logic. Logic and reason are only used to design an excuse to justify our behaviour".[93]

This woman in the *Songs*, like all human beings, has a need to feel significant. In the past she had satisfied that need through her relationship with a man whom she loved, and with whom she could share mutual trust.

Remember; without trust there cannot be any real intimacy. But now the intimacy is a bit jaded, and she seems to have recognised it is probably largely her own fault. So she will make the move towards this man in an effort to restore some sense of warmth and intimacy into the relationship. And we will see what happens.

---

93. Dr. Paul Tournier, *The Meaning of Persons* (1957), p56.)

ACT 6 RESTORATION

Songs 7:1 to 8:4

7:1 How beautiful your sandaled feet, O prince's daughter! Your graceful legs are like jewels, the work of a craftsman's hands.
2 Your navel is a rounded goblet that never lacks blended wine. Your waist is a mound of wheat encircled by lilies.
3 Your breasts are like two fawns, twins of a gazelle.
4 Your neck is like an ivory tower. Your eyes are the pools of Heshbon by the gate of Bath Rabbim. Your nose is like the tower of Lebanon looking toward Damascus.
5 Your head crowns you like Mount Carmel. Your hair is like royal tapestry; the king is held captive by its tresses.
6 How beautiful you are and how pleasing, O love, with your delights!
7 Your stature is like that of the palm, and your breasts like clusters of fruit.
8 I said, "I will climb the palm tree; I will take hold of its fruit." May your breasts be like the clusters of the vine, the fragrance of your breath like apples,
9 and your mouth like the best wine.
    May the wine go straight to my lover, flowing gently over lips and teeth.
10 I belong to my lover, and his desire is for me.
11 Come, my lover, let us go to the countryside, let us spend the night in the villages.
12 Let us go early to the vineyards to see if the vines have budded, if their blossoms have opened, and if the pomegranates are in bloom-- there I will give you my love.
13 The mandrakes send out their fragrance, and at our door is every delicacy, both new and old, that I have stored up for you, my lover.
8:1 If only you were to me like a brother, who was nursed at my mother's breasts! Then, if I found you outside, I would kiss you, and no one would despise me.
2 I would lead you and bring you to my mother's house-- she who has taught me. I would give you spiced wine to drink, the nectar of my pomegranates.
3 His left arm is under my head and his right arm embraces me.   [NIV]

8:4 She:
    Daughters of Jerusalem, please heed this warning!
    Do not ever stir up passion as powerful as this until it can be safely and appropriately satisfied!"   [author paraphrase]

ACT 6

RESTORATION

Having recognised that the quality of their relationship and the sense of intimacy between herself and her husband is not what it should be, the wife now plans to take some action. But she does not resort to whingeing complaints or nagging and criticism. Although she obviously lived several hundred years before the imaginative Marabel Morgan[94], nevertheless we find that in response to this potential conflict issue, those two women might have a lot in common!

However, I also have to admit at this point that I have been criticised for making favourable reference to Marabel Morgan's writings.

But in defence of Mrs Marabel Morgan I believe that, in writing as she did, she made herself very vulnerable. She had discovered, at a critical point in her own marriage, that holding anger and resentment in her heart was no way to make a happy partnership. But there are successful ways to restore the excitement, the love, and the sense of intimacy into our marriage relationships. Mrs Morgan was merely trying to share the things she had discovered, <u>illustrated from</u> her own experiences.

94. Author of *The Total Woman* (1975).

ACT 6 - RESTORATION

She is not alone is these discoveries. In her book entitled *If You Really Loved Me*, Counsellor/Psychologist Toby Green[95], who describes herself as "a liberated woman who has solved the problem of getting her needs met by the male in her life," points out that it is the "victim mentality" which really does women the most harm. Although there are plenty of case histories describing how women have been improperly treated by the men in their lives, persisting with an us-against-them attitude has never been a successful way of resolving conflict. It does not really succeed in the work-place or the boardroom, nor is it successful in the domestic scene or the bedroom.

If we feel we have been wronged then we need to take the initiative to communicate, to talk about our expectations and our disappointments where these expectations have not been met. But this must be done in a manner that does not allow the other person to feel threatened in any way. This is called dialogue, and is an essential ingredient for any happy relationship. Improving our skill in dialogue was the main focus of the 'Marriage Enrichment Seminars' that Rose and I were once involved with.

Toby Green and Marabel Morgan have both shared their experience in an effort to convince us that it is possible to work through our disappoint-ments, our shattered dreams and expectations, and our conflicts in general, and end up with a relationship of genuine love and harmony. But we don't achieve this by constant negative criticism.

There is a Law of Relationship involved here. As Jesus of Nazareth said to Peter when he swiped off the ear of one of the soldiers who had come to arrest him, "put your sword back in its place, for all who draw the sword will die by the sword". (Matt 26:52 and John 18:11). It follows that those who try to win the battle by holding bitterness and resentment in their heart will be destroyed by the very "weapons" they try to use.

---

95. Toby Green, *If You Really Loved Me* (1996), p43.

He also taught that those who seek only their own interests in life will never find true happiness. On the contrary they will lose what little contentment they have. (Read the comments made by Jesus of Nazareth in Mark 8:35-38; and Luke 9:24-26).

The road to harmony in marriage starts with reconciliation and the resolution of our conflicts. And the resolution of conflict is often dependent on our seeking and offering forgiveness. In human terms, that means forgiveness from both parties. Resentment and bitterness are not part of the pathway to paradise, and without forgiveness we will never find paradise. But Mrs Morgan was game to do better than just trying to re-establish communication with her stressed-out lawyer husband. She added a bit of sexy sparkle to the process, and that sort of grabbed the man's attention. This woman in the *Songs* made use of a similar technique.

No person who has spent the day trying to deal with difficult and unhelpful people, or even troublesome equipment in the workplace, wants to come home and be greeted by a spouse who also gripes and complains, or who seems to be trying to make everyone else in his or her life feel like a failure.

There was once a popular proverb which said something like "The squeaking wheel gets oiled first." But in my experience in the aviation industry the "squeaking wheel" (or noisy bearing) would be simply discarded, and replaced with a unit that works smoothly, or works "without grumbling and complaining". As a marriage partner we need to use some creative imagination and invent or discover ways to get our needs met without resorting to grumbling and complaining, or oppressive nagging.

Modern relationship counsellors tell us that there are at least four methods we could use to improve the intimacy in a marriage relationship:-

1. The SOUL to SOUL approach, where we arrange to spend time together to simply talk and discuss our hopes, dreams,

and expectations; to talk about our real goals in life. Many Christians would include in this some shared times of prayer together.

2. The SUPPORTIVE approach, where we communicate to our partner, often through non verbal methods, a sense of encouragement, possibly through the use of playfulness and good humour. The couple in the *Song of Songs* have done this more than once with their playful games suggestive of hide-and-seek. A playful balance of seduction and withdrawal. To use this technique does require some measure of understanding and trust before you begin. But then trust, understanding, and intimacy should be enhanced as you play out your "games".

3. The SENSUAL approach, where we awaken our partner's senses in a gentle and delicate way by using some or all of the five senses. Examples of this could be massage and other non-sexual touching, or relaxing together in a hot tub, or writing and singing songs to each other. At the same time we also give expression to our own feelings.

4. The SEDUCTIVE approach, where we enjoy expressing our own sensuality and feelings as we communicate with our partner through movement or dance, and also perhaps with gentle word and touch.

Of course in all of the above techniques we may make ourselves vulnerable, but then intimacy requires that we allow ourselves to be vulnerable. That is why trust and faithfulness are such important factors in love and intimacy. And, in real terms, we must acknowledge that achieving good communication in the first approach is not always as easy as we may have expected.

It needs practice, and a good deal of patience, which is why some people are more comfortable starting with some other method of reconciliation.

As we have already noted, this woman in the *Songs* has chosen to use the seductive approach. So in order to attract the attention of her husband she begins to dance, and the only description we have of her dance routine is the song her husband sings as he looks upon her with increasing interest and attention.

> 7:1-9 How beautiful your sandaled feet, O prince's daughter!
>
> Your graceful legs are like jewels, the work of a craftsman's hands. Your navel is a rounded goblet that never lacks blended wine.
>
> Your waist is a mound of wheat encircled by lilies. Your breasts are like two fawns, twins of a gazelle. Your neck is like an ivory tower.
>
> Your eyes are the pools of Heshbon by the gate of Bath Rabbim.
>
> Your nose is like the tower of Lebanon looking toward Damascus. Your head crowns you like Mount Carmel.
>
> Your hair is like royal tapestry; the king is held captive by its tresses. How beautiful you are and how pleasing, O love, with your delights! Your stature is like that of the palm tree, and your breasts like clusters of fruit. I said, "I will climb the palm; I will take hold of its fruit."
>
> May your breasts be like the clusters of the vine, the fragrance of your breath like apples, and your mouth like the best wine. May the wine go straight to my lover, flowing gently over lips and teeth. [NIV]

This time the description of the woman starts at her feet, suggesting that the husband is still lying on a low couch or on his sleeping mat. Also the description of her body is far more sensuous and sexy than any previous descriptions, and the dance itself seems to be very sexually suggestive. So obviously this is not their first night together. You will remember that they were both

ACT 6 - RESTORATION

a little shy and nervous on that occasion, and they used humour and playfulness to defuse any sense of embarrassment. But now we have a much more confident and sensuous woman who, in the presence of her wonderful husband, is quite unashamed of the power of her sexuality.

Under no circumstances should we confuse this woman's performance with any suggestion of pornographic display. The problem some readers may have is that we live in a society where sex and lovemaking have become so degraded that we become preoccupied with the physical and may miss the profound meaning of the message here.

This is a wife re-establishing communication with her husband after she has become aware that somehow their precious sense of unity and intimacy has been lost.

In this "dance" (however you may imagine the activity to be) she is expressing her desire for a return to that beautiful sense of togetherness where two hearts beat as one – that delicious melting together of two individuals into "one".

This is a precious and intensely personal dialogue between two lovers. In a spiritual sense this is the "I surrender all" expression of rededication and commitment. Her nakedness is simply an outward expression of an inner attitude of heart. It means unashamed transparent honesty where there are no hidden agendas. This is an expression of absolute trust. It is a non-verbal way of saying, "I am prepared to make myself vulnerable in your presence because I believe that you can be trusted and will accept me completely as a person, and not reject me." It means, "I trust you to treat me with love, dignity and respect."

In this context it is an invitation to intimacy. It is not a crude flaunting her body. And if you want to spiritualise this we need to recognise that nothing is hidden from the eyes of God, for we read elsewhere that "All are naked and bare before the eyes of the one to whom we must give account." (Hebrews 4:13).

The inability to accept nakedness even in the bathroom or the bed-room is based on fear, not modesty. The fear of nakedness is the fear of being vulnerable. It is the fear that someone may take advantage of us or that we may be abused, laughed at, rejected, or condemned for not being perfect in every way. All of these symptoms indicate a violation of the laws of relationship. There can be no violation of these laws in paradise. This is why the comment that the man and the woman in the paradise of Eden were both "naked and not ashamed" is so significant. The laws of relationship had, at that point in time, not been violated so there was no reason for fear. They lived in an environment of perfect trust and of mutual acceptance and respect.

We should not find anything offensive in the suggestion of husband and wife enjoying such naked communication together.

And yet we know that there are people who cannot accept such a simple matter-of-fact statement. We have even heard of individuals who are scared to enjoy soaking naked in a hot spa. And the reason they give is, "What would happen if the LORD comes back and I have no clothes on?"

These people are confused. Job recognised that we leave this world just as naked as we entered it.[96]

Both the apostle Paul and the writer of Ecclesiastes tell us that when we leave this world we can take nothing at all that can be held in the hand.[97] And that includes every stitch of clothing to which these people so fearfully cling. But there is no need to fear embarrassment in Heaven.

Nearly all the recorded visions of Glory tell us that all the people there are either clothed in brightness (sunshine?) or clothed in dazzling white linen. In describing his vision of Heaven John explains that this white linen is a symbol of righteousness.[98]

---

96. Job 1:21
97. Ecclesiastes 5:15, and 1 Timothy 6:7
98. Revelation 19:8.

ACT 6 - RESTORATION

Jesus taught that anyone who does not have this "robe of righteousness" will not be permitted to enter Heaven.[99]

But, as many New Testament writers tell us, this robe of righteousness is a gift that is freely available to all who, having recognised the sinful attitudes of their own heart, approach God in confession and repentance asking for forgiveness and cleansing.[100] So we can rest assured: there will be no more embarrassment or shame in the paradise of Heaven than there was before the fall in the garden of Eden.

Many people are aware that in John's description of Heaven he mentions streets of gold (Revelation 21:21). But they seem to overlook the fact that John also tells us that "the entire city is pure gold, *clear as glass*" (Rev 21:18). Even the golden streets are described as being transparent as glass. The emphasis of this scene is not on material wealth but on purity.

In their writings the ancient Hebrews often use refined gold as a symbol of purity. But, like the king in the account of Archimedes, they were aware that gold can be alloyed with impurities. Now perhaps I need to mention again at this point that in biblical teaching purity does not necessarily mean there is a total lack of any normal healthy interest in sex. But it does mean that there is no ulterior motive, no dishonesty, no unfaithfulness. It means that there is no deceitful desire to exploit, to manipulate, to possess and control, or to simply use another person to satisfy our own lust for power, prestige or pleasure.

In order for paradise to be paradise it must be a place where **all** motives are absolutely pure. In his description of Heaven,

---

[99] This is clearly taught in the parable recorded in Matthew's Gospel, chapter 22.
[100] In much of his writing the Apostle Paul explains that this righteousness is not something we can earn but it is a gift from God, and for each individual is dependant on their own personal relationship of faith and trust in the LORD. Even the prophet Isaiah was aware of this for he also wrote, "I will greatly rejoice in the LORD. My whole being shall exult in my God; for He has clothed me with the garments of salvation, He has covered me with a robe of righteousness, as a bridegroom decks himself with a garland, and as a bride adorns herself with jewels." (Isaiah 61:10).

John was trying to emphasise the essence of purity in that place. In paradise there can be no dishonesty or unfaithfulness, no liars, nor any creature with ulterior motives and hidden agendas. So, once again, we can be quite certain that there will be no shame, and no cause for shame, any more than there was in the Garden of Eden before the fall.

We must understand that paradise is a *safe* place and if we want our marriage, or any other relationship, to be a truly enjoyable experience then we should try to follow the principles of paradise – an environment where *agapé* love is the norm. In such an environment it is safe to allow oneself to be vulnerable. *Agapé* love creates a safe environment to grow – a place where there is no ridicule or scorn; a place where we can find help in times of need; where any acknowledgement of imperfection or failure is met with empathy, understanding, and encouragement (and not criticism).

This, of course, should be a characteristic of any Christian group and, incidentally, was the reason why Christians of the first few centuries were able to accept the practice of nude baptisms without any fear of becoming a victim of crude comment or lustful looking.

The comments which the husband makes here in reference to her thighs has troubled many students of these lyrics. Those who write from a technical knowledge of the Hebrew language seem to struggle in particular with the adjective that is used here to describe this part of the woman's body. The word implies not just roundness, but rather some concept of rotation, or moving in a circle. Probably the real reason is simply that the wording is too hot for some translators to handle.

The NIV says, your *graceful legs*. The RSV reads, your *rounded thighs*. The Good News Bible and the Jerusalem Bible both read, *the curve of your thighs*.

Perhaps it is not exactly the thigh that is being referred to in this case. The Hebrew word *yarek*, translated here as "thigh", is commonly used in reference to the reproductive organs. Examples of where the word is used in this way are found in the following verses where we read:

> All the souls that came with Jacob into Egypt, which came out of his *loins* (Hebrew *yarek*), besides Jacob's sons' wives, all the souls were threescore and six;
> Genesis 46:26, [KJV]

And also,

> All the souls that came out of the *loins* of Jacob were seventy souls: for Joseph was in Egypt already.   Exodus 1:5 [KJV]
>
> Gideon had threescore and ten sons of his *body*: for he had many wives.   Judges 8:30 [KJV]

In chapter five of the book of Numbers there is the description of a test which was used to determine whether or not a woman had been unfaithful to her husband.

In the King James version we read that the woman is warned, if the test is positive, "Your *thigh* (Heb. *yarek*), will rot." (Numbers 5:21). But a footnote in the NIV indicates an alternative reading should be "Your *womb* will become barren". The NRSV for this verse reads "Your *uterus* will drop." So in those translations the reference would seem to be to some form of venereal disease or disorder of the reproductive organs.

However, a more believable translation of 7:1 could be that the reference is to the circular movement of the woman's pelvis as she dances. The inference therefore seems to be that she is rotating her pelvis in a sexually suggestive manner, and her husband expresses words of praise to the One who designed and crafted something of such beauty.

He then says, "Your navel is like a round goblet, which never lacks wine:" Many commentaries point out that the word "navel" is an incorrect and unduly restrained translation of the original language, because the word more correctly refers to the reproductive organs. The description of a rounded goblet (literally *crescent shaped bowl*, or *bowl of roundness*) gives an indication that the whole scene really is sexually suggestive, yet the writer is still making use of poetic language.

So we would seem to be justified in believing that the wife's dancing is a very provocative invitation to her husband. When he says that this goblet *never lacks wine* he probably means that this part of his bride is a constant source of pleasure, or that she has no problems that might inhibit her sexual arousal. The word *never* is emphatic in the Hebrew.

The imagery of a palm tree suggests a graceful swaying movement as this woman dances, like a tall palm tree in the wind. The inference is of one who is tall, slender, and supple, and the woman's breasts are likened to two bunches of dates on this gracefully moving tree. The husband then says, "I will climb the palm tree and lay hold of its branches."

The word translated *branches* is from a root which refers to something that tapers to a point, hence "branches" or even arms. However in this context it could possibly be an appropriate word to use in reference to the woman's breast. But then the fellow suddenly decides to change his imagery from two bunches of dates to a vine with two delicious bunches of grapes. Now a bunch of dates tends to be rather floppy, although this fitted in with the imagery of the palm tree, but a bunch of grapes can be much firmer and will hold its conical shape much better. Also grapes swell and become rounded and smooth as they ripen, similar to a firm well shaped female breast.

Many people are puzzled by her belly being likened to a heap of wheat set about with lilies. The word translated as "*belly*" actually refers to the womb, so he is probably making some reference to fruitfulness, or the conceiving and bearing of children.

The word translated as "set about" can also mean to "hem in" or "hedge in", and we have already discovered that "lilies" may be a reference to the labia at the entrance to the vagina. Hence, in more clinical terminology, we could perhaps paraphrase this to read, "Those lips surround the entrance to a fruitful womb."

Even as recently as the 1950's many Christians would have had real problems accepting any suggestion that what we read here should be taken as a role model for the legitimate invitation to sexual intimacy for a married couple. You have probably heard the (cynical) remark, "My church did not approve of sex, they thought it might lead to dancing."

The Christianity we were taught in the earlier part of the twentieth century was really more a Stoic philosophy of emotional repression rather than a Hebraic acceptance of emotional expression. Even at the dawn of the twenty-first century I wonder how many Christians can accept this.

I could think of many congregations who would sing with enthusiasm, "When the Spirit of the LORD is in my heart I will dance like David danced." The reference in this chorus is to King David dancing before the LORD as the Ark of the Covenant was being brought into Jerusalem. The Bible record tells us that:

> David ... brought the Ark of the LORD to the city of David with a great celebration. After the men who were carrying it had gone six paces, they stopped and waited so that he could sacrifice an ox and a fat lamb. And David danced before the LORD with all his might, and he was wearing [only] a linen ephod (priests' clothing - like an apron). So Israel brought home the Ark of the LORD with much shouting and blowing of trumpets.
>
> But as the procession came into the city Saul's daughter Michal watched from a window and saw King David leaping and dancing before the LORD; and she was filled with contempt.   2 Samuel 6:14-16 [TLB]

Then at the conclusion of the story we read David's response to Michal's reaction:

Michal came out to meet him and exclaimed in disgust, "How glorious the king of Israel looked today. He exposed himself to the girls along the street like a common pervert!"

David replied, "I was dancing before the LORD who chose me above your father and his family and who appointed me as leader of Israel, the people of the LORD! So I am willing to act like a fool in order to show my joy in the LORD. Yes, and I am willing to look even more foolish than this, but I will be held in respect by the girls of whom you spoke.

2 Samuel 6:20-23 [TLB]

Although there are thousands of Christians who would sing, with enthusiasm, the chorus "I will dance as David danced," I have not as yet met one whom I believe would actually put the words into practice, and dance with the uninhibited enthusiasm which David expressed on that occasion. There may be some who would dance, but they would insist on wearing something more than just an ephod (apron). Perhaps we still do not really believe just how freely these Hebrew people gave expression to their feelings of joy.

Kaufmann Koehler, in the *Jewish Encyclopaedia*, tells us that no other language has as many words for joy and rejoicing as are found in the Hebrew tongue. In the Old Testament alone there are some twenty-seven different words used to describe various aspects of joy or joyful participation in religious worship. The whole Hebrew concept of worship involved the expression of joy and gladness, for they regarded the act of praising and thanking God to be the supreme joy of life.

As the psalmist says, "In your presence there is fullness of joy; in your right hand are pleasures forevermore" (Psa 16:11). Since they recognised that their sexuality was part of God's perfect creation it is reasonable to assume that they would have applied a similar enthusiasm to their husband-wife lovemaking. Yet there have been times in our own culture when it would have been considered improper to even suggest that married couples follow some of the examples which this delightful pair have role-modelled for us.

As I have already indicated, within the context of the *Song of Songs* this woman's dancing must not be confused with crude exhibitionism, and neither should her behaviour be described in any way as immodest. Perhaps at this point we need to explain that there is a difference between exhibitionism and entertainment, and also between modesty and shame.

Quite apart from the type of activity involved, the main problems with the exhibitionist are with the motive and the focus of attention.

With a good entertainer the motive is to get the audience involved so that they either laugh or become emotionally caught up in the proceedings. The focus of attention is therefore actually in the audience and with a desire to leave them feeling that they have indeed been entertained. But with an exhibitionist the focus of attention is with himself, and the underlying motive is that he is allowed to feel significant by becoming the centre of attention. The exhibitionist wants to get attention whereas the good entertainer is happy to give (or provide) entertainment. The exhibitionist operates out of emotional emptiness ("I *want* for me") while the entertainer operates from emotional abundance (hence, in effect, "*I give you* the right to enjoy".) Thus the exhibitionist makes us feel burdened with care, concern, embarrassment, inadequacy, or fear, whereas a good entertainer leaves us with a feeling of light-hearted release.

Note that the same principles apply here as apply in the case of healthy relationships. The exhibitionist (who is often considered to be offensive) is self centred, whereas a good entertainer is other centred. So it is with relationships: If our motive in forming a relationship is primarily to satisfy self (I want something for me) then the relationship will never grow. But if the motive is other centred (I love, therefore I am prepared to give) then the relationship can blossom and flourish. The exhibitionist's attitude says, "I do not really care about you, I just want to be the centre of attention". But the attitude of the entertainer, as with the wife at this point in the *Songs*, says in effect, "I **do** care about you, and I care about our relationship. This is the reason why I would appreciate your attention, affirmation, and acceptance".

Therefore, if you feel too embarrassed to appear naked in the presence of your marriage partner, then it would be wise to ask yourself why this is so, and why you feel ashamed. We must understand that **modesty and shame are not the same.**

The confusion we sometimes experience in trying to understand these two words becomes evident when we begin reading books in an effort to deal with the problem of shame. Dr. Sandra Wilson, in her book *Released From Shame*,[101] defines shame as "a strong sense of being uniquely and hopelessly flawed . . . of being different and less than other human beings." A different writer quoted by Dennis Smith in his book *Growing up Without Shame* defines modesty as being "a feeling of acute self-consciousness due to appearing unusual or different from those around us."[102]

Note that the two definitions which I have quoted for two different words have a significant similarity and both carry overtones of the fear of being rejected on the grounds that we think we are different or that we are somehow "less perfect" than everybody else. But the two words should really be understood as describing two very different conditions.

Shame is a totally negative emotion that may be related to feelings of guilt or, more often, to some feeling of inadequacy and failure, and the associated fear of condemnation or rejection. True **modesty,** by contrast, develops out of a positive attitude that is related to humility and a healthy sense of being accepted.

---

101. Dr. Sandra Wilson, Released From Shame (1990) pages 10 & 25
102. Dennis Smith, *Growing Up Without Shame* (1986) p107.

Note the important difference between the fear of rejection on the one hand and the confidence of being accepted on the other. A person who lacks the security of being loved and accepted may sometimes behave in an immodest way just to gain attention. Real modesty is the opposite of such exhibitionism.

Shame may be the result of poor parenting. Dr Sandra Wilson, author of the books *Released From Shame* and *Shame Free Parenting*, mentions the case of a ten-year old boy who was deeply wounded by shame when he was criticised for failing to do a perfect job after being told to trim a hedge. Nobody had ever shown the lad how to even hold a set of hedge-clippers, let alone showing him how the task of trimming the hedge should normally be tackled. Where he should have been commended for at least making some attempt he was instead only criticised for achieving a less than perfect result. A sense of shame and personal failure was the logical outcome.

Many a wife complains that her husband is clumsy and inept in love-making skills. But when asked, "Have you discussed with him your expectations in this regard?" they reply, "Of course not! If I have to tell him what to do then I can't enjoy it."

Do we see here a repetition of the boy with the hedge-clippers? Shame builds upon the feelings of confusion and failure which in turn have been caused by the lack of proper instruction and information. Eventually we create a problem that needs to be discussed, but one that can scarcely be mentioned, for the emotional wound is now too painful to touch.

Yet some people have even made the mistake of describing shame as a virtue.! While modesty may be a virtue, **shame is more often a symptom that something is wrong with the relationship**. It may be a symptom that guilt, fear, a sense of failure, or a lack of trust and faithfulness has destroyed any hope of real intimacy.

To some people their understanding of the word modesty simply means that there are certain parts of our bodies which must always remain hidden or, as other people have expressed it, "We try to pretend that there are some parts of our body that don't really exist".

Most of us recognise these parts of our bodies as very private and personal. But these are the parts which may be involved in the most intimate expression of relationship between husband and wife – an intimacy which, as I have already mentioned, is described in the Bible as "one flesh".

These are also the parts that are involved with the conception of a new life where mere humans have the awesome privilege of being partakers with God in an act of creation! And, in the case of the human female, with the subsequent physical and emotional nourishment of this "miracle".

Note that the writer of the *Songs* treats these parts of the body as sacred and holy, therefore worthy of honour and respect. They are not treated as indecent, obscene or unmentionable.

Modesty accepts what God has designed and, because it is not focussed on self, is able to give appropriate honour to the Creator for His amazing design. **Shame,** being more focussed on self, withdraws in fear when faced with the evidence of personal failure or of some perceived imperfection. Shame corrodes and destroys intimacy. True modesty is able to accept human sexuality with a sense of reverent awe and, because it is not so self-conscious, is able to make a positive contribution towards intimacy.

The writer of the *Songs* has emphasised the importance of intimacy and of healthy relationships, rather than empty or exploitative ritual.

Within the intimacy of marriage we should be able to accept the physical openness modelled by this couple as healthy and normal. Since the Hebrew prophets used the concept of a healthy marriage relationship as an illustration of the intimate spiritual relationship which YHWH desires to have with his people then it follows that such physical openness must have been recognised as desirable. The naked body, in this context, should therefore be accepted as part of God's wonderful design and every part of it treated with dignity and respect.

The utter moral sickness of our present-day society is shown by the way we react to intimacy. For many people the reaction is one of fear – they are too ashamed or embarrassed to even talk comfortably about the subject, and instead of treating the sexual parts of the human body with reverence and honour they are treated with contempt or something unmentionable.

Likewise there are people who make a mockery of prayer. Note that prayer is an expression of spiritual intimacy. And instead of accepting the female breast as a symbol of a mother's ability to provide both physical and emotional nourishment for her offspring (hence a means of developing appropriate parent-child bonding) our modern-day censors treat this part of the human anatomy as obscene, and therefore claim that it is immodest for a woman to breast-feed her infant child in public.!

But when we lived in Papua New Guinea during the 1960's I saw hundreds of bare-breasted women unashamedly breast-feeding their infant children in church, in the market-place, and even as passengers on my aircraft. Yet these women were always extremely modest in every way. There was not even a hint of exhibitionism in their behaviour.

By contrast to these "half naked" (but extremely modest) women, Rose and I have seen many people in more industrialised countries, legally clothed by the standards of their own society, whose body-language and dress style could only be described as immodest. Their clothing, obviously designed for titillation while not quite breaking the laws on "decency", seems to shout the message, "I would rather be chased than chaste."

To pursue this topic a little further it could even be argued that any society which denies a woman the right to breastfeed her baby in public has, in principle, accepted the idea that sexual exploitation and immodest or immoral thought patterns are "normal". Remember, Leviticus 18:6 states that it is the *lustful looking that is sinful*. The problem is in the mind of the beholder! So to put sexual connotations on any woman who exposes her breast to feed her baby is a violation of that law!

I trust that I have made the point that modesty is not defined by clothing (or the lack of it) but by behaviour, context, motive, and what is going on **in the mind of the beholder** = the person who is looking.

"Clothed" does not necessarily mean "modest", and "naked" (even totally naked in some contexts) does not necessarily mean "immodest".

Just a brief personal comment on this. In the country where I was born military training was compulsory for all physically fit 18yr old men. So, sometime after my 17th birthday I received notification to present myself for an Army medical. After the usual preliminaries of being asked, name, place and date of birth etc, one of the two doctors casually said, "Okay lad. Get your gear off and let's have a look at your body." I knew that in some situations "naked" simply meant strip down to underwear. So I simply asked with one word, "Everything?" The doctor sighed a sort of unspoken "not another one" and then in a very friendly voice said, "Listen lad. No one here is going to make fun of you or molest you in any way. Our job is to determine whether on not you are fit enough for military service. Yes, everything." And after more than 40 years of more medical checks for pilot's license etc, I still say that was the most thorough and least embarrassing medical check I ever had. There was nothing immodest or embarrassing about it at all.

Confusion in the minds of some newlyweds on the question of modesty and nakedness reminds me of a story that I read several years ago. It involved a large hotel which specialised in accommodation for couples on honeymoon. It was not only very popular for newlyweds but also with those couples who are able to afford a second honeymoon. Part of the facilities in each private unit included an above-ground spa-pool built to look like a huge champagne glass. At breakfast one morning a shy young couple appeared in the dining room. They had been married just the day before, and this was to be their first breakfast together as a married couple.

As part of a cheerful greeting somebody loudly asked, "Did you enjoy the spa?" To which the new husband naively replied, "Aw, shucks no. Would you believe, we forgot to bring our bathers!" To their great embarrassment this comment was greeted with hoots of laughter from every corner of the room.

I hope, for their own sake, that this couple have since discovered why everyone else in that room considered it so amusing that a married couple should think it necessary to hide themselves in bathing costumes when sharing a private spa-bath together. Nakedness in such a situation should not be considered immodest. On the contrary nakedness for husband and wife should be considered a perfectly normal and healthy expression of mutual trust, acceptance, and intimacy.

And let's face it. The word *bathing suit* is an oxymoron! Normally when we take a bath it is in order to wash or cleanse our entire body. Why would any sensible person wrap themselves in tight-fitting clothing that would make it impossible for them to achieve what the water in the bath was supposed to do – to wash away all the sweat and dirt after a hard day at work – A swimming costume, maybe. But a bathing suit – are you crazy?

There must be something seriously wrong with a society that encourages or condones experimentation with a number of different partners in the name of "sex education" but professes to be upset by any hint of a married couple sitting naked together in a spa pool, or the sight of a woman unashamedly breastfeeding her infant-child in a shopping mall. Modesty does not condemn such activity, it simply requires that such things be done in a way that those involved do not deliberately make themselves the centre of attention. To deliberately draw attention to oneself in such a situation means we are back with the problem of the exhibitionist.

Just as much as we should try to avoid unnecessary behaviour that might cause offence to others, so also it follows that we must allow other people the right to do necessary things, such as breastfeeding a baby, without causing them to feel that they are in any way the focus of unwanted attention. This consideration for the rights and feelings of other people is also an aspect of modesty. Put in very simple terms, which even a child should understand, it means "don't stare!"

The writer of the *Songs* is aware of this, for her comment, "Why would you gaze upon the Shulammite?" implies an appeal to not be the subject of a gawking crowd of onlookers. This is not immodest exhibitionism.

Her dancing in this context is simply an invitation to deeper intimacy – an intimate and private expression of feelings shared between a wife and her husband in the privacy of their marriage relationship, and in the privacy of their own home. This woman lived in a culture where dance was freely accepted as a means of self-expression..

The wife now gives voice to a simple but profoundly important declaration:

7:10 "I am my beloved's, and his desire is for me."

The woman who wrote these songs has learned a few things that she believes are worth sharing with the world at large. Did you notice how the wife has changed her attitude to the relationship?

Back on the honeymoon night she sang, "My beloved is mine" (2:16). Back then she thought that she "owned" her husband. When anyone begins to think that way about their marriage partner there is a danger that they will take that person, and their relationship with that person, for granted.

It works both ways. Men and women may both be guilty of this. But now she realises that it is a privilege and an honour just to be loved by this man. She had begun to take him for granted, yet when she treated him with neglect he did not force his attention. He did not make demands, for true love does not demand. No, instead he waited for her to invite him back into a more intimate relationship. And it worked!

As she considers how things now are between them, with the current misunderstanding, she reassures herself of some important truths. Firstly, she acknowledges their mutual commitment, and secondly that they are both persons of equal worth in a precious relationship. So, she now sings, "I belong to my lover, and my lover is mine." (6:3). Note that rather than claiming possession she now expresses her joy at simply belonging.

But she also recognised that if there was to be an end to this misunderstanding then she would have to take some initiative. Hence her "Dance of Mahanaim", where she expressed an invitation for renewed intimacy and her desire for an end to the separation.

But have you noticed that after the intimacy has been restored, and after she has finally recognised what an almost unbelievably wonderful, sensitive and thoughtful husband she has actually married, and after she realises how close she came to losing his adoration and love for her, she seemed to almost weep in humility as she declared, "I belong to this wonderful man, and his desire is for *me*." (7:10).

Many people have found great comfort in the spiritual application of this verse. When I finally recognise that, in spite of my awful arrogance, pride and failures, God loves me. And with tears of penitence I can declare, "I belong to my Lord, and He cares about me – of all people, God cares about me."

When we go through an experience like this we then recognise that there is no basis for pride or self-glorification of any sort. I am unworthy of His love, yet He loves me. Part of the miracle is that this realisation does not produce a soul-destroying sense of shame. Instead there is a healthy humility, which leaves some measure of dignity.

The phrase "*I belong to my lover and his desire is for me*" (7:10) can also be translated to read, "*... he reaches out toward me,*" or "*he extends himself* (on my account, as an expression of his love)." The reference is thus to a sense of belonging in a relationship of genuine love. This is not exploitation or possessive lust. This is emotional security. This is the essence of a happy marriage and a healthy family.

In the light of this verse (7:10), consider also Ruth's request to Boaz where she asked,

> "Spread (or extend) the corner of your garment over me, since you are a kinsman-redeemer." (Ruth 3:9, NIV)

The "garment" in this context symbolises the protection which Boaz could offer. And again in the book of Revelation we read,

> He who sits on the throne will spread (or extend) his tent [the symbol of God's protection] over them. Never again will they hunger; never again will they thirst. ... For the Lamb at the centre of the throne will be their shepherd; he will lead them to springs of living water. And God will wipe away every tear from their eyes. (Revelation 7:15-17, NIV)

All these references speak of a *shalom* peace, and also of one who cares, provides, and protects. This is the essence of paradise.[103]

---

103. The word *shalom* is often translated into English as "peace", but it means much more than just an absence of conflict. The root meaning of the word is related to wholeness, and the word can mean "peace, completeness, welfare, and health." It is often used in the context of relationship between two or more people. [Ref. Vines Expository Dictionary of Biblical Words (1985) p173]. It is perhaps also worth explaining here that the angels' message of "Peace on Earth" as recorded by Luke in his Gospel record

As married individuals we sometimes need to get past our own arrogance and pride and recognise that in spite of our own personal shortcomings and failures we have been privileged to live in an intimate relationship with the wonderful person whom we chose to marry. Then we respond with humility, love, and genuine appreciation. Then, and only then, does the marriage become based on a solid foundation.

Perhaps this is the most important lesson we need to learn from this entire study of the *Songs*.

Having obviously gained her husband's undivided attention, the wife now offers an interesting invitation:

> 7:11 - 8:2 "Come, my beloved, let us go out into the fields, and spend time in the henna bushes; let us go out early to the vineyards, and see whether the vines have budded, whether the grape blossoms have opened and the pomegranates are in bloom.
>
> "There I will give you my love.
>
> "The mandrakes give forth fragrance, and over our doors are all choice fruits, new as well as old, which I have laid up for you, O my beloved.
>
> "O that you were like a brother to me, who nursed at my mother's breast! Then, if I met you outside, I could kiss you, and no one would despise me. I would lead you and bring you into the house of my mother, and into the chamber of the one who bore me [or – the room where I was conceived].
>
> "I would give you spiced wine to drink, the juice of my pomegranates."

(Luke 2:15) did not mean that there will be no more war, as this would contradict the many prophecies referring to war. The reference is to the birth of a Redeemer who would make possible a restoration of the healthy relationship between God and individual co-operating human beings. The promise speaks of a renewed covenant.

8:3-4

She: "His left hand is under my head, and his right hand embraces me!

"Daughters of Jerusalem, please heed this warning! Do not stir up passion as powerful as this until it can be safely and appropriately satisfied!" [author paraphrase]

The invitation, "Come, my beloved, let us go out into the fields and spend time in the henna bushes." sounds like a request from the wife to go and check some of the crops in their garden - or may be it is to spend the night somewhere in the open air, or at least in some different place, for the word translated *henna bushes* can also mean *villages*. Hence the NIV translation reads, "Let us spend the night in the villages". But after this very sexy presentation to gain the attention of her husband does this woman simply want to go and check the garden or take a look at some Real Estate?

Surely not! The word is definitely plural, so does not mean one particular village. Why ever would she want to spend the night travelling from one village to the next? There must be another interpretation. We need to take a closer look at the broader meaning of some of these words.

A comment on verse 7:11 in *The Interpreter's Bible* indicates that henna bushes or henna flowers is the more likely correct interpretation here.

The word translated "*countryside*" is from a word root meaning "*to spread out*", and is more correctly translated as "*flat ground*". If we then accept the interpretation of "henna bushes" rather than "villages" we may bring to light some very interesting symbolism.

As already explained in the comments on 1:14 and 4:13, the word henna has connotations of "covering", hence its word-root connection with the word village, being a sheltered, protected or covered place.

ACT 6 - RESTORATION

You might also remember that the crushed leaves of henna bushes are used to produce an orange/red coloured dye which can be also used as a hair dye. Beverley and Vidal Sasoon in their book *A Year of Beauty and Health*[104] tell us that not only is henna one of the oldest known natural colourings, but it can be used to give some remarkably beautiful lights to black hair, and it can be used to put a glow like polished rosewood into otherwise drab brown hair. Bronwen Meredith, in a publication entitled *Vogue Natural Health and Beauty*,[105] tells us that the colour lasts several months and is completely non toxic, so this dye can be safely used on pubic hair!

Strange, perhaps, that this is one hair dye which modern beauty therapists tell us can be safely used on pubic hair. But this got me thinking.

Is it possible that the reference to henna bushes in this context may be a poetic allusion to pubic hair? Firstly, of course, there may be some poetic justification in using the name of a bushy shrub to describe this patch of hair which itself is often bushy in appearance. But there may be much more than that in the writer's use of *henna* in this context.

Have you ever wondered why it is that the sexually mature human body develops this growth of hair around the external genital organs?

Please allow me to digress from the *Songs* story for a few paragraphs. Some people have said that this is evidence which proves that we have evolved from apes. However that argument is not at all logical. Most fur-covered animals do not have an extra dense covering of fur or hair in the area of their genitals. If anything the hair is less dense in this area. And, if our human bodies have ceased to grow hair all over because we habitually wear some form of clothing, then pubic hair would have been the first to disappear, since many of the virtually naked races

---
104. Beverly and Vidal Sasoon *A Year of Beauty and Health* (1975), p77.
105. Bronwen Meredith Vogue *Natural Health and Beauty* (1980), p206.

of humans have usually worn some covering over their genital organs.

Also, when observed under a microscope, it becomes obvious that the construction of pubic hair is unique. When seen in cross-section it is oval in shape and not circular like other hair from the body (or the hair from fur covered animals). It does not grow as long as the hair on our heads and tends to be crinkly rather than smooth, like the hair from our heads normally is.

Some people have therefore suggested that we have been provided with this patch of hair for lubrication and padding. Its purpose is thus to prevent any chaffing of the skin or bruising of the flesh over the pubic bone during the close physical contact of sexual intercourse. Hence sexually immature children do not need and do not have this growth of hair.

Yet others have suggested that pubic hair has to do with the matter of pheromones – that aspect of body odour which is supposed to give us "sex-appeal". Scientists have recognised with many animal species that this is an important factor in attracting a mate at breeding time. Or it may even be possible that God designed human beings with pubic hair for purely sensuous reasons. To just run your finger tips through your partner's pubic hair, with your fingers not quite touching the skin beneath, can give rise to some very pleasurable sensations. If this is the case then it is obvious that our creator God intended for us to enjoy our sexuality and our husband-wife expressions of physical and sexual touching.

There may be some truth in all of these ideas. But it is also possible that this hair can serve for other purposes. There is evidence in Scripture that body hair may have spiritual significance. A priest was required to take special care of his hair.[106] For Samson his uncut hair was a symbol of his Nazarite vow. (Chapter 6 of the book of Numbers gives details of the conditions for a Nazarite, such as applied to Samson, and emphasises the holiness

---

106. Leviticus 21:5-10; and Ezekiel 44:20.

of the Nazarite's hair). In some cases rituals of purity required shaving the entire body.[107] The Apostle Paul shaved off his hair in relation to some vow he had made.[108] We have also discovered, from experience, that when a person has been released from some form of spiritual bondage, sometimes one of the first things they will do is to get rid of their bizarre hairstyle and adopt a more "normal" appearance.

Another account which may have some significance here is that of Adam and Eve. Have you ever wondered why, when this couple tried to hide in the Garden of Eden, they covered their genitals instead of their faces?

In our culture we may speak of people hiding their face in shame, but Adam and Eve covered their loins, not their faces. Was it because they recognised the reproductive organs are in some way connected to the very core of the personality, and thus, for both sexes, this part of the physical body is significant in a very powerful and binding covenant?

Consider also the following points: We know that *henna* is used as a symbol of redemption – a ransom, or covering to atone for sin. In the minds of ancient Hebrew people there was some connection in thought between redemption and the covenant of marriage. It is also obvious that the genitals of both man and woman are involved in this covenant relationship. Remember that the woman's Mound of Venus was described as the "Mound (or mountain) of the Covenant". (2:17 in the Jerusalem Bible). The reproductive organs of the man were also recognised as being involved in a sacred covenant relationship, for we know that the Hebrew people used circumcision (the removal of the foreskin from the male reproductive organ, the penis) as a mark of their covenant relationship with YHWH.

Linguists and anthropologists also both point out that there is a word-root connection between the words "*testes*", "*testify*",

---
107. Numbers 8:7; and Deuteronomy 21:11.
108. Acts 18:18.

and "*testament*", and the words *testament* and *covenant* both mean the same thing.

So in all these ways we see the recognition of covenant relationship expressed through the sex organs.

It is therefore possible that the idea of describing pubic hair as "*henna bushes*" may have some special symbolism. Perhaps this patch of hair is not just there for aesthetic reasons. Perhaps it should also be considered as a reminder that this part of our body is not there just for party games. Perhaps pubic hair should also be seen as a reminder of covenant relationship, and an important factor in any covenant is faithfulness.

Even today we recognise that our reproductive organs are, in some mystical way, attached to the very heart or core of our personality. This is why we tend to keep them out of sight, and as with our most personal and private feelings, we may feel awkward, embarrassed, or even fearful, in the presence of someone who could misuse access to this part of our being. I have noticed that even old English laws relating to the reproductive organs use the euphemism "*person*" in place of the word "*genitals*".

Therefore, since this story in the *Song of Songs* deals with the covenant relationship of a husband and wife, the woman's invitation could be interpreted as something like, "Let us go to some place where we can spread out together and start playing in the 'henna bushes'." Or, perhaps she may be expressing some thought such as, "Our intimacy has now been redeemed (or restored), let us spend the night rejoicing in the restoration of our covenant relationship."

This interpretation continues to make sense when we consider the following comments made by the woman. She continues her invitation with, "Let us go early to see if the vines have budded, and the pomegranates are in bloom." Do you remember the comments about vines budding and pomegranate blooms in reference to 6:11, and how these words were used as a poetic

ACT 6 - RESTORATION

reference to the normal changes in the woman's body as she becomes sexually aroused?

She says, "Let us go early ..." In the original language these words actually imply a sense of enthusiastic anticipation. I am ready, and very eager to make love with you!" Mandrakes were considered to be an aphrodisiac, and were associated with fertility, and hence with sexual intercourse.

Having just expressed something of her intense desire, in words and in dance, this amorous wife then admits how frustrating she finds the cultural prohibition on showing husband-to-wife affection in public. She is permitted to kiss her brother in public, but not her husband. So she says,

> 8:1 I wish that you were like a brother to me ... Then if I met you in the street, I could kiss you and no-one would be offended."

Throughout the various cultural groups in our world there are some very different attitudes to the expression of husband-wife affection in public. In some countries you may even be arrested for kissing your spouse in public, although one is permitted to kiss a close relative in greeting.

If you think that is rather narrow minded then be aware that even the European pioneers of the USA have not been immune from such ultra-conservative prudery.

According to Isaac Asimov, in his *Giant Book of Facts and Trivia*, two hundred years ago a Boston ship captain, who had just returned from a three-year-long voyage, kissed his wife in greeting. But this was done in a public place, and it was a Sunday! He was charged with "lewd and unseemly behaviour" and made to sit in the stocks for two hours. !!!

But here in the *Songs* the wife also adds,

> "I would ... bring you to my mother's house, who would instruct me." (AV)

And then,

"I would give you spiced wine to drink, the nectar of my pomegranate."

This verse may require some explanation, and one writer suggests that the bride is hinting that her mother would give her (or the NIV infers 'has already given') instruction in the art of lovemaking. In some cultures that could be acceptable, and the idea is not inconsistent with Paul's instruction that the older women (ie: mothers) should teach the younger women (ie: daughters). Others suggest that it is the husband who will do the instructing, but they don't say why this should be in the mother's house.

However, the phrase *"who would instruct me"* is lacking in some very ancient manuscripts, such as the Septuagint, Old Latin, Syriac, and Origen's Greek Old Testament. Instead these manuscripts have the words, *".. into the chamber of her that conceived me"*. Hence the RSV translation,

"I would lead you and bring you into the house of my mother, and into the chamber of her that conceived me."

But we are still not given any reason why they should go to the mother's house in preference to their own "bridal chamber" (2:4).

Craig Glickman[109] explains this as simply being an extension of the bride's wish of 8:1. Thus, having assumed the role of the groom's sister (for this would allow them to kiss in public), she would then lead him to her (their) childhood home.

In Egyptian love poetry the mother can either support or reject the relationship of the Lover and Beloved. In the *Song of Songs* her attitude is obviously a supportive one. However, it may also be significant that Genesis 2:24 states quite clearly that it is the responsibility of the man to leave the protection and supervision of *his* parents in order to be united with his wife. No such requirement is made for the female member of the

---

109. Craig Glickman, *A Song For Lovers* p168, footnote.

marriage partnership. Some have interpreted this to mean that, in the biblical concept of marriage, the wife can still call on her parents for protection if her husband mistreats her in any way. The husband is then always accountable to his parents-in-law for the way he treats their daughter.

What does she mean when she says, "I would give you spiced wine to drink, the nectar of my pomegranate."? Many of the words used in the Hebrew text for this verse allude to banqueting, but we have already noted that the tree, fruit, and blossom of the pomegranate may be used in reference to the sex organs, (4:13 & 6:11).

The word translated to drink is the Hebrew *shaqah* (*Strong's* ref. H8248) which may mean "to give drink", but can also mean "to moisten", and is closely related to *shakar* meaning "to satiate with a stimulating drink or influence."

As for the actual "drink" which she mentions, the word nectar usually refers to the juice of some fruit which has just been squeezed. But spiced wine refers to fermented wine, or to some spicy or perfumed effervescent drink. So she seems to be simply using poetic words in reference to some enjoyable experience. In the context of her reference to delights both old and new we are probably safe to assume that she is promising some expression of love that is the result of renewed thinking on her part.

The scene then closes with the familiar refrain,

> Daughters of Jerusalem, I charge you: Do not stir up or awaken such powerful passion as this until it can be properly satisfied.

This repeated refrain not only indicates the close of this scene, but also tends to confirm that the couple did not go on a chariot ride around the villages. Instead they are celebrating their covenant relationship in the way that most husbands and wives do after a period of separation with some intimate "playing in the henna bushes"

ACT 7 REVELATION

Song of Songs 8:5 to 8:14

NIV

8:5 Who is this coming up from the desert leaning on her lover? Under the apple tree I roused you; there your mother conceived you, there she who was in labor gave you birth.

6 Place me like a seal over your heart, like a seal on your arm; for love is as strong as death, its jealousy unyielding as the grave. It burns like blazing fire, like a mighty flame.

7 Many waters cannot quench love; rivers cannot wash it away. If one were to give all the wealth of his house for love, it would be utterly scorned.

8 We have a young sister, and her breasts are not yet grown. What shall we do for our sister for the day she is spoken for?

9 If she is a wall, we will build towers of silver on her. If she is a door, we will enclose her with panels of cedar.

10 I am a wall, and my breasts are like towers. Thus I have become in his eyes like one bringing contentment.

11 Solomon had a vineyard in Baal Hamon; he let out his vineyard to tenants. Each was to bring for its fruit a thousand shekels of silver.

12 But my own vineyard is mine to give; the thousand shekels are for you, O Solomon, and two hundred are for those who tend its fruit.

13 You who dwell in the gardens with friends in attendance, let me hear your voice!

14 Come away, my lover, and be like a gazelle or like a young stag on the spice-laden mountains.

KJV

8:5 Who is this that cometh up from the wilderness, leaning upon her beloved?
I raised thee up under the apple tree: there thy mother brought thee forth: there she brought thee forth that bare thee.

6 Set me as a seal upon thine heart, as a seal upon thine arm: for love is strong as death; jealousy is cruel as the grave: the coals thereof are coals of fire, which hath a most vehement flame.

7 Many waters cannot quench love, neither can the floods drown it: if a man would give all the substance of his house for love, it would utterly be contemned.

8 We have a little sister, and she hath no breasts: what shall we do for our sister in the day when she shall be spoken for?

9 If she be a wall, we will build upon her a palace of silver: and if she be a door, we will enclose her with boards of cedar.

10 I am a wall, and my breasts like towers: then was I in his eyes as one that found favour.

11 Solomon had a vineyard at Baalhamon; he let out the vineyard unto keepers; every one for the fruit thereof was to bring a thousand pieces of silver.

12 My vineyard, which is mine, is before me: thou, O Solomon, must have a thousand, and those that keep the fruit thereof two hundred.

13 Thou that dwellest in the gardens, the companions hearken to thy voice: cause me to hear it.

14 Make haste, my beloved, and be thou like to a roe or to a young hart upon the mountains of spices.

ACT 7

REVELATION

Main Themes: The value of love, and childhood reflections.

8:5 Who is this coming up from the desert leaning on her lover?

He: "Under the apple tree I roused you; there your mother conceived you, there she who was in labour gave you birth."
[NIV]

This song opens with a theme (probably sung by the choir) that is similar to one we have heard before. "Who is this coming up from the desert leaning on her lover?" We encountered the imagery of coming up from the desert in 3:6, and it was suggested then that the reference may be to moving from a dry and barren place to a place of fruitfulness. In this new experience of course she is supported by her husband, hence "leaning on her lover".

We then hear the husband singing, "Under the apple tree I aroused you. There your mother conceived you, there she who was in labour gave you birth." Do we take this literally? Was this woman conceived and born under an apple tree? And have this couple just been lovemaking in a similar location? Why not? It may be possible to accept this as it reads.

ACT 7 Scene 1

In Egyptian poetry the shade of a tree is often the place where a couple discreetly make love.[110] And we have to acknowledge that throughout Scripture there are many references which indicate that sexual intercourse took place "on every mountain top and under every green tree" as a normal part of fertility cult rituals.[111] When we check these references, it is clear that the condemnation expressed by the Hebrew prophets was because of sexual activity in the context of prostitution, adultery, or pagan festivals, and not for the setting itself.

In the context of this reference to lovemaking under an apple-tree there is another Bible story which may be significant. In Genesis chapter 26 we read that on one occasion King Abimelech looked down from a window in his palace and saw Isaac and Rebecca making love (Genesis 26:7-11).

Now you and I know that Isaac and Rebecca were a married couple, but Abimelech had been told that they were brother and sister, so he had good reason to wonder just what on earth was really going on between these two. Perhaps, then, we also have good reason to ask just what Isaac and Rebecca were doing, apparently in open view somewhere in the palace grounds. The KJV says that Isaac was *sporting* with Rebecca; the RSV translation tells us that Abimelech saw Isaac *fondling* Rebecca; The Living Bible tells us that this Philistine king saw Isaac *petting* with Rebecca; the NIV translation tells us that he saw Isaac *caressing* her; and the Good News Bible says that they were *making love*.

In order to gain a better understanding of the meaning of any word in a foreign language it seems a good idea to compare how the same word has been translated in other places where it is used.

---

110. J F Craghan C SS R *Commentary on The Song of Songs and The Book of Wisdom* (1979).
111. 1 Kings 14:23-24; 2 Kings 16:4; 17:10-11; 2 Chronicles 28:4; Isaiah 57:5; Jeremiah 2:20; 3:6-13.

ACT 7 - REVELATION

The word translated variously as making love, caressing, fondling, etc. in the Hebrew text is a form of the verb which means *"to laugh"*. The same word is translated as *laughter* in Genesis 17:17 and 18:12-15, where we read that the aged Abraham and Sarah both laughed in disbelief when told that Sarah would give birth to a son in her old age.

The same word occurs again, and this time with some definite sexual connotations, in Exodus 32:6 where we read an account of what the people of Israel were doing after Aaron made that golden calf, when Moses was up on Mount Sinai. The story tells us that the people all "sat down to eat and drink and [then] got up to indulge in *revelry*". We know from Paul's comments in his letter to the Corinthians that this party did involve sexual activity, although in that case it was unlawful activity (1 Cor. 10:7-8).

Although we may not know exactly what Isaac and Rebecca were doing on the palace lawns the word used to describe their behaviour can certainly have sexual connotations and it is obvious from Abimelech's questioning of them after the event that they had been engaged in some very definite husband-wife activity. So, even apart from Adam and Eve in the Garden of Eden, who in their unashamed nakedness were told to go and reproduce (Gen 1:28), the concept of enjoying some form of love-play in a garden setting is certainly not unheard of in Scripture, and in many cases it was more than just foreplay.

Now of course I am not suggesting that we should all abandon the bedroom and move our lovemaking sessions to the front lawn. Such a public performance would not only be unlawful, it would be definitely inappropriate. And we can be quite certain that the lawns and gardens around Abimelech's palace would have been enclosed within a high stone wall, so Isaac and Rebecca's performance was not a public display.

Likewise there is no reason to assume that the apple tree referred to in these songs was in public view. But I would like to make the point that any ideas which suggest that sessions of husband-wife lovemaking must only ever be confined to "under the bedclothes, after dark, behind locked doors with the light out" do not have a good biblical basis.

There is, of course, another possible interpretation to the reference to an apple tree in this particular song. You may remember that I have already mentioned how the apple tree is sometimes used as a symbol of love and that the word *fruit* may refer to sweet words of praise and adoration (page 37-38, and *Songs* 2:3). So once again this could be a purely symbolic or poetic reference here and is intended to remind us that sexual arousal and the conception and birth of any child should always be under the protective umbrella of genuine agapé love.

The writer of these songs has obviously selected specific incidents in the life of a married couple (or from her own personal experience) in order to teach some lessons about relationships and love. She now concludes this musical presentation with a few significant comments, all of which relate to the value of true love and the importance of setting personal standards:

> 8:6 Place me like a seal over your heart, like a seal upon your arm: for love is as strong as death; and jealousy as relentless as the grave: it burns like a blazing fire, like the fire of the LORD. [NIV]

This verse, sung by the wife, is an appeal for a committed and faithful relationship between herself and her husband.

In Hebrew thought the heart indicates not only the seat of affections but also of moral decision making. The arm indicates strength. A seal was the symbol of ownership, the "signature" of the owner by which possessions could be identified. Elsewhere in the Old Testament the word "seal" is also used to represent something of great value.[112] So she asks for a faithful relationship, "Place me as a seal over your heart." In other words, "Please remember me. Do not let your heart go astray"

---

112. As, for example, in Haggai 2:25 and Jeremiah 22:24.

She then sings of the power of love and passion, but in so doing she makes a reference to death and the grave. Death is like a victorious hero who conquers all – no-one escapes. But what about jealousy? We are told that jealousy is sinful and dangerous. Well, some tell us that the word should be better translated as "passion" or "zealous love".[113] So the NRSV probably gives a better translation where we read, "For love is strong as death, passion as fierce as the grave." This is more consistent with the parallelism of Hebrew poetry, where the same idea is repeated using a slightly different imagery. In this case the writer would seem to be reinforcing her message regarding the almost irresistible power of sexual passion once the flame has been ignited. But, if she is referring to jealousy, then the message could be to the effect that, just as the grave (Sheol) will not give up the dead, so she will not give up (or abandon) the one she loves.

It is certainly appropriate to ask, "Is jealousy a healthy emotion?" Love should be possessive, but in the sense of being intensely concerned for the wellbeing of the one who is loved. When we really love a person we should be jealously concerned for their welfare or wellbeing and happiness. Anything less than that is not love, it is either indifference at one extreme or possessive lust at the other. The wife here is not extolling the sort of jealousy which desires to possess for the purpose of "using" another human being. Hence the Good News Bible translates this verse as:

> **8:6** Close your heart to everyone else but me. Love is as powerful as death; passion is as strong as death itself.
>
> It bursts into flame and burns like a raging fire.   [GNB]

In the Hebrew text the reference to "a raging fire" conveys the idea of an intense all-consuming flame, and seems to imply some form of super-natural power.

---
113. *The Interpreter's Bible* Vol V p143.

The comments which this woman makes here stand in contrast to the indifference which she had expressed at the beginning of Act 5 (5:3).

Perhaps, having written this story (from her own personal experiences?) including her experience of how she discovered that love does require some measure of discipline and commitment, she now wants to reassure us of the immeasurable value of real love. To this end we are presented with some wisdom statements, similar to those which are to be found in the book of Proverbs:

> 8:7 Many waters cannot quench love, neither can floods drown it. If one offered for love all the wealth of his house, it would be utterly scorned.   [NIV]

We are not told that no flood waters will ever come, but we are told that no flood waters will overcome. To expect to live without any trials or hardships in life is surely unreasonable, but a relationship that is founded on true love will not be destroyed by these "floods". Where true **love** exists, no opposition can destroy it.

Because real love is of such infinite value, to try to set a finite price for it would be to insult the one who offers love. Mere sensual pleasure can be purchased with money, but true love can only be freely given. Love cannot be purchased, and love that is freely given should create a sense of emotional security and healthy self-esteem within the one who is loved. Therefore the song says, "If a man would give all the substance of his house for love, he would be utterly scorned." Conditional love leads to feelings of insecurity, and the pressure to perform may undermine the very foundations of love.

There is of course a spiritual message for the Christian in this verse. The Apostle Paul went to great lengths in many of his letters to carefully explain that our redemption or salvation is offered as a *free gift* from God. Any suggestion that we can somehow buy this gift of love indicates an attitude of arrogance and is an insult to God. In writing to the Christians in Ephesus Paul explains that it is because of his great grace that God offers salvation as a free gift and this must be received by faith – it is not the result of human effort because if it were then men might boast about their achievements and this would then pander to human pride. (Ephesians 2:8-9).

Of course this does not mean that we simply reach out to take the gift while continuing to live a life of deliberate sin. And yet there were some who, deliberately trying to misinterpret what Paul was preaching, were saying that they could do just that. You can almost hear the exasperation in the apostle's voice when he challenged his friends in Rome with the question, "Shall we continue in sin that grace may abound?" Then answers his own question with the emphatic statement, "Of course not!" or, "By no means!" (Romans 6:1).

I recommend that you read Paul's letters for yourself if you wish to follow through on what he has to say about this wonderful demonstration of God's love.

The emphasis here on love and the appropriate response to love should also remind us that it is relationship that touches the heart of God. It is not some adherence to religious ritual or even human achievement. The empty repetition of any form of ritual, religious or otherwise, that is not focussed on developing a personal and intimate relationship is offensive to the heart of God.[114]

> *The intensity and eternity of the king's jealous concern for his wife is the same quality as the love which God has for His people. Nothing can extinguish it.* [source unknown]

---

114. Isaiah 1:11; Jer. 6:16-20; 7:21-26; Hosea 6:6; Amos 5:21-23, etc.

ACT 7 Scene 2

The scene then changes to the vineyard where this woman once worked with her family. People who conduct pre-marriage training courses for engaged couples often encourage those participating in the course to take a look at their own family background to determine how this has affected their expectations of marriage and also how it has shaped their own personality as an adult. This woman has also recognised the importance of doing this.

In a brief flashback scene of her childhood we are introduced to her family of origin. Apparently her older brothers filled this role, for they tell us,

> **8:8** We have a young sister, and her breasts are not yet grown. What shall we do for our sister for the day she is spoken for?"
>
> If she is a wall, we will build towers of silver on her. If she is a door, we will enclose her with panels of cedar.   [NIV]

This is obviously a reference to the beloved's childhood, for the words *she has no breasts* indicate a young girl who has not yet reached puberty. When she was a child her family were obviously concerned for her future, and for the development of her character and personality. And so they ask, "What shall we do for our sister?" The phrase, "In the day when she shall be spoken for" refers to the day of her betrothal. For Hebrew people the day of betrothal, although not the actual wedding day, was very important. Betrothal for these people, from what we have been told, was far more binding than our Western concept of engagement.

Although the contract had not as yet been consummated with any sexual act, to break a betrothal was almost equivalent to a divorce. After a minimum of a one year period of betrothal the couple were normally expected to marry, and only then was the contract formally consummated with sexual intercourse. This idea of betrothal would not be all that strange to some Europeans, as even today there are communities in Europe where a similar practice is still followed for couples who desire to get married.

The family explain their resolve with the words, "If she is a wall, we will build upon her a palace of silver: but if she is a door, we will enclose her with boards of cedar."

It may help us to understand what is being discussed here if we realise the different concept of time that may be used in Hebrew writings. The brothers sing in the present tense because the story is told from a viewpoint of the girl's childhood. Some story tellers use a similar idiom even today. For example, a particularly significant event may be introduced with, "So here I am, sitting in this car in peak hour traffic, and nothing will work. ..."

The expression, *If she be a wall*, refers to the need for establishing personal boundaries. Solomon himself taught the importance of personal boundaries in Proverbs 25:28 when he wrote, "Like a city whose walls are broken down is a person who lacks self control". So, in effect, the family of this young girl are saying that if she establishes and maintains her own definite boundaries and guide-lines for behaviour, then they would honour her. But if she proves to be weak in character, and in danger of being easily seduced or led astray, (ie: *if she is a door*) then they would need to restrict her freedoms. Thus they declare, "We will enclose her with panels of cedar."

Perhaps an acceptable modern paraphrase of the brothers' declaration could read something like this,

> If she proves to have it all together, and obviously knows how to behave properly, then we will honour her boundaries. But if she proves to be promiscuous, or irresponsible in her behaviour, then we will take action to restrict her activities, so that (or until) she becomes firmly established in the important issues of living. [author paraphrase]

The woman unashamedly tells us that,

> 8:10 "I am a wall, and my breasts are like towers: Thus I have become in his eyes as one who brings contentment."
>
> [NIV]

Now, as a mature woman and very obviously feminine *(my breasts are like towers)*, she tells us that she understands the importance of personal boundaries *(I am a wall)*, and this was a significant factor in her personal attractiveness. Her own choice for responsible behaviour, instead of having it forced upon her by others, indicated a strength of character that appealed to her "king".

Translators differ as to whether she is the one who **brings** peace and contentment or one who **finds** peace. The original language is ambiguous, but the message is still significant. It is also significant that the last part of her statement is emphatic in the Hebrew. "**Thus** I became in his eyes as one who brings contentment." It was because she demonstrated this strength of character that she found favour in the eyes of the man who is now her husband.

The word translated here as "peace" is the Hebrew *shalom*. Unfortunately the English words do not really give the full rich meaning of the original language, for the Hebrew word *shalom* encompasses far more than just a lack of conflict. The word has overtones of wholeness, welfare, and satisfaction, and thus represents the greatest measure of contentment to be found in life. So this is (almost) paradise, and it sounds very much as though this woman is telling us that she and her husband are both totally satisfied with their marriage relationship.

There may also be an important play on words with the phrase *one who brings peace*, and this may explain why the lover is referred to as "Solomon". The girl's name in Hebrew, when pronounced, sounds like Shulammith. The name Solomon, in original Hebrew, sounds like Shulamoh, and the Hebrew word for peace is *shalom*. Thus the woman is telling us that either, "Shulammith found *shalom* with Shulamoh," or conversely, "Shulamoh found *shalom* with Shulammith."

We are then presented with this strange little parable.

8:11 "Solomon had a vineyard at Baal-hamon; he entrusted the vineyard to keepers; each one was to bring for its fruit a thousand pieces of silver." [NRSV]

The wife here is making reference to one particular cultural practice and using this as an explanation of another. It was not uncommon for the owner of a vineyard to lease the property to vine-keepers, who in turn received a percentage of sales returns in payment for their labour. "Solomon's" vineyard, which was apparently leased to her brothers, is thus used as an illustration of her situation and her own person.

8:12 "But as for my own vineyard, you, O Solomon, shall have my thousand pieces of silver and I will give two hundred pieces to those who cared for it." [TLB]

She was, for a time, under the care and protection of her brothers. But her own vineyard (ie: her own body, as in 1:6 and 2:5) is now under her own authority and control, but she freely gives this completely and exclusively to her husband (king), who is the source of her *shalom*-peace.

Since caretakers of the vineyard normally received twenty percent of the sales in a normal business contract, she asks her "Solomon" (ie: the one who shares her peace and satisfaction) to give her family 200 shekels (20% of 1000) for their efforts in caring for her, and ensuring that she developed into a person of worthy character. This may be some allusion to bride-price, possibly cultural at the time, or simply a request that he acknowledge and express appreciation for the part her family have played in her upbringing. By recording this event (8:6-12) the writer has told us something of the development of this woman's character, and of the love that binds this marriage together.

The writer now concludes this love-drama with an interesting challenge from the husband and an appropriate response from the wife:

8:13-14

> **He:** "O you who dwell in the gardens, my companions are listening for your voice; let me hear it."
>
> **She:** "Make haste, my beloved, and be like a gazelle or a young stag upon the mountain of spices!" [NRSV]

Having made this necessary visit to the bride's family, the bridegroom now says, in effect, "These people are all listening to hear what you have to say to me about all this, and about our marriage contract."

So, in the hearing of her family (or everyone), she boldly replies, "Make haste, my beloved, and be like a gazelle or a young stag upon the mountain of spices."

This statement, with its reference to the "mountain of spices", as we discovered in 2:17, is a very specific invitation to sexual intimacy, and by saying this the woman has unashamedly declared — by her invitation to perform the sacred marriage rite — that she is now the wife of this man.

Healthy Boundaries, Healthy Relationships

The bride made the statement, "I am a wall," and we are also told that this was a significant attribute of her character which her husband-king found attractive about her. So what does she mean when she says, "I am a wall"? We know of many teenage boys who are confused by this question, because to them a wall means a flat surface, and how can this woman say, "I am a wall," and then immediately contradict herself by saying, "My breasts are like towers."

When we and our children had the privilege of building the house in which we could all live, one of the first things we did, after establishing the foundations and putting up the basic framework and installing roofing iron, was to complete the construction of the walls. I did not plan to do this because I am fascinated by flat surfaces, but this was done for protection. Those walls were necessary to keep the cold winter winds out, and to keep the warm air in. Walls were also necessary to prevent certain people from entering our property and removing things which did not belong to them. You see, walls are necessary to keep the good things in and to keep the bad things out, and the most common interpretation of her expression, "I am a wall" is that the woman was referring to personal boundaries.

Clearly defined boundaries give us the power and the authority to set our own values, and to help us take control of our own lives and to stop others from forcing us to do what they would like us to do, too often for their own personal gain. Any confusion of responsibility, control, and ownership in our lives is a problem of *boundaries*. Without healthy boundaries we don't really have freedom; instead we simply become victims of other people's exploitation or abuse.

Boundaries are not there to stop us from enjoying life. They are there to enable us to keep the good things in and the bad things out.

They allow us to invite into our social circle those people with whom we feel safe, and allow us to form a close bond of friendship with them, while keeping the unsafe people (negative, critical, abusive, exploitative) at a safe distance. Just as home-owners use some method of indicating the limits of their property, so also we need to set mental, physical, emotional, and spiritual boundaries for our lives, to help us distinguish what is our responsibility and what is not our personal responsibility.

People who do not respect boundaries are dangerous, but when we are allowed to set our own boundaries and the people with whom we associate respect those boundaries we set, then we have some hope of growing in a healthy relationship. If a person does not feel they have the freedom to say "No" then they do not really have the authority to say "Yes" either, because they are obviously being confronted by a "boundary buster", and boundary busters do not make safe companions.

Anyone who believes the myth, "No means maybe, and maybe means yes," cannot be trusted, and *is not fit to have as a companion!!*

However, the boundaries we establish need to be realistic and we may need to allow room for error. Unfortunately it is a fact of life that many of us allow our boundaries to be violated. Almost any of us may be seduced over a period of time if we persistently allow ourselves to be in places where we are vulnerable and in the presence of people who are not entirely trustworthy. Sometimes this may be the result of our own foolishness, or incautious action, but we also need to be aware that we may be the victim of deliberate deceit, as happened in the following story.

Lisa was an attractive woman who had a sad tale to tell. When she met Tom, one of the things that appealed to her was that he told her he would not drink alcohol. They were married after a brief courtship, but only a few months later, on his way home from a party, the vehicle Tom was driving left the road and he was killed. An autopsy indicated that Tom had an excessively high blood alcohol level at the time of his death. Lisa was distraught and perplexed. How could she explain to their child, who was born several months after the accident, that his normally sober father was accused of a fatal drink-driving accident. This evidence created confusion and embarrassment for her. It was years later that Lisa discovered the truth. A friend who had been at the same party let it slip that Tom had thought he was drinking only coffee, but his "mates" had been spiking the drinks with vodka.

This is a typical case of unacceptable boundary violations. Tom had made a decision that he would not drink alcohol. His workmates did not respect that boundary when they deceitfully laced his coffee with vodka. But worse than this, not one of those so called friends had the moral courage to face their own responsibility, to deal with issues within their own boundaries, by going and confessing their foolishness to the grieving widow. I object to calling such creatures "men". They were despicable boundary busters!! A person who does not respect boundaries cannot be trusted, and such behaviour does not create "men". But Tom's action, in choosing to set his own boundaries and in having the courage to be different in spite of peer-group pressure, would have been a pathway to real manhood, if he had been allowed to live.

We know from the ancient law as stated in Deuteronomy 19:14 that the Hebrew people were taught to respect property boundaries, and the entire Levitical law indicates that they were also to respect personal boundaries. Have you noticed that one of the characteristics of Paradise, wherever such a place is described in the Bible, is the respect for boundaries. However, there is a significant difference between ancient Levitical law and modern teaching about boundaries.

Modern relationship counsellors seem to emphasise the need for us all to be more assertive and more prepared to be in control of our own relationship issues so that others will have less chance of violating our personal boundaries. Hence, consistent with this approach of "learn to defend yourself", we are instructed to lock our doors so that the thief cannot enter our property. But in Levitical law the emphasis is the other way around. ANY individual who violates another person's boundary either has to make restitution if the violation was accidental or, in some cases, forfeits his own life if the violation was deliberate and malicious.

Some of the significant features of Heaven that are given in the book of Revelation indicate that Heaven is a place where boundaries will be respected. There will be no boundary busters in Paradise, for we are told that NO person who is unfaithful, who is immoral, who is a liar, who is a vile person, a rapist, or a murderer, will be permitted to enter. [115]

The paradise of Heaven will be a safe place where no-one will ever take advantage of another person. So there will be no reason for anyone to be afraid. But we are also told that there will be no cowards in Heaven. Why are cowards denied entry into Paradise? It is because these people do not deal appropriately with matters that are within their own boundaries, and which are therefore within their own personal area of responsibility. Even the Garden of Eden story implies the importance of respect for boundaries in character development.

What can we learn from the story of Adam and Eve in the Garden of Eden? Why was the forbidden tree left in an accessible place, instead of being protected by a solid stone wall? Probably because the Creator wanted Adam and Eve to recognise the importance of maintaining boundaries of their own personal discipline, and thus grow in character and develop a loving relationship based on trust. Unfortunately they failed the test. Respect for personal boundaries develops character.

Some time ago we watched a film entitled *Coming to America*. Although it is pure fiction, the story that is told in this film is of a young African prince, the son of an important tribal king, who wants to travel and "see the world" before getting married and having to settle down with his inherited responsibilities. The part of the young prince, Akeem, is acted by Eddie Murphy, and before he is allowed to leave home his father introduces him to the woman who has been chosen as his future bride.

At the introduction Akeem asks his prospective bride, "What is your favourite music?" She bows demurely and says, "Whatever you wish, my lord." Somewhat perplexed at this lack of personal opinion he then asks, "What is your favourite food?"

---
115. (Heb 13:4; Rev 21:8; Rev 22:15.

ACT 7 - REVELATION

Again she bows and replies, "Whatever you wish, my lord." In utter disappointment the young prince dismisses her, and she leaves the room. In his eyes this woman is a mindless puppet. She cannot even determine the boundaries of her own personality. She has no character. He wants the challenge of getting to know a woman who has a mind of her own. In contrast to that film story, the bride in the *Song of Songs* did have an honourable personality and character of her own. But, as we saw, this did not prevent her from adapting to meet the needs of her husband.

Consider the following simple rules for living and think what society would be like if everyone lived according to these boundaries:

1. Wouldn't is be nice if we lived in a society where there was no greed or envy, but instead there was always a respect for other people's right to be successful.

2. Wouldn't it be nice if we lived in a society where there was no lying and false accusations, but instead, a respect for integrity.

3. Wouldn't it be nice if we lived in a society where we could leave things "unlocked" with no fear that they would ever be stolen. A place where there is respect for every individual person's property.

4. Wouldn't it be nice if we lived in a society where people could always be trusted, and where they were always faithful to every agreement and contract they entered into. A society where covenant agreements were treated with honour and respect.

5. Wouldn't it be nice if we lived in a society where there was no hatred, no desire for revenge, and no murder? A place where we could live in peace without fear of violence.

6. Wouldn't it be nice if we lived in a society where children always treated their parents with honour and respect.

7. Wouldn't it be nice if we lived in a society where every week we could be sure of at least one day free of work, when we could

simply rest and praise the Creator who made this beautiful world.

8. Wouldn't it be nice if we lived in a society where no-one ever used profanity, and if they said they honoured God then we would know that they really are a trustworthy person.
9. Wouldn't it be nice if we lived in a society where people recognised that there is a Creator who loves us and cares for each one of us as an individual, and where every individual person recognises that one day we will all have to give account for every thing we have done and for every word we have spoken.

As you have probably recognised, that list is simply the Ten Commandments, in reverse order. They were not given to stop us having fun, they were provided for the protection of innocent, peace-loving people. The perversity of our society today is that our legal system seems to be more preoccupied with appeasing the boundary breakers than with protecting the boundary keepers. But, in the ancient standards handed down to Moses, God's attitude seemed to be, "You violate the boundaries my man, and you are out of the game."

If we were ever to attempt to create such a place as paradise on earth then everyone would have to agree to play according to the rules, and recognise that there must be boundaries, otherwise it would never work. As soon as we allow into paradise even just one individual who would wilfully violate the boundary of another person then that place immediately ceases to be paradise. It is no longer possible to guarantee the safety of everybody or anybody. We would therefore need to establish some rules and guidelines governing acceptable behaviour, and some rules to tell us what sort of things may be forbidden in order that we may know where the boundaries lie.

We may eventually even have to produce a list of "Thou shalt not's." But paradise is supposed to be a place of love, not of

ACT 7 - REVELATION

rules and lists of forbidden activities. Yes, that may be true. But any parent can tell you it is a far greater blessing to see a child whose attempts to do-the-right-thing are motivated by love and respect for the parent rather than one who is driven by the fear of punishment. This is why Jesus of Nazareth told his disciples, "If you love me you will do what I ask" (John 14:15).

We have to admit that the evidence of real love will be seen in more than simply obeying a set of rules, or in the keeping of some tedious ritual.

So if paradise is to be understood as a place of perfect peace, harmony, and love then it cannot mean that everyone is expected to act like mere puppets under the control of some harsh dictator. Nor can it be established by a legalistic adherence to some tiresome ritual. But neither can it mean the wishy-washy acceptance of any and every conceivable alternative lifestyle, or a place where almost anything and everything is tolerated. The hippies of the 1960's tried this, and they were certainly not the first to do so.

But it is significant to note that such ideas have never proved to be so successful that they replaced the traditional concept of the nuclear family, nor have they ever been adopted by any society on a long-term basis. Even Plato's concept of an ascetic community where wives and children are all shared in common has never really found enthusiastic acceptance.

As I may have already mentioned, when Marcia Seligson[116] set out to explore some of the alternative lifestyles of the 1960's and 70's she was determined to prove that monotonous monogamy, as she called it, was a lost cause. But at the end of her book she frankly admits that she was caught off-guard when a teenage boy thew her a question about relationships and she surprised herself by responding with the first thought that came to her mind. She then recognised that, in spite of all her own ideologies and observations, when it came down to gut-level feelings she still believed that for her a faithful monogamous relationship of

---
116. Marcia Seligson, *Options*, 1977

marriage was the only acceptable option. And in many of the case histories which she presented it also became obvious that those folk had more rules and less real satisfaction and contentment in life than a lot of couples in faithful long-term monogamous relationships.

It may also be significant to note that the most common reason given for the failure of many of the hippy communes was that so many of their members formed an exclusive pair-bond with one opposite-sex member of the commune and then they both left the commune to live together as husband and wife.

There is something written deep into the human psyche that keeps telling us that sexual intercourse touches the very heart of our being and as such it should be more than just a casual party-game. Such a close and intimate expression of togetherness must be seen as a sacred celebration of a special relationship. For this reason it is not uncommon to find that for those who have cheapened their sexuality through a series of brief and casual affairs where there was no real commitment then life became very cheap, empty, and meaningless. We should not be surprised when we find that modern societies which encourage teenage promiscuity have also seen a rapid increase in the incidence of teenage suicide.

In the physical world in which we live there are many invisible forces such as gravity, magnetism, electricity, heat, light, sound, ... all of these forces operate in accordance with predictable and known laws which we refer to as physical laws or The Laws of Physics. Just as there are laws of physics so also there are laws of relationship. Although these principles may not have been so clearly documented (yet) as have the laws of physics this does not mean that they do not exist. The law of gravity existed long before Isaac Newton was hit on the head by a falling apple and the man stopped to ponder what force has caused that apple to fall. Scientists have studied and recorded many of the physical laws which relate to the world in which we live but we don't try to deny, challenge, or refute these laws. Instead we use our knowledge of them to design and create some wonderful machines.

Pilots who fly those dare-devil aerobatic manoeuvres know and understand the laws of physics which affect the operation of their aircraft. Because they know and understand those laws, they know the limits of the performance they can achieve. But, by knowing the limits, they are able to do things that other pilots would never attempt. So it is with human relationships. When we play it according to the rules we actually have a greater measure of freedom and can have so much more fulfilment and enjoyment in life, because we know where the boundaries are, and why they are there.

Two important factors that will determine our success or failure and our happiness or otherwise in life are the decisions we make and the belief system and value systems which we choose to accept.

Jesus of Nazareth taught that those who live their life in selfishness, concerned only for their own comfort and wealth, may loose what little they already have, but those who show a genuine concern for others and who give to those in need will find that provision will be made for all of their own need. Some of his statements are well known, such as his commissioning of the twelve disciples where he instructed them to, "give as freely as you have received." (Matt. 10:8); and again where he said, "If you try to live your life for yourself you will lose it ... What good will it be for a man if he gains the whole world, yet forfeits his own soul? (Matt. 16:26). He counselled a rich man, who had asked how he may find eternal life, with this advice, "If you wish to be perfect, go, sell your possessions, and give the money to the poor, and you will have treasure in heaven; then come, follow me." (Matt. 19:21; Mark 10:21; Luke 18:22).

It is obvious that, as human beings, we have been designed with a desire to live in relationship with other people and God has really given us some excellent resource material to teach us how we can do this and, of course, the most significant relationship of all is the one which we can have with God Himself.

Over the years many people have experimented with all sorts of alternative lifestyles but the evidence all suggests that if we want to find anything like the *shalom* peace and contentment of paradise, even in this twisted world in which we live, then it works best if we follow the Designer's instructions.

Summary

We have learned that paradise is not determined by the material things that we possess or by our success in business, but by the relationships that exist between all the persons involved. We have seen that the theme of the *Song of Songs* is relationships and that this little book can teach us much about maintaining a relationship of *shalom* peace:

- We have seen how the couple in the *Song of Songs* express their love and acceptance of each other through the frequent use of words of affirmation and encouragement.
- We have learned that marriage is a covenant relationship, and that the heterosexual union of the man and woman is a special and sacred celebration of that relationship.
- We have seen that the Bible does offer some very positive input on the subject of human sexual love and the type of communication needed to keep a marriage in good working order.
- We have seen that there should be an unashamed acceptance of the physical human body and of a married couple's right to celebrate their emotional and spiritual unity through physical and sexual communion.
- By the end of this story the couple's relationship is no longer

inhibited by feelings of guilt, embarrassment or shame. So, in a way, they have come close to regaining something of the paradise that once existed in the Garden of Eden.

- We have also discovered that some aspects of the sexual union of a married couple have significant similarities to the intimate communication of prayer. An ideal marriage relationship therefore presents a picture of the spiritual relationship between God and His people, or between Christ and the Church.
- We have seen that if any concept of paradise is to work we must all obey all the rules and also respect our own boundaries as well as those of other people. This is love put into action.

APPENDIX 1

Is Eros Evil?

A brief history of Judaeo-Christian attitudes regarding sex and marriage

There has obviously been some considerable influence throughout the history of our culture to persuade people to believe that a really spiritual person will never really enjoy sexual activity. There are still remnants of the idea that sex, even within marriage, is somehow sinful or shameful.

Much of this confusion may be the result of anti-Christian propaganda which has deliberately misquoted statements of church leaders, but the records do show that over the centuries leaders within the Christian church have taught many strange and sometimes unbiblical ideas about the subjects of sex, marriage, and the acceptance of the human body.

Origen (182-251 AD), brilliant scholar though he was, is reported to have said, "Adam did not have any sexual relationship with his wife until after the Fall. If it was not for the Fall the human race would probably have been propagated without sex and therefore without sin."

He obviously had not registered the significance of the creation record in Genesis 1:27-28 where we read:

> Male and female he created them. God blessed them and said to them, 'Be fruitful and increase in number'.

It is obvious from the context that the male and female aspect of God's creation was for the purpose of reproduction. For some reason Origen equated sexual activity with sin, even within marriage. This saintly man castrated himself in a frenzied attempt to attain greater spiritual heights.

In the fourth century AD a group of Christians in North Africa sought to return to the innocence of Adam and Eve in the Garden of Eden. Calling themselves Adamites, they ate no meat, wore no clothes, and insisted on total abstinence from all sexual activity. Predictably, the group was doomed to extinction.

In the year 305AD the Church Council of Elvira enacted that, "All concerned with the ministry of the altar must practice abstinence from their wives ... or forfeit their positions." By the end of the 4th century all priests were forbidden to marry.

Yet this is contrary to the teaching of Leviticus 21:14 and Paul's specific instructions to Timothy where he states that leaders within the Church must be married men who have first proved their leadership skills within their own household and family. (1 Tim. 3:4-12).

Bishop Ambrose (340-397AD), expressed attitudes typical of his time when he said that, "Married people ought to blush when they consider the sort of lives they live." Eight hundred years later Thomas Aquinas (1225-1274) taught that the Christian life could be lived at two levels - the higher, truly spiritual level of the unmarried celibate, or the lower, less spiritual level of those who married.

By the mid 16th century leaders in the Church of Rome were insistent that the state of unmarried celibacy was spiritually superior to the married state. These attitudes stand in utter contrast to the Hebrew and biblical understanding of human sexuality as God designed and intended it to be.

Although there are now marriage counselors within the Christian church who are desperately trying to repair the damage these doctrines have caused, and are still causing today, this understanding is only shared in the privacy of the counseling room. Until a clear, positive attitude to human sexuality is boldly preached from our pulpits we will continue to be troubled by these confused ideas.

Hebrew Theology of Sexuality

The Talmud views marriage as the only legitimate means of fulfilling the biblical command of procreation which is given in Genesis 1:28. And therefore, in contrast to the recorded ideas of men like Origen, Ambrose, and Thomas Aquinas, the Hebrews were strongly opposed to celibacy.

Genesis 2:18 states clearly that "it is not good for man to be alone". The Talmud declares, "He who has no wife is not a proper man" (Yev. 63a); He lives "without joy, blessing, goodness, protection, and peace". (Yev. 62b).[117] Another rabbi went even further in saying, "He who remains single diminishes the image of God."[118]

Possibly the best known example of the ancient Hebrew acceptance of the beauty of God's creation and of human sexuality is found in the Genesis account of creation. The story is significant because it sets the stage for the unfolding drama of redemption that is presented throughout the rest of the Bible, but also for the way the creation story itself is presented.

Most other accounts of creation involve a pantheon of gods and lesser gods, often fighting and quarrelling for a position of

---

117. Quoted by I. H. Fishbein, *Dictionary of Pastoral Care and Counselling* p679.
  [Subject Heading: Marriage (Jewish Theology)] Nashville: Abingdon Press, 1990.
118. Quoted by Dr. David R Mace in *The Christian Response to the Sexual Revolution* p29

superiority. In many of the creation stories as taught by Greek philosophers the supreme God could not have created the world because the world is so evil that such a Holy Being could have nothing to do with it. We will see later how these ideas had a damaging effect on the early Christian church.

The Genesis account tells us in simple unashamed language that God himself created the earth and placed mankind upon it. Genesis chapter 1 tells us that:

> "God created man in His own image [this refers to his character, not his physical appearance] ... male and female He created them. And God blessed them and said to them, 'Be fruitful and increase in number; fill the earth and subdue it.' ... And God saw all that He had made and behold it was very good."
> (Genesis 1:27–31. NIV)

In Genesis chapter 2 we are presented with a second account which explains why God created us as male and female. This factor of the design was to provide for both a sense of companionship as well as a means of reproduction.

Chapter 2 then ends with some significant statements:

> "For this reason a man will leave his father and mother and be united to his wife and the two shall become one-flesh. Now the man and his wife were both naked and they felt no shame."
> (Gen 2:24-25. NIV)

Incidentally the phrase translated *no shame* or *not ashamed* can also be translated "not disappointed". In other words, everyone involved in the scene was perfectly happy with the whole situation.

So we have a scene of perfect contentment where there was no embarrassment, no guilt, no shame, and no fear. The weather was perfect with no need for clothing to protect against frostbite or sunburn. There was perfect trust, and we find no mention of locked doors. This was *shalom* peace. In a word, this was Paradise.

So the ancient Hebrew (Genesis) account has told us that the Great Creator YHWH Elohim was Himself personally responsible for the design and creation of mankind. We are told that sex was part of that design. We are told that so long as they lived at peace with God the couple were not ashamed of their naked bodies. We are told that God looked upon this world He had created, including the naked man and woman, and declared the entire scene very good. And we are told that this same God told the naked couple to go and reproduce (Gen 1:28). Since this instruction follows immediately after the statement referring to the sexual aspect of the design we can be quite certain that this was a specific instruction to engage in sexual intercourse. Note also that there is no mention of "only do it after dark, under the bedclothes and with the light out".

In other words, this creation story clearly teaches that the God of creation is not embarrassed about the sight of naked bodies, nor even of a married couple engaged in sexual intercourse, because that is the way He designed it.

Further evidence that God intended husbands and wives to enjoy their sexuality is found (as already mentioned) in Deuteronomy 24:5, where we are told that it is the responsibility of the husband, during the first year of marriage, to learn to make his wife happy. This ancient biblical law states,

> "If a man has recently married, he must not be sent to war or have any other such duty laid on him. For one year he is to be free to stay at home and bring happiness to the wife he has married." (Deuteronomy 24:5)

All Hebrew men were expected to marry and raise a family. Even priests were expected to marry, the only restriction being that they were to marry a virgin from their own clan. Leviticus 21:14-15 tells us that a priest *"must not marry a widow, a divorced woman, or a woman defiled by prostitution, but only a virgin from his own people* (ie: from the tribe of Levi), *so he will not defile his offspring among his people."* Note that this restriction was for racial purity, for only men from the tribe of Levi were permitted to serve as priests in the temple.

Hebrew women believed that their ultimate goal and purpose in life was to be a wife and a mother. A woman's whole purpose in living was to produce children in fulfillment of the instruction given in Genesis 1:28.

Since the ancient Hebrews had such a matter-of-fact acceptance of their sexuality we obviously need to address the question, "Why do some people believe that the Bible contains anti-sex teachings?"

So let me explain: Many ancient cultures, and apparently the Hebrews were no exception, believed that the male semen was the substance which actually formed the foetus in the womb of the woman. The male had to provide sufficient "seed" (semen) to actually develop into a foetus. They believed the woman contributed nothing to the blood-line of the child, being merely an "incubator" in which the foetus developed. Missionary anthropologists working in Papua New Guinea during the 1960's have told me that they encountered similar beliefs amongst some of the tribes-people of that country.

So these people believed that a woman who had any sexual intercourse with a man other than her husband could give birth to a contaminated child who was not solely of her husband's "seed". This evidently was the background to the double standard which allowed men to be promiscuous (with a recognized prostitute - never with another man's wife, as that would dishonor the other husband) but required absolute fidelity for all married women. Of course this belief also required that a woman must remain a virgin until married to ensure that her first child was the sole product of her husband's seed. Otherwise she may give birth to a contaminated or adulterated child. It also follows that in a marriage where the wife was barren it was considered acceptable for the husband to impregnate one of his wife's servant girls who would thus bare a child on behalf of the barren wife.

It will also be helpful if we understand a little about the attitudes regarding women, sex, religious beliefs, and prostitution in the nations who lived alongside these people in Old Testament times. As you read these notes you will begin to understand why YHWH warned his people to have nothing whatever to do with the tribes who previously lived in the Land of Canaan.

Harlots were of two kinds. The common prostitute, although officially rejected and condemned, seems to have been quietly tolerated in practical terms. Because the social welfare system of those times was dependent on the structure of the family there were no specific organizations to which widows and orphans could turn for support. Thus, for an unattached woman or a widow who had no husband or male relative to provide for her welfare, prostitution was often the most readily available means of earning money or other resources to buy food and clothing. There is no apparent condemnation of the Patriarch Judah visiting a woman he thought was a prostitute after the death of his own wife (Genesis 38:15).

But the role of a cult prostitute was a very different matter. Her activities were part of the worship of pagan gods. As already mentioned in an earlier chapter, followers of these pagan fertility cults believed there was some form of sympathetic magic connecting human sexual activity with the new life in nature that is observed every Spring. So in order to ensure good crops and an abundant harvest the devotees of these cults engaged in religious rituals which involved sexual activity.

It was also for this reason that all women in those pagan lands were expected to engage in some form of religious prostitution. In some parts of Canaan, in order to bring new strength into the clan, woman were all encouraged to become pregnant to a total stranger at least once in her lifetime, as part of these ceremonies.

Herodotus tells us that in the land of Babylon:

APPENDIX 1

> The foulest custom ... is that which compels every woman of the land once in her lifetime to sit in the temple of Aphrodite and have intercourse with some stranger. ... When a woman has once taken her place there she goes not away to her home before some stranger has cast money into her lap and had intercourse with her ... so she follows the first man who casts and rejects none. After their intercourse she has made herself holy in the sight of the goddess and goes away to her home...[119]

Ceremonies such as these probably account for the behavior of Gomer, the unfaithful wife of the prophet Hosea, who bore at least three children, only one of whom was fathered by her husband. Similar customs existed in other parts of Western Asia, in North Africa and islands around the Mediterranean, and also in Greece.

The Temple of the goddess Aphrodite in the city of Corinth employed about one thousand sacred prostitutes dedicated to her service. In many parts of the world these cults also practiced child sacrifice. We know from the writings of the Hebrew prophet Jeremiah that, in the land of Canaan the ashes of these children were placed in urns which were then buried in a special cemetery known as "Topheth" (Jeremiah 7:31-34). It was only after presenting such an offering, and thus consecrating her reproductive system to Molech (a Canaanite fertility god), that a young woman devotee of this particular cult was permitted to marry.[120]

Jewish law condemned all of these practices. (Leviticus 18:21; 20:2-3; etc.) For a Hebrew man to be involved with any of these ceremonies was a serious spiritual and religious offence rather than just a sexual offence. So it was no accident that required every Hebrew man to be circumcised and thus carry on his penis the mark of his identity as a member of the people of YHWH.

---

119. Hans Walter Wolf, Hermeneia, A Critical and Historical Commentary on the book of Hosea, translated from German by Gary Stansell. (USA: Fortress Press, 1974), p 86-87.
120. R.D.Barnett, Illustrations Of Old Testament History, p37.

As soon as he appeared in one of these pagan festivals he was identified as being out-of-bounds.

For the Hebrew man, circumcision was a religious symbol dedicating him to use his reproductive organ for the glory of God. It was not to be used in some orgiastic pagan ceremony. Far from being obscene, the man's penis was the most sacred part of his whole body.

It was also for this reason that Moses was very careful to warn the Children of Israel to never become involved with these fertility cults. And YHWH clearly warned His people, through Moses, that the abundance of the Promised Land would not be the result of any sort of sexual license, but it would be dependent on the faithfulness of their relationship with Him. (Deuteronomy 11:9-14, 12:2-3).

And we do need to remember that within the Hebrew culture crimes such as adultery with another man's wife, rape, or the seduction of a virgin outside of marriage, carried very severe penalties. Their laws may seem harsh to our modern day standards, but they were there to prevent the exploitation and abuse of women, such as was happening in the surrounding nations.

Do you begin to understand what was being condemned here? Wherever we read of the condemnation of sexual activity in the Old Testament it is a condemnation of these heathen practices. The motive was for religious purity, the stability of the family, respect for women and respect for covenant relationships. There is no condemnation of sexual lovemaking within marriage. As Dr David Mace expressed it, "In the Old Testament we find no trace of the sexual asceticism which later dominated the Christian church".[121]

There is big difference between the religious beliefs of the fertility cults and the belief systems of the Hebrews. The Hebrew people placed great importance on covenant relationships; and

---

121. Dr David Mace, Christian Response to the Sexual Revolution. p29

individuals persons were treated with dignity. To the Hebrew people the specific relationship between YHWH and each individual person was also very important.

But in the religions of the fertility cults we find a swirl of creatures involved in a whirlpool of sensuality where individual persons loose their significance. These people believed that, as a group, they must stir up feelings of ecstasy in order to impress, or control, the spiritual forces around them, and thus persuade the gods to respond to the will of the community.

When this activity was directed towards the gods of fertility then all the males in the group were expected to contribute, and all the females were obliged to help stir up the appropriate desire within the men and, perchance, to conceive a child in honor of the gods. Individuals don't count in this sort of society. People dance and swirl about, hoping that the "pattern" they create will be pleasing to the gods. But who cares about an individual person. Women became merely things to be used.

In contrast to these crude activities, within the Hebrew culture women, sex, and marriage, were all, for the most part, treated with dignity and respect. Where we do find evidence that women seem to have been treated unfairly, by what we might consider an acceptable standard today, we need to remember the social, cultural, and religious environment in which these people lived. As Dr B. Ward Powers wrote:

> The status of women in Judaism was higher than anywhere else in the ancient world. Whenever we read these Old Testament laws we need to remember the culture and environment in which they were drafted. There are many laws and regulations which exist even now, even in our own country, which are less than perfect and ideal by absolute standards of fair-dealing. But changing the customs and practices of any people can be a long and difficult task. Anyone who thinks it can be done by the stroke of a pen on paper is out of touch with reality. The true measure of the Mosaic law is not the deficiencies we may be able

to find with it now ... but how it handled the situation which prevailed beforehand and how it compares with alternatives being enacted by other contemporaries.[122]

New Testament Teaching on Sex and Marriage

Jesus of Nazareth obviously approved of marriage. We read about his support of the marriage feast at Cana in Galilee,[123] and Matthew tells us that he obviously enjoyed celebrating.[124] He was no religious freak living in ascetic isolation. He treated all women with dignity, including the unfortunate Samaritan woman who had suffered five failed marriages,[125] the woman caught "in the very act of adultery"[126], and even ex-prostitutes.[127]

In his "Sermon on the Mount" Jesus taught,

> "... if any man looks lustfully at any woman he has already committed adultery with her in his heart." (Matthew 5:27-28)

To the Hebrew mind this was nothing new.

Levitical law, as spelled out in Leviticus chapter 18, condemns gazing with lustful intention at the body, or genitals, of any close relative. Jesus was simply saying that any man who looks with lustful intention at *any* woman has fallen short of God's standard and is thus guilty of sin. This is not condemning the legitimate mutual sharing of sexual pleasure within marriage, neither does it condemn simply admiring a woman for her natural beauty. But it is a condemnation of those who view any woman as nothing more than an object or a sex toy. The emphasis of this teaching is not that the physical (sexual) body is obscene, but rather it is

---

122. Dr B Ward Powers, Marriage and Divorce, p275 (used with permission)
123. The Gospel according to John, chapter 2
124. Matthew 11:29
125. John 4:7-26
126. John 8:1-11
127. Luke 7:36-50

APPENDIX 1

the matter of accountability. Actions should be traced back to the basic motivation and thoughts in the mind of the beholder, and it is the thoughts of many people that are obscene.

In teaching about divorce Jesus said, "Some are eunuchs (ie: have no sex-drive or desire) because they were born that way; others were made that way by men; others have made themselves eunuchs (ie: renounced marriage) because of the kingdom of heaven. The one who can accept this should accept it." (Matthew 19:12). But Jesus is not saying here that every man needs to behave like a eunuch, only that we should accept that some people choose to live that way.

St Paul left us in no doubt about his respect for marriage when he used it as a symbolic image of the relationship between Christ and His church. However, many people run into problems when they read Paul's first letter to the church in Corinth, especially chapter seven of that letter. It helps if we understand something about the people to whom Paul was writing on this occasion. And the questions about divorce was probably asked by men who, even in those days, were beginning to think that unmarried "celibacy" would be a more "spiritual" lifestyle.

One of the significant elements of Greek philosophy is what theologians call "dualism". The basis of this teaching was that God, who is absolute holiness, created an ideal world (the "world" of the soul) but he employed subordinate beings to create the physical world in which we abide as physical flesh and blood beings. It is the soul that is good, but all physical matter is inherently evil. A holy God could have no contact with this evil world in which we live.

This concept of dualism (the soul is good but the body is evil) was an element in many religious philosophies of the world in which the Christian church first developed, and these ideas seriously affected the church during the first century. One of the major problems was the development of a sect, or heresy, known as Gnosticism. Within this sect two entirely contradictory lifestyles developed. At one extreme was a very austere or ascetic lifestyle, and the other extreme was "total freedom" or libertinism. Many of the New Testament passages referring to "sexual immorality" are directed against the excesses of this cult.

The church in Corinth was seriously affected by these teachings, and there were elements of both extremes in this congregation. Those who followed the libertine extreme believed that the body and the spirit were so separate that, provided their followers had the correct "knowledge", it did not matter what they did with their physical body. These people had also twisted Paul's teachings of salvation-by-grace and freedom-from-the-law, and as a result were teaching that they were now free to indulge in all sorts of sexual and moral license. They believed that it was quite acceptable for them to attend celebrations at the pagan temples, and to involve themselves with the associated festivities, which included a lot of adulterous and immoral sexual activity (*porneia*).

Remember that in Corinth alone the temple of Aphrodite employed something like one thousand sacred prostitutes (*porné*). One Commentary writer stated that their adultery and other acts of immorality were so blatant that even the censors of the bawdy Roman Empire were appalled by their behavior.

There was also in Corinth an element of the ascetic extreme who were teaching that those who were married were lowering themselves to an inferior spiritual standing, and these people were therefore encouraging husbands and wives to withhold conjugal rights from each other, and they were teaching betrothed couples to refrain from ever sexually consummating their marriage.

So Paul was faced with a problem. Should he choose to endorse the opinions of the ascetic extreme, with their renunciation of sex, then he would be effectively downgrading the status of women, and could be understood as condoning attitudes that treated marriage with contempt. But at the same time he had to be careful that he was not understood as approving of the licentious

APPENDIX 1

behavior of the libertine group, who were already claiming Paul's approval of their viewpoint because he had said that Christians are not bound by the law of Moses. Therefore, to the libertines he writes:

> You say, "I am free to do anything". Yes, but not everything is for my good. ... it is not true that the body is for lust; it is for the LORD. ... Do you not know that your bodies are limbs and organs of Christ? Shall I then take from Christ his bodily parts and make them over to a harlot [in a pagan ceremony]? Never! You surely know that anyone who links himself with a harlot becomes physically one with her, for the Scripture says, "The two shall become one flesh"; but he who links himself with Christ is one with him spiritually. ... You do not belong to yourselves; you were bought with a price. Then honour God with your body. (1 Corinthians 6:12-20. NEB)

Throughout the rest of this letter Paul also deals with other matters, such as the issue of involvement with idol feasts in general (chapter 8-10). In his remarks to the ascetics he writes:

> Since there is so much immorality, each man should have his own wife, and each woman her own husband. The husband should fulfill his marital duty to his wife, and likewise the wife to her husband. The wife's body does not belong to her alone but also to her husband.
>
> In the same way, the husband's body does not belong to him alone but also to his wife. Do not deprive each other except by mutual consent and for a time, so that you may devote yourselves to prayer.
>
> Then come together again so that Satan will not tempt you because of your lack of self-control.
> (1 Corinthians. 7:2-5. NIV)

What he has done, in effect, is to point out the errors and dangers of both extremes, and declare that both are a distortion of God's design. Although he acknowledges that married couples will have to face many problems in life, Paul specifically states more than once in his following comments that it is no sin to be married, and marriage obviously implies an active sexual relationship, for he also wrote, "Do not deprive each other … so that Satan will not tempt you." (1 Cor. 7:5 NIV). Note also that Paul's emphatic statements to the effect that a wife must not separate from her husband, and a husband must not divorce his wife, are within this context. These people were not wanting to divorce because of irreconcilable conflict, but in their confusion they were being persuaded that living a 'single' or celibate life would be a means toward more holy living.

The Apostle Paul would probably have been appalled to learn that later theologians would use the teaching in his Corinthian letter to support their doctrine that marriage was "nothing more than a contemptible refuge for the morally weak."

Those who have studied church history will also be aware that some of those confused theologians held lengthy and heated debate regarding whether or not a woman even possessed a soul! By contrast, Paul had elevated the status of woman by suggesting that the wife has part-ownership of her husband's body. To the culture of his time, this was radical teaching.

In his letter to the young pastor Timothy, Paul states explicitly that those who forbid people to marry are teaching *"doctrines inspired by devils"* (1 Timothy 4:1-5). He also tells Timothy that those chosen to be bishops or leaders of the congregation must be married, and first prove their pastoral skills by the way they treat their own family.[128] And in his letter to the Christians in Corinth, Paul made reference to the fact that the half-brothers of Jesus, now also evangelists, are married men, as also was the disciple Peter.[129]

---

128. 1 Timothy 3:2-5. Note especially v5. An unmarried man would not have children.
129. 1 Corinthians 9:5

APPENDIX 1

The writer of the letter to the Hebrews wrote, "Let marriage be held in honour and thus let the marriage bed be undefiled".[130] The Greek word translated as "marriage bed" is *koitee (koité)* from which we get our English coitus.

The words "let" and "be held" are not in the original Greek text. So this verse could be translated literally as, "Marriage is completely honourable and coitus does not defile," in which case we have a clear statement defending marriage against any suggestion that celibacy is a more holy or spiritual state.

Throughout the entire New Testament marriage and sex within marriage are held in honour and respect, as also is the status of women. To quote from no lesser authority than the *Dictionary of Pastoral Care and Counseling*:[131]

> "Nowhere in the New Testament is sexual intercourse understood to be exclusively for the procreation of children; the one-flesh bond of marriage is normative."

A second significant difference between Hebrew and Hellenistic philosophies was their concept of God. To the Hebrews YHWH was a God of love, mercy, and compassion. After the Genesis account of creation and the fall we read that when:

> "the LORD saw how great man's wickedness on the earth had become, and that every inclination of the thoughts of his heart was only evil all the time [He] was grieved, ... and his heart was filled with pain." (Genesis 6:5-6 NIV)

The Hebrew people would have understood that it was because of His desire for a personal relationship with each man and woman that the Creator's reaction, in response to this foolish behavior, was one of intense grief. He is obviously a God who has emotional feelings.

---

130. Hebrews 13:4.
131. *Dictionary of Pastoral Care and Counselling* p678

The Gospel writers frequently tell us that Jesus of Nazareth was moved with *compassion*, and the word they use (*splagchnitzomai* or *splagchnitzestai*) is the strongest word used in the Greek language to describe the feeling of compassion. It means an emotion which moves the man to the very depths of his being.[132] With three exceptions this word is only ever used of Jesus, and those three exceptions are parables which he told to describe the compassion of God the Father. (Matthew 18:33, Luke 10:33, Luke 15:20.)

So the Hebrew people understood YHWH to be a God of justice, but also a God of compassion. And since man is made in the image of God it follows that people are designed to have emotions and feelings.

We have already noted how the Hebrew people regarded the act of praising and thanking God to be the supreme joy of life. As the psalmist says, "In your presence there is fullness of joy; in your right hand are pleasures forevermore" (Psa 16:11).

By contrast, according to the Stoics, who were supposed to be the highest philosophical Greek thinkers of the time, the essential characteristic of God was *apatheia*. Not *apathy*, but *apatheia*, which simply means His incapability of feeling any emotion. They reasoned that if God could feel sorrow or joy because of what a person does, then that person has some measure of power or control over God. But, they reasoned, it is not possible for a person to have power over God, so they concluded that God must have no feelings (or no emotional reactions).

The grim thing about these pagan ideas is that the Stoics taught that man should seek to make himself like God. Barclay summarizes the teachings of the Stoic philosopher Epictetus with the words:

> "See your nearest and dearest die, and say, 'It doesn't matter. I don't care [because I have no feelings]'". [133]

---

132. William Barclay, *New Testament Words*. p276ff
133. William Barclay *New Testament Words*. p280

APPENDIX 1

The aim of perfect manhood then, was to attain a life from which all feelings of joy or grief, pleasure or compassion, and all sense of personal desire and passion were totally and utterly banished. The emotions stirred by sexual love (eros) are powerful indeed, but, like all other feelings, they must be eliminated from the heart and mind. Such was the Hellenistic (ancient Greek) concept of sex and love.

We must recognize that many of the early church fathers had been seriously influenced by these Hellenistic philosophers. And their concept of sex and sexual love was very different from the simple Hebrew acceptance of God's sexual design. Aristotle taught that a woman's place in life was merely "to serve and obey."

I have already mentioned Plato's theory that the nuclear family should be abandoned and replaced by a form of communal living where wives and children would all be shared in common. But remember that the reason he gave for this idea was to eliminate any possibility of people being motivated by some form of exclusive "love".

Where Plato had regarded the pursuit of women and physical pleasure as a distraction from the pursuit of "truth," some early church leaders saw this as a diversion of man's service to God, and therefore a cause of sin. Once the link between sin and sexual desire (in any context) was established, "good" women were expected to be uncontaminated by any hint of sexual desire. Their "purity" was to be modeled on that of Mary, mother of Jesus.

Perhaps I need to here reinforce a point which has already been mentioned. The reference to "Purity" in the New Testament writings does not necessarily mean the person is devoid of a normal healthy interest in sex. But it does mean that their motives are not contaminated by any form of self-interest; It means that their real motive is a genuine concern for the welfare of the other party. Any act motivated by greed, and any form of exploitation or manipulation is therefore "impurity." It seems that some of these early church fathers may have been confused on this point.

The belief that contact with a woman will cause a man to be spiritually defiled, or unclean, is a characteristic of many pagan religions, and yet once this idea was accepted by leaders within the Christian church the logical conclusion was that such activity would make a person unfitted for God's service. For some leaders in the early church, the story of the virgin birth was interpreted to mean that sexual intercourse was of itself a sinful business. This led to the doctrine of the perpetual virginity of Mary.

According to some of those scholars, Mary the mother of Jesus was totally devoid of all sexual desire and remained a virgin throughout her entire life. This idea was taught in spite of the fact that Matthew clearly implies Mary and Joseph lived a normal married life when he wrote that Joseph "had no union with her *until* she gave birth to a son" (Matt 1:25). Matthew also refers to Jesus as the firstborn son of Mary, not the only son. Both Matthew and Mark even give us the names of Jesus' four brothers - James, Joseph, Simon and Judas, and tell us that he had sisters as well.[134] The New Testament book of James was written by James the brother of Jesus.

In addition to this (very questionable) teaching about the perpetual virginity of Mary, the celibacy of John the Baptist and Jesus, were taken as evidence that the renunciation of sex and a life of celibacy were the only way to a truly spiritual life. Those who marry therefore sink to an inferior spiritual level.

Hence, as already mentioned, in 305AD the Church Council of Elvira issued the ruling that "All who are concerned with the ministry of the altar must practice abstinence from their wives or forfeit their position." The logical extension of this ruling was that any person involved with "the ministry of the altar" must remain unmarried. Yet this teaching is directly opposed to Paul's specific instructions to Timothy (1 Timothy 3:2-5) that leaders

---

134. Matthew 13:55-56 and Mark 6:3

in the church must be married men who have first proved their leadership skills by the way they treat their own children, and it contradicts the teaching of Hebrews 13:4, as well as Leviticus 21:14-15.

When Emperor Constantine became a Christian he issued an edict (313AD) granting everyone the right to choose their own religion. The official persecution of Christians thus came to an end. But unfortunately many of the people who now joined the church did not entirely abandon their pagan philosophies. Instead they brought many of these ideas with them into the church. Augustine (354-430 AD) had problems accepting that God could have created men and women with such powerful emotions as those which accompany the act of sexual intercourse, and he taught that such pleasure, even within marriage, was always tainted with sin.

But then he had been so persuaded to believe that anything pleasurable was sinful he even questioned whether it may be sinful to enjoy a good meal, simply because the food tasted good. More than a century later, Gregory the Great (C540-604) modified Augustine's ideas slightly by suggesting that coitus was not sinful of itself, because it was necessary for the conception of children, but it would be sinful if the couple enjoyed it.

Several years after Constantine, Emperor Theodosius (378-395) made Christianity the State Religion of the Roman Empire, and church membership (for people in positions of authority) was made compulsory. Thousands of unregenerate people now joined the Church and did little to abandon their immoral lifestyles. For some folk the natural reaction against this influx of immorality was to go to even greater extremes in their ascetic teaching. As we have already noted, far from supporting the God ordained relationships of marriage and of family these ascetic teachings served only to produce an increasingly lower opinion of the role and status of women and of motherhood.

While Tertullian (160-220) and Cyprian (200-258) had both urged women to remain virgins as the only way to escape the consequences of "the fall", Jerome (C347-420) argued that marriage was acceptable, but only because it was the means by which more virgins would be born. Bishop Ambrose (340-397) described the loss of a woman's virginity as a defacement of creation.

Now that the ideal woman was virtually defined as a permanent virgin, and the image of Christian manhood was understood to be unmarried and celibate, then an even greater contempt for human sexuality was the inevitable result. Instead of accepting sexual intercourse between a husband and wife as a sacred celebration of their special relationship the sex drive was now seen as some kind of a demon. And if sex was sinful then female sexuality was thought to be particularly evil. Eve became the temptress who had caused Adam to sin. So all women were to be treated with suspicion and avoided as "a subtle and dangerous temptress, always inclined to beguile men and inflame them with evil desires."

Where Jesus had taught that the problem of sexual immorality and defilement starts in the mind of the *man* whose basic motive in life is his own self-serving pleasure, these people were trying to place the blame with the woman, simply because she exists as a woman. We can hardly call such attitudes Christ like or pro-family.

Nevertheless, there were some men who opposed these ascetic trends, but they struggled to be heard, and their writings were most probably destroyed by the more powerful and militant ascetics. Helvidius, Vigilantus, and Jovinian are known to us, but only from the writings of Jerome, who attacked these men with such sarcasm that even Jerome's own supporters began to protest.

It was not only sexual activity that was condemned by the ascetics. It was anything that could be described as pleasurable. Antisthenes, a Cynic philosopher, was so horrified at the thought of a life wasted on pleasure that he once said he would prefer madness to pleasure. Some monks in the fourth and fifth centuries even made a cult of discomfort. These men trained themselves to do with a minimum of food, sometimes only two meals a week, and a minimum of sleep. Adolus never slept except for the three hours before dawn. Sisoes spent nights on a jutting crag, so that if he fell asleep he would fall to his death. Pachomius never lay down, but when he did sleep he did so standing in his cell.

There were others for whom the sensuous pleasure of washing was abhorrent. The dirtier they were the holier they felt. It was said of Simeon Stylites, as a mark of his great holiness, that his body dropped vermin as he walked. Jerome congratulated nuns for never allowing water to touch their bodies, and wrote to Paula (who, although she had two daughters of her own, was leader of a community of virgins), "Why should Paula add fuel to a sleeping fire by taking a bath?" A Roman lady named Melania boasted that after her conversion she never allowed water to touch her body, except the tips of her fingers, in spite of her doctor's advice. One wonders how these people accepted the Christian and biblical idea of baptism, and what their thoughts would have been on the requirements for frequent washing, as spelled out in Levitical law.[135]

I have read somewhere that, "The true ascetics are those who succeed in converting all of their erotic drive into cultural activity" [or into art or productive work]. But these people seem to have been confused. Surely Jesus' criticism of the Pharisees who had put aside God's commands and were following the teachings of men (Mark 7:8) could have equally well been directed at some of these fanatics.

So it was in these ways that the men in leadership within the Christian church had allowed pagan philosophies to affect their teaching. As Geoffrey May says:

---

135. Exo 30:20; Lev 13:6b; Lev 16:223-24; Num 19:7; 1 Sam 25:42. These are just random samples of the Levitical laws on frequent washing.

"Within a period of four centuries, Christianity had exchanged its attitude of emotional expression for an attitude of emotional repression." [136]

We must understand then that the anti-sex doctrines all had their origins in pagan philosophies, and the end result of such teaching was to further undermine the sanctity of marriage and the status of women.

We do well to remember that, whilst pornography may be degrading to women and to man-woman relationships in general, excessive prudery and shame also produce attitudes that are degrading to woman, and are thus harmful to marriage and to family life. Both of these extremes should be equally condemned, because they are both an insult to the Creator.

It is not sex or the sex-drive that is evil when it is expressed within the God-ordained context of legitimate marriage. Neither is sensual pleasure necessarily sinful of itself. Nor is nakedness necessarily evil.

What is evil is the degradation of something that ought to be a beautiful, holy and God-designed celebration of mutual surrender and an expression of love between a husband and wife who are in the special relationship of marriage. This degradation of something sacred is offensive in the same way and for the same reasons that we feel deeply offended when somebody makes a mockery of prayer or of some celebration of divine worship.

As the ancient Hebrew proverb expressed it;

"If it were not for the sex drive no man would ever marry a wife, build a house, or raise a family."

---

136. Geoffrey May, *Social Control of Sex Expression*. London, Allen and Unwin 1930 p43.

APPENDIX 2

Other Interpretations of the Song of Songs

There are probably as many interpretations of the *Song of Songs* as there are people who have studied the book. However a brief glance at some of the many possible interpretations which have been suggested in the past may be helpful here, as this should help us to appreciate the breadth of teaching which can be found in this book, and also to decry the opinion that human love is not a fit subject to be included in holy Scripture.

Some of the common interpretations include:

- This is a religious love-drama.
- This is simply a book about love.
- The book is a protest against polygamy.
- This is a collection of secular love songs.
- This is a collection of Judean wedding songs.
- This is a Jewish allegory of the history of Israel.
- This is a story of Solomon and one of his wives.
- This is part of the liturgy of a Syrian wedding ceremony.
- This is an allegory of the relationship between God and Israel.
- This is an allegory of the relationship between Christ and His bride, the church.

- The book is intended to provide teaching about the relationship between Christ and any individual believer. Many people take this in a very personal way, and apply it to their own personal experience.
- This is a collection of ancient New Year liturgies which celebrated the reunion and marriage of the god and goddess of fertility, and therefore owe their origin to the ancient fertility cults. These cults are not without some surviving remnant even in our own day, as evidenced by celebrations of Easter with eggs and Easter Bunnies. These New Year festivals may possibly be equated with ancient May Day celebrations, or Springtime festivals, in some parts of Europe.
- For Jews, at least part of the Songs featured in the liturgy for the Passover or the Feast of Unleavened Bread. (The modern Christian equivalent of this is, of course, Easter).
- This is simply a book which teaches God's approval of sexual love within marriage.

Possibly one of the main reasons for identifying the *Song of Songs* as **an allegory of the Nation of Israel** is the similarity to the parable of the vineyard as described by Isaiah (Isaiah ch.5). However the various allegorical interpretations all meet with the difficulty that the writing itself offers no clues for identifying scenes or characters. Moreover there is no indication within the text that the writing is intended to be allegorical, and the sometimes contradictory results of those who try to interpret the book this way would seem to indicate that this is not its primary purpose.

Also, there is no mention of the *Song of Songs* in the New Testament. Most members of this school of interpretation seem to hint very strongly that they consider human physical/sexual love is not a worthy subject to be included in sacred literature, and it is for this reason that they prefer to find some other, in this case allegorical, interpretation.

APPENDIX 2

The **literal school** interprets the *Song of Songs* as simply a collection of love songs or poems which reflect the various moods of lovers in different situations. Adherents to this school claim there is no unity throughout the writings. If the book is simply a collection of lyrics of folk origin they claim that this would explain its apparent lack of unity. Its purely secular, erotic character could be explained as being the text of songs sung by dancers at wedding ceremonies, where an appropriate subject was the portrayal of love. Its inclusion in the canon of sacred Hebrew writings could then be explained by the fact that the singing and dancing belonged to festivals of good religious standing.

In contradiction to the "literal" interpretation I hope I have given enough evidence to prove that there IS a unity and progressive theme throughout the entire text.

The **cultic school of interpretation** finds here the myth of the dying and rising god of fertility. In winter all fertility ceases because the god of fertility is dead. In spring all fertility resumes because the god of fertility is revived by his beloved. Evidence for this interpretation is found in the many references to nature - flowers, spices, animals, etc. Against the cultic view we must acknowledge that no divine name is ever specifically mentioned in the text, and also that this book was included in the canon of ancient Hebrew Scripture. It is inconceivable that the Jewish fathers would have admitted to their sacred canon a series of lyrics which had blatant and obvious connections with pagan fertility cults. The allusions to the world of nature, the erotic imagery, and particularly the games of hide-and-seek, are more plausible if understood as a simple love story from a writer with an Egyptian background, such as Solomon's wife, the daughter of Pharoah.

But let us not be too distressed that some interpreters find references to symbolism from the fertility cults. Our sexuality is part of God's design, and expressions of sexual love within marriage are part of that design. When some enemy, or predator, wishes to pervert or destroy that design he creates a counterfeit.

In order to deceive people he makes his counterfeit appear as much as is possible like the original. Therefore many aspects of the fertility cults may be similar to a genuine God-ordained expression of sexual love within marriage. For this reason it is possible that the writer has occasionally alluded to cultic symbolism to help describe a word-picture, without necessarily condoning the activities of those cults. As already mentioned, we have done a similar thing in our own culture by accepting eggs, a fertility cult symbol of new life, as part of our celebrations of Easter and also gifts under a tree at Christmas time probably have a pagan origin.

The **dramatic school** sees the *Song of Songs* as a play, with a plot and characters. Those who reject this interpretation argue that the Hebrews never used drama as a means of teaching or communicating ideas. It was the Greeks who established theatres in the lands they conquered, and then used drama and the theatre as a means of teaching their culture and religious ideas. The use of drama, we are told, only became popular after the time of Alexander the Great. However I could have believed that the prophet Ezekiel used a form of drama to get his message across, and so did Hosea, in effect. They also claim that no real plot develops throughout the *Song of Songs*, and that there is no clear division of scenes, and no stage directions. But, as I have tried to explain in the previous pages, there are distinct characters and there is a definite theme and there is a logical progression of storyline presented throughout the entire book.

One of the more popular **spiritual interpretations** sees the *Songs* as a drama involving three characters: The Shulammite representing the individual Christian; The Shepherd representing Christ; and King Solomon, with all his splendour and wealth, representing "the world".

However I personally find this interpretation offensive and difficult to accept. The idea that this book, which is almost the centrefold of the entire Christian Bible, should be interpreted as

APPENDIX 2

a seduction scene where some wealthy (sleazy?) worldly monarch is trying to seduce an innocent country lass and persuade her to join his harem seems somewhat unsuitable for Holy Scripture. I definitely prefer to see the *Song of Songs* as a beautiful honest-to-goodness love story, but a story which, because of its God-given beauty, does also contain some valuable spiritual and practical teaching.

Although absolute irrefutable proof regarding the original writer and original purpose of the *Song of Songs* may forever remain a mystery, one thing is certain – these are lyrics about love and about relationships. This is poetry, and as such we need to permit all the textual liberties which poetry demands.

To understand and appreciate such a work of art we must always remember if or when we try to examine and analyse individual words or phrases in minute detail (as it were under a microscope), that we should never loose sight of the big picture. We must always see the entire production as a living whole.

Remember: the *Song of Songs* is poetry. It was never intended to be a scientific lecture or technical thesis.

BIBLIOGRAPHY

Anand, Margo. (1990). *The Art of Sexual Ecstasy.* London UK: Aquarian Press.

Augustine, *Confessions.* (E B Pussey D.D., trans. 1907) London: J M Dent & Sons.

Barclay, William. (1971). *Ethics in a Permissive Society.* UK: Fontana Books.

Barclay, William. (1964). *New Testament Words.* London UK: SCM Press.

Barnett, R D. (1966-68). *Illustrations of Old Testament History.* British Museum Publ.

Barnhouse, Ruth T. & Urban T.Holmes, (Eds). (1976) *Male and Female - Christian Approaches to Sexuality.* New York: The Seabury Press.

Biddulph, Steve. (1994-95) *Manhood,* Lane Cove NSW: Finch Publishing.

Blitchington, Peter W. (1981). *Sex Roles & The Christian Family.* Wheaton: Tyndale.

Brecher, Ruth and Edward (Ed). (1968) *An Analysis of Human Sexual Response.* London UK: Panther Books.

Bremness, Lesley. (1998) *Fragrant Herbal.* London, England: Quadrille Publishing Ltd.,

Bullough, Vern L. (1994). *Science in the Bedroom.* New York: Basic Books.

Calderone, Mary S; & Eric Johnson, (1989-91) *The Family Book About Sexuality.* New York: Harper and Row.

Clarke, Dr. Magnus (1982). *Nudism in Australia.* Geelong: Deakin University Press.

Clinebell, Howard and Charlotte. (1974-81) *The Intimate Marriage.* New York: Harper and Row.

Cloud, Dr Henry; & Dr John Townsend, (1992) *Boundaries.* Sydney: Strand Publishing.

Collins, Gary R. (1988) *Christian Counselling: A comprehensive guide.* Dallas: Word.

Collins, Gary R (Ed). (1991) *Case Studies in Christian Counselling.* Dallas: Word.

Comfort, Dr Alex (Ed). (1974-86). *More Joy of Sex.* Dee Why, NSW: Rigby.

Comfort, Dr Alex. (1986-91). *The New Joy of Sex.* London UK: Mitchell Beazley.

Crabb, Dr Lawrence. (1991). *Men and Women, Enjoying the Difference.* USA: Zondervan.

Crabb, Dr Lawrence. (1987). *Understanding People.* London UK: Marshall Pickering.

Crabb, Dr Lawrence.(1982-86). *The Marriage Builder.* USA: Zondervan.

Craghan, John F., C SS R. (1979). *Old Testament Reading Guide - The Song of Songs and The Book of Wisdom.* Minnesota: The Liturgical Press (Order of St Benedict).

Curran, Dolores. (1983). *Traits of a Healthy Family.* San Francisco: Harper and Row.

Dewberry, Ps Harold. Tape recorded lectures on The Song of Solomon. Alfa Loma CA, USA: Dewberry Ministries.

Dillow, Joseph C. (1977). *Solomon on Sex.* Nashville: Thomas Nelson.

Dix, Rev Gregory (Ed). *Treatise on the Apostolic Traditions of St Hippolytus.* Connecticut: Moorhouse Publ.

Dobson, Dr James. (1987). *Love for a Lifetime.* UK: Word Publishing.

Dupont, Marc. (1997). *Walking Out of Spiritual Abuse.* Kent, UK: Sovereign World.

Enroth, Ronald M. (1992-93). *Churches That Abuse.* Michigan USA: Zondervan.

Glickman, S Craig. (1976). *A Song for Lovers.* USA: InterVarsityPress.

Gray, John, PhD. (1993). *Men are from Mars Women are from Venus.* London: Thorsons (Harper Collins).

Green, Toby. (1996). *If You Really Loved Me.* NSW Australia: Random House.

Guyon, Jeanne. *Song of Songs.* New Kengsington, PA: Whitaker House, 1997.

Hamrogue, John M C SS R. (1987). *Sex and Marriage - A Catholic Perspective.* Missouri: Ligouri Publications.

Hite, Shere. (1976-66). *The Hite Report.* Dee Why NSW: Summitt/Paul Hamlyn.

Hughes, Selwyn. (1983-86). *Marriage as God Intended.* Eastbourne UK: Kingsway.

Hurnard, Hannah. (1983-90). *Mountain of Spices.* UK: Kingsway.

Jordan, Professor W G. *Peake's Commentary of the Bible.*

Juan, Dr Stephen. (1990). *Only Human.* Milsons Point NSW: Random House.

Kitzinger, Sheila. (1983). *Woman's Experience of Sex.* New York: Putnam's Sons.

Mace, Dr David & Vera. (1977) *How to Have A Happy Marriage.* Nashville: Abingdon Press.

Mace, Dr David R (1982). *Love & Anger In Marriage.* Grand Rapids: Zondervan.

Mace, Dr David R. (1958-85). *Success in Marriage*. Nashville: Abingdon.

Mace, Dr David R. (1971). *The Christian Response to the Sexual Revolution*. London UK: Lutterworth Press.

Mace, Dr David R. (1988). *When The Honeymoon's Over*. Nashville: Abingdon.

Mace, Dr David R. (1953-63). *Whom God Hath Joined*. London: Epworth.

Mackay, Hugh. (1994). *Why Don't People Listen?* Sydney NSW: Pan Macmillan Publ.

Masters, Dr William & Virginia Johnson. (1970-81). *Human Sexual Inadequacy*. New York: Bantam Books.

May, Geoffrey. (1930). *Social Control of Sex Expression*. London: Allen and Unwin.

McDonald, Paula and Dick. (1978). *Loving Free*. Dee Why: Paul Hamlyn. Note: This book was also published in New York by Ballantine Books (Random House) 1973-75, using the pseudonyms Jackie and Jeff Herrigan.

Meredith, Bronwen. (1980). *Vogue Natural Health and Beauty*. Penguin Books.

Morgan, Dr G Campbell. (1912). *Living Messages of the Books of the Bible*. London: Pickering and Inglis.

Morgan, Marabel. (1979). *The Total Woman*. Sevenoaks UK: Hodder and Stoughton.

O'Conner, Dagmar. (1989). *How to Put the Love Back Into Making Love*. New York: Doubleday.

Overman, Christian. (1998). *Assumptions That Affect Our Lives*. Simi Valley, California: "Micah 6:8" - Growing Families International.

Penner, Dr Clifford & Joyce. (1981-86). *The Gift of Sex*. UK: Word Publishing.

Powers, Dr B Ward. (1987). *Marriage and Divorce.* Petersham NSW: Jordan Books.

Powers, G. P., & Wade Baskin, (Eds). (1969). *Sex Education in a Changing Culture.* London: Peter Owen.

Renn, Stephen, (1989). *Bible Probe - Song of Songs.* NSW, Australia: ANZEA (Scripture Union).

Robinson, Constance. (1965). *Passion and Marriage.* London UK: S.P.C.K., Holy Trinity Church.

Rosenau, Dr Douglas. (1994). *A Celebration of Sex,* UK: Word Publishing.

Sasoon, Beverley & Vidal. (1975). *A Year of Beauty and Health.* Angus and Robertson.

Scott, George Ryley (1963) *Curious Customs of Sex and Marriage.* London UK: Ben's Books.

Seamands, Prof. David A. (1981). *Healing for Damaged Emotions.* Wheaton: Victor Books / SP Publications.

Seligson, Marcia. (1977). *Options.* New York: Charter Books / Random House.

Smith, Dennis; & Dr. William Sparks. (1986). *Growing Up Without Shame.* Los Angeles: Elysium Growth Press.

Sutherland, Frank N. (1973). *Beyond The Sexual Revolution.* Dee Why: Tempo Books.

Tannen, Deborah. (1991). *You Just Don't Understand.* Random House. Australia.

Tiefer, Leonore (1979) *Human Sexuality.* Melbourne: Thomas Nelson Australia.

Tournier, Dr Paul. (1957-74) *The Meaning of Persons.* London SCM Press.

Van der Hoeven, Rev J H. (1989). *Song of Songs - Outlines on Song of Solomon,* (A study book translated by Het Hooglied.) Australia: League of Free Reformed Women's Bible Study Societies in Australia.

Weatherhead, Dr Leslie D. (1931-64) *The Mastery of Sex Through Psychology and Religion.* London: SCM Press.

Wheat, Ed MD. (1981). *Intended For Pleasure,* USA: Fleming H Revell Co.

White, Dr John. (1977-86). *Eros defiled.* UK: InterVarsity Press.

White, Dr John. (1993). *Eros Redeemed.* USA: InterVarsityPress.

Wilson, Sandra D. (1998). *Into Abba's Arms,* Wheaton: Tyndale House.

Wilson, Sandra D. (1990). *Released From Shame,* Illinois: InterVarsityPress.

Wilson, Sandra D. (1992). *Shame Free Parenting,* Illinois: InterVarsityPress.

Wolf, Hans Walter, (Gary Stansell trans., 1974). *Hermeneia - Hosea, a critical and historical commentary.* Philadelphia USA: Fortress Press.

Young, Roger & Rosemarie. (1993). *The "Naked" Marriage - learning to live and love without the mask,* Wendouree Australia: Family Reading Publications.

Young, Wayland. (1964-68). *Eros Denied,* London UK: Corgi Books.

Zimmerman, Carle C. [Harvard University] (Feb. 1947) *Family and Civilization,* Harper & Brothers NewYork, USA.

Reference Works

Dictionary of Pastoral Care and Counselling. (1990). Nashville: Abingdon Press.

Encyclopaedia Brittanica, 1962 edition.

Encyclopaedia Brittanica, 1994 edition.

Halley's Bible Handbook, 22nd edition (1959). London: Oliphants.

Holman Bible Dictionary (1994).
Peake's Commentary of the Bible.
Strong's Exhaustive Concordance of the Bible. USA: Hendrickson Publishers. (n.d.)
The Interpreter's Bible. Nashville: Abingdon Press (not dated)
The New Bible Commentary (Revised, 1973). InterVarsityPress.
The New Jerome Bible Commentary. (1990). Englewood Cliffs NJ: Prentice Hill.
Vine's Expository Dictionary of Biblical Words, (1985). Nashville: Thomas Nelson.
QuickVerse For Windows [Computer software]. (1996). Hiawatha, Iowa: Parsons Technology.

Magazine Articles

"Baptism in the Early Church" Larry Amyett, USA: Naturist Life International #19. 1997.

"Childhood Nakedness Reconsidered" Paul Bowman, USA: Naturist Life International #13. 1995.

"Children Having Children - Teen pregnancy in America," Time, December 9th 1985.

"Healthy Boundaries Healthy Relationships," Dick Innes, Encounter, June 1995.

"Isn't Sex Supposed to be Fun?" Dr Cliff & Joyce Penner, Marriage Partnership, Spring 1991.

"Keeping The Spark Alive," Dr Cliff & Joyce Penner, Marriage, Jul/Aug 1997.

"Now for the Truth About Americans and Sex," Time, Oct 17th, 1994.

"Sex and the Song of Songs," David Jackson, On Being, November 1992.

"Sexuality and Spirituality," Michael Frost, On Being, June 1996.

"Teen Sex: Not for Love," Christianity Today, May 1989.

Audio Cassettes and Tape Recordings

Wheat, Ed MD. (1975). "Sex Techniques and Sex Problems in Marriage".

Wheat, Ed MD. (1979). "Love Life for every married couple".

Wheat, Ed MD. (1982). "Before the Wedding Night." [tape recorded messages] Arkansas: Scriptural Counsel Inc.

Video Presentations

"Where Did I Come From - The Animated Video" 29 mins VHS tape (Rated "PG") Written by Peter Mayle, Produced by Steve Walsh. Distributed in Australia by Roadshow Home Video. Cooke, Helen (Writer) and Pritchard, M. (Director). (1993)

"The Adam and Eve Factor". [Series of four 35min tapes. Rated "E" Exempt from classification.] A series of role-plays and discussion, dealing with the issues of Commitment, Conflict, Intimacy, and Servanthood, in marriage. Amersham, Bucks, UK: Scripture Press, and International Films and Video.

Dobson, James with Dr. Dave Hernandez [55 mins]. "Sex and The Family." A series of clips from Focus on The Family TV programs covering the topics:

"Sex Education at Home",

"Teaching Male and Female Roles", and

"Sex In Marriage".

This video was released in Australia through Gospel Film Ministry.

Silvoso, Ed. (1992). "How to Have Intimacy in Marriage". [55min.] Ed Silvoso, well known for his teaching on Spiritual Warfare, speaks to a group of church leaders. His message is entertaining, very practical, and easy listening. Oakbrook, Il, USA: Institute of Basic Life Principles.

"Sex Pleasuring - an enrichment series", Vol. 1, 2 & 3 New Age Video Inc., New York USA 1981 Used worldwide by leading professional sex therapists. This 2hour video includes three 40 minute sessions:

Vol 1 = Exploring the art of touching using Masters & Johnson Sensate Focus program.

Vol 2 = Techniques to help overcome problems of premature ejaculation in the male.

Vol 3 = Foreplay and intercourse.

Originally produced by EDCOA, USA, 1976

Copyright (1981) now held by New Age Video, New York.

NOTE: Because of the explicit nature of material in the "Sex Pleasuring" series, and because the producers chose to use real married couples instead of cartoon drawings to illustrate the techniques discussed, this video has an "X" for explicit classification.

www.ingramcontent.com/pod-product-compliance
Lightning Source LLC
Chambersburg PA
CBHW050307010526
44107CB00055B/2136